# American Literature Readings in the 21st Century

Series editor
Linda Wagner-Martin
University of North Carolina
Chapel Hill, NC, USA

American Literature Readings in the 21st Century publishes works by contemporary critics that help shape critical opinion regarding literature of the nineteenth and twentieth centuries in the United States.

More information about this series at
http://www.palgrave.com/gp/series/14765

Kathryn Wichelns

# Henry James's Feminist Afterlives

Annie Fields, Emily Dickinson, Marguerite Duras

Kathryn Wichelns
Department of English, University of New Mexico,
Albuquerque, NM, USA

American Literature Readings in the 21st Century
ISBN 978-3-319-71799-9 (hardcover)    ISBN 978-3-319-71800-2 (eBook)
ISBN 978-3-319-89107-1 (softcover)
https://doi.org/10.1007/978-3-319-71800-2

Library of Congress Control Number: 2017963646

© The Editor(s) (if applicable) and The Author(s) 2018, First softcover printing 2019
This work is subject to copyright. All rights are solely and exclusively licensed by the Publisher, whether the whole or part of the material is concerned, specifically the rights of translation, reprinting, reuse of illustrations, recitation, broadcasting, reproduction on microfilms or in any other physical way, and transmission or information storage and retrieval, electronic adaptation, computer software, or by similar or dissimilar methodology now known or hereafter developed.
The use of general descriptive names, registered names, trademarks, service marks, etc. in this publication does not imply, even in the absence of a specific statement, that such names are exempt from the relevant protective laws and regulations and therefore free for general use.
The publisher, the authors and the editors are safe to assume that the advice and information in this book are believed to be true and accurate at the date of publication. Neither the publisher nor the authors or the editors give a warranty, express or implied, with respect to the material contained herein or for any errors or omissions that may have been made. The publisher remains neutral with regard to jurisdictional claims in published maps and institutional affiliations.

Cover illustration: Glasshouse Images / Alamy Stock Photo

Printed on acid-free paper

This Palgrave Macmillan imprint is published by Springer Nature
The registered company is Springer International Publishing AG
The registered company address is: Gewerbestrasse 11, 6330 Cham, Switzerland

*In memoriam:*
*Susan R. Barnard*
*(1969–2000)*

An early version of Chapter 3 was published in *The Emily Dickinson Journal* 20.1 (2011). It appears here by permission of Johns Hopkins University Press.
An early version of Chapter 4 appeared in *Comparative Literature* 67.1 (2015). It appears here by permission of Duke University Press.

# ACKNOWLEDGMENTS

Like all books, this one reflects the contributions of many. I want particularly to thank the students, professors, friends, and colleagues who have been most instrumental in my approach to specific aspects of this project, in ways large and small: Aaron Aguilar, Jesse Alemán, Aaron Alter, Brooke Beloso, Stéphanie Boulard, Frank Boyle, Shelby Crosby, Amy Cunningham, Ken Dauber, Richard Giannone, Christopher GoGwilt, Jason Goldbarg, Alyosha Goldstein, Elizabeth Grosz, Oliver Herford, Philip Horne, Susan Howe, Lynne Huffer, Dalia Judovitz, Mary Lannon, Chad Lavin, Sarah Lewis, Elissa Marder, Elias Marenco, Olivia McGinnis, Christanne Miller, Michael Moon, Gerry O'Sullivan, Elizabeth Petrino, Adriana Ramirez de Arellano, Cindy Rankin, Bárbara Reyes, Jill Robbins, Joyce Rowe, Neil Schmitz, Rebecca Schreiber, Shane Vogel, Daniel Worden, and Greg Zacharias.

Two anonymous reviewers for Palgrave Macmillan gave invaluably specific and thorough feedback. In addition, my editors at Palgrave, Allie Bochicchio and Emily Janakiram, have served as advocates and consultants throughout this process.

Librarians are at the foundations of every scholarly project. The staffs of the Miller Library at Colby College, the Houghton Library at Harvard University, the Huntington Library, the Maine Women Writers Collective at the University of New England, and the Massachusetts Historical Society have provided access to, and input on, the unpublished and archival material that helps support the arguments in Chaps. 2 and 3. The staff of the Interlibrary Library Loan Office at the University of New Mexico's Zimmerman Library has bent over backwards over the last couple of years, in an increasingly impossible budget climate, to get copies of far-flung texts sent, with remarkable speed, to the U.S. Southwest.

I also thank the members of my various incarnations of family—biological, legal, and chosen—who continue to inspire me with their courage in the face of mortality, parenthood, and other unthinkables: Adrian, Dan, George, Grace, Jenny, Jerry, Katy, Nancy, Sarah, and Trish.

# Contents

1 Introduction: On James, Mastery, and Transgression  1

2 "Those Who Know": Henry James and Annie Adams Fields  15

3 Emily Dickinson's Henry James  57

4 Henry James, French Feminist: Marguerite Duras's *La Bête dans la jungle*  85

5 Gender, Colonialism, and Italian Difference: Duras and *The Aspern Papers*  113

6 Conclusion: Towards a Queer Feminist James  143

Works Cited  153

Index  171

CHAPTER 1

# Introduction: On James, Mastery, and Transgression

This book approaches the thorny, much-debated question of Henry James's negotiations with his own period's ideas about gender, sexuality, class, nation, and literary style tangentially—through the responses of three women authors who have never substantively been examined in light of their relationships to James or his work. Writing in very different times and places, Annie Adams Fields, Emily Dickinson, and Marguerite Duras nevertheless share ambivalent responses to notions of womanhood and authorship. Henry James's correspondence with Annie Fields—a writer and women's rights activist whose "Boston marriage" with Sarah Orne Jewett influenced James's complex sympathy with her—and Dickinson's and Duras's revisions of James's fiction, offer a new avenue for understanding what I argue are gender-transgressive elements of James's project.

Just to clarify at the outset: my goal is not to present James himself as a feminist of a sort that we would easily recognize. As the title suggests, I regard James throughout this book through a series of feminist frames—each representative of a specific time and place, sometimes incompatibly distinct from the others. Yet I also argue that scholarly views on James's depictions of women, and his relationship to women's rights, have suffered from incomplete attention to available documents, including but not limited to his letters to Fields. In part, this oversight reflects the influence of twentieth-century canonizations of James as the "master" who bridges the realist and modernist periods, best understood through his relationship to literary aesthetics, and even then primarily via his late novels. Scholarship since the 1990s has done a great deal to chip away at the foundations of this version of James, as I will discuss briefly below, but surprising gaps remain. In *Henry James's Feminist Afterlives* I examine James as seen by three women writers who approach him from outside of our own inherited sense of what matters most in his work. For them, he is a male author who closely explores women's inner lives, as they negotiate existing ideas about gender and selfhood during the unprecedented transformations brought about by the late nineteenth-century period. Read in this light, James's critical preoccupation with questions of class, gender, and power becomes the defining aspect of his corpus.[1]

James's relationship to what his contemporaries called "the woman question" both is and is not consistent with his era's conventions. Most infamously, in two separate letters, written in March 1912 to Edith Wharton and William Dean Howells respectively, James's lack of sympathy for the "mortally tedious" movement for British women's suffrage is palpable. At the same time, scholarly readers of the 1912 letters often fail to note the context in which they were written. James condemns Emmeline Pankhurst and the other middle-class "window-smashing women" both because they break gender- and class-specific rules of conduct and because he considers their cause to be insensitively abstract during a period of unprecedented income inequality, known to historians as the Great Unrest. In March 1912, when Pankhurst had resumed a campaign of breaking windows in London and James was writing his letters to Wharton and Howells, a million coal miners had just begun what remains one of the most important strikes in British labor history, in protest over the government's failure to pass minimum wage laws (Anesko 456–457; Hobsbawm 116–129, 306; Kelly). On March 13, he writes to Wharton of "the coal strike and its mass of attendant misery" just prior to turning to Pankhurst and her fellow activists, who "add a darker shade" to the communal despair (James *Letters Vol. II*, 227–229). This in part—and only in part—is a critique of the women's methods and timing, which to him seem tone-deaf; of course, Pankhurst also is violating what James presumably saw as natural and necessary standards of feminine selflessness, during periods of collective hardship. While twenty-first century readers (including me) tend to look more favorably on Pankhurst than on James in this instance, Annie Fields would have shared his views. Another women's suffrage activist, she also served for James as an exemplar of appropriately private and genteel feminine behavior—one who, for the entire three decades of their correspondence, lived and thrived outside of heterosexual paradigms. Indeed, as British and

American feminist speeches and writings of the period consistently indicate, it was *through* their very privacy, domesticity, modesty, and separateness— and the greater capacity for spirituality, selflessness, and love for which those innately "feminine" attributes served as an outward sign—that (white) women were seen as deserving of the vote.[2] To James, Fields, and their (white, upper-class, Anglo-American) contemporaries, these two sets of beliefs about women would not have seemed in the least bit contradictory.

*Henry James's Feminist Afterlives* represents a close conversation between two recent traditions: feminist and queer theoretical readings of James's work, life, and/or influence. While these approaches are not, and perhaps should not be, aligned in many contexts, deploying either one separately in the face of James's writing strikes me as reductive. Early feminist and queer theoretical readings of the author, in the 1980s and 1990s, at times seemed to collaborate on little more than sounding the death knell of the asexual, aesthetic figure that emerged from earlier scholarship. Feminist work on James from this period sometimes doesn't seem to square with the writer who responded so negatively to Emmeline Pankhurst's protest campaign in 1912.[3] That work gave way, at least in terms of prominence, to the various queer theoretical readings that followed Eve Sedgwick's 1986 essay "The Beast in the Closet" (republished in 1990's *Epistemology of the Closet*). Sedgwick's ground-breaking opening salvo in this discussion would come to be productively nuanced by others (Haralson, *Henry James*; Lane; Looby; Moon; Ohi; Savoy; Stevens). Leo Bersani's psychoanalysis-influenced queer theoretical investigations of aesthetic subjectivity have inspired various readers to explore James the male artist as sympathetic towards alternatives to conventional masculine roles (*Future* 128–155).[4] The figure that this alternate subjectivity takes for James often is feminine, but this doesn't necessarily make him a feminist (or, indeed, *not* feminist)—again, reading him in either way may actually blind us to his negotiations with ideals of masculinity and femininity, as representative of and indistinguishable from ideologies of capitalism, class, individual selfhood, sexuality, nationality, and authorship. Kevin Ohi's contribution to queer theoretical James studies enables me to argue, quite differently, that what he describes as James's "queerness of style" just as clearly can be understood as a gender-transgressive approach to writing and authorship. Three decades after the first flowering of feminist and queer theoretical readings of James, an extended examination of the author that critically deploys both theoretical lenses, without either declaring the primacy of one over the other or compromising their differences, arguably still remains to be done.

For nineteenth-century subjects, what today we call gender and sexuality were not divisible: same-sex desire would have been understood as a form of spiritual "hermaphroditism," as scholars from Michel Foucault to Elizabeth Reis have extensively demonstrated.[5] To put this distinction in very basic terms, twenty-first century readers understand that it is both homophobic and misogynistic to conflate gay men with (heterosexual) women; we know that lesbians are not "actually" male, in some way only explainable through recourse to long-dead pseudosciences. Legal apparatuses exist, in some countries, to acknowledge that genitalia and gender are not always necessarily aligned. It seems self-evident to point out that our concepts are just as historically-contingent and -situated as James's, Fields's, and Dickinson's (as well as Duras's): that does not make them any less real. Yet in reading work from earlier eras we sometimes do not fully consider the fundamental incompatibility between their ideas and our own; equally problematic is our tendency to condemn historical figures for their period-specific notions. The historiographical approach that winds through *Henry James's Feminist Afterlives* most resembles Jack Halberstam's "perverse presentism," as first presented in 1998. Halberstam describes the quandary faced by scholars of queer and feminist history: seemingly, they must choose between "untheoretical historical surveys" that effectively erase non-normative sexualities and genders from the record, and "ahistorical theoretical models" that impose anachronism through their reliance on essentialized notions of sexual identities. As a resolution to this conflict, Halberstam offers a model that "avoids the trap of simply projecting contemporary understandings back in time, but one that can apply insights from the present to conundrums of the past" (46, 52–53). In short, rigorous attention to the profound alienness of nineteenth- and early twentieth-century notions of what we now call sex, gender, and sexuality provides us with more balanced understandings of the work of James and other authors who lived in the period.

A number of women writers from James's time and afterwards have, of course, been read extensively in light of their responses to him: Willa Cather, Edith Wharton, Gertrude Stein, and Constance Fenimore Woolson, to name a few. Until most recently, studies of James's relationships with women and women authors have tended to emphasize his (masculine) stylistic or artistic authority, rather than what I suggest is the specifically gender-transgressive aesthetics that his writing models for others with ambivalent relationships to their own period's ideas about gender and voice.[6] Readings of James's relationships to gender and writing, and the real women he knew or the fictional ones he depicted, often have missed the complex gender ambivalences and identifications inherent to his project. Tessa Hadley and Jonathan Freedman have presented useful correctives to earlier critiques of James's treatments of women, but each regards James's examinations of feminine subjectivity as based in a fundamentally more optimistic relationship to the mechanisms of late nineteenth-century capitalism than I think is accurate. Most useful for my purposes are three studies by Lyndall Gordon, Leland Person, and Victoria Coulson. In 2007's excellent *Henry James, Women and Realism*, Coulson uses his relationships with Edith Wharton, Constance Fenimore Woolson, and his sister Alice to argue that James is "subject to, and the compelling artist of, a potent ambivalence about the social authority of conservative gender patterns." For Coulson, this is a sign of James's "conservative resistance," or what she also terms "ambivalent realism" (8, 11, 19–23). I agree with most of Coulson's argument about James's complex, multivalent authorial relationship to gender and subjectivity: in *Henry James's Feminist Afterlives*, I add a different set of names to the growing list of women writers who recognized what Coulson and I both argue is his ambivalent resistance to his society's notions of femininity. Unlike Coulson, though, I think that this kinship really can best be explored via the theoretical avenues and tools made available by contemporary queer feminisms.

Annie Fields has served as a brief reference in scholarly interpretations of James's early work for 100 years, but James's letters to her have never fully been considered by scholars. This lacuna partly reflects the fact that a complete, accurate, multi-volume edition of James's epistolary writing is only now, as I write, in process.[7] Earlier editors of James's letters evidently did not consider missives to Fields in which James discussed matters other than his own literary production to be relevant. Reading his still largely-unpublished letters to her together, in conversation with each other, Chap. 2 begins to fill one of the numerous scholarly gaps resulting from the influence of outdated assumptions about gender, genre, and cultural influence. Working against the long legacy of those assumptions, in readings of James and his potential relevance to feminist literary scholarship, is one of the central motivations for this project. Although a published author, Annie Fields predominantly expressed herself through her letters and diaries. Her secondary position—from a twentieth-century scholarly viewpoint—as a Boston literary hostess, and the widow of an influential editor of the *Atlantic Monthly*, in fact actually enabled James's partial identification with her. Chapter 2 focuses on the ways that his own examinations of gender, privacy, and "queer" community come forth, in unique form, in his letters to her.

I hope that my chapter on Emily Dickinson's references to James's *The Europeans* will open the way for more substantive discussions of resonances between their larger corpora. While several scholars have pointed out sympathies shared by both writers, I argue that Dickinson's brief epistolary deployments of James's novel establish the foundation for a fuller comparison. Similarly, Marguerite Duras's theatrical adaptations of two of James's shorter fictional works have served solely as scholarly asides and footnotes. There are a few brief, French-language readings of the plays themselves by Duras scholars, but none that focuses on the wider implications of Duras's revisions of James, or explores his influence on her examinations of sex, sexuality, and gender in these pieces (or, indeed, throughout her extensive body of work). In short, in *Henry James's Feminist Afterlives* I parse the version of James that emerges via Fields, Dickinson, and Duras—one that in my view offers readers the beginnings of a systematically feminist analysis of James's equivocal, expatriate identification with nineteenth- and early twentieth-century Anglo-American ideals of womanhood and privacy. Across distinct time periods, biographies, genres, and notions of authorship, Fields, Dickinson, and Duras all seem to recognize in Henry James a close engagement with class- and nation-specific gender expectations. For each, James's writing reflects her own ambivalence towards what we might call both feminist and anti-feminist versions of womanhood, as those ideas are understood in her own period.

Reading James through the ways that these three women writers understand and sometimes appropriate his voice allows us new insights into his relationship to his period's ideas about femininity, which often serve as a means of also examining the related issues of manhood, nationality, sexuality, subjectivity, and the cultural role of the author in the *fin-de-siècle*. James's consistent attention to womanhood and femininity may seem suspect to us: we necessarily balk at the idea of men "speaking for" women. What I suggest is that James's complex identification with (normative) femininity reflects the distinctive forms of resistance available to him, as a male author who was both "queer" and, just as significantly, formed in a nineteenth-century, upper middle-class, and Anglo-American cultural context. While the gender-transgressive elements of his project therefore are only inconclusively "feminist," they invite and indeed require feminist analysis; and while they may not reflect the notions of queer resistance available in our period, I argue that they manifestly reflect James's own.

During the trip to Cambridge, Massachusetts described in 1907's *The American Scene*, James visited the cemetery where his beloved sister, Alice—an invalid, who had a long-term intimate relationship with Katharine Loring, who also served as her caretaker—had been buried. In his *Notebooks*, he writes of being deeply moved by the epitaph, a quote from Dante's *Paradiso* chosen for Alice's tombstone by their older brother, which he terms "William's inspired transcript." However, in remembering the lines James leaves out the pronoun that had rendered its subject (Alice) feminine. As Sharon Cameron suggests in her provocative reading of this moment, "through the subsequent ambiguity of gender James makes himself also into the object of the line's reference" (*Notebooks* 239–240; Cameron, *Thinking* 14–15).[8] Although she notes the gender transgression this requires, Cameron's focus is on the ways that James's account of this event provides insights into his relationship to writing and consciousness. Cameron convincingly argues that the published version of this memory is displaced and deferred: in *The American Scene*, Alice's gravestone is described only by substitution and without its important epitaph, in the form of the "flat memorial slab" on Soldier's Field in Cambridge "that waits to be inscribed" (54). I want to emphasize two elements that Cameron identifies but does not fully explore. First, and most obviously, James blurs clear gender identifications, recognizing himself in a familial other who is marked as both female and "queer." Second, in transforming his private memory into published form, James displaces his relationship to "the old Cambridge ghosts" (53), his sister foremost among them, onto a shared public memory and a national grief: Alice's gravestone becomes the uninscribed memorial at Soldier's Field. This says a great deal about James's relationship to both writing and thinking, as Cameron argues. More to the point, for my purposes, it provides insight into the ways that he uses writing—and particularly the simultaneously public and private forms of the epistle, the travel essay, and the memoir—to confound clear boundaries between personal, public, and national identities. As Cameron lets us infer but does not entirely suggest, the fact that James identifies with his only sister via Dante, at her tombstone, may imply not only that he recognizes the gender-specific nature of Alice's lifelong struggle but also that he considers himself, in that family, somehow also to be marked as foreign and other. In that particular personal, as well as the wider historical context, the most obvious signifier of a secondary status would have been Alice's femininity. Alice James's probable hysteria has been examined at length by feminist scholars (see Sontag, Strouse, Yeazell) who argue that her invalidism resulted from deep personal frustration: she was a woman struggling with the gender-specific imperatives of her own family, and with a period-specific class identity that discouraged women from pursuing their intellectual or artistic interests. As another brilliant but disappointingly female James child, Alice would have been the member of the family most negatively marked by these dynamics.[9]

In Chap. 2, I focus on James's responses to a different woman writer: also "queer," also representative for James of his resistant identification with his own Anglo-American origins. Over the course of their 35-year correspondence, Henry James's letters to Annie Fields render her a symbol of nineteenth-century American literary culture as well as the city of Boston, as its center. Both his personal letters to Fields and his later memorial essay, 1915's "Mr. and Mrs. James T. Fields," reveal the processes by which James makes a personal relationship simultaneously central to and displaced from public and national frames of self-understanding. Just like Alice James, Annie Fields does not entirely conform to James's private/public writing of her—and that very slippage provides fodder for his unresolved focus on her and what she represents for him.

I begin with Annie Fields because of her personal relationship with James, but also because the long span of their correspondence enables *Henry James's Feminist Afterlives*, at its inception, to resist periodizations of his work. I explore what I describe as a gender-transgressive aesthetics that cuts across the different decades of his life: periodization blinds us both to that point of consistency and to the ways that that consistency changes to reflect material, historical shifts in ideals of gender and privacy from James's earlier to his later writing. Much existing feminist and queer theoretical scholarship on James follows a periodization model; or, alternately, focuses on a specific genre of his work. Periodization does little to dislodge ahistorical ideas of James's artistic development; although this methodology has been necessary in some instances and useful in a number of ways, among other consequences it risks suggesting James's one-sided influence on other writers. Like Emily Dickinson and Sarah Orne Jewett, Marguerite Duras engages critically and tactically with James, as an interlocutor rather than a literary daughter; she rewrites him in order to render his voice more unequivocally feminist, as that concept is understood in her own time. An emphasis on James's stylistic development also is unhelpful for the purposes of this book because it implies a focus on his later fiction, and on publicly-recognized (and canonical) influences. James's response to Annie Fields does not fit neatly into this model. It is evidenced largely through letters; and in any case, Fields is not considered to be a great author. His relationship with her generally has been understood as private and therefore not artistic, despite evidence to the contrary. As I have suggested, his unresolved identification with specific versions of womanhood is expressed differently, in different times and places (from Boston to Rye, from the 1870s to 1915), via the letters to Fields and his writing about her. None of these is more significant or interesting—because earlier or later; American or British or transatlantic; post-Civil War or pre-World War I—than the others. Literary scholarly methods that rely on either period or genre do not work for my approach, as they create blind spots that can be illuminated when we use historiographical (rather than literary-historical) approaches, which emphasize the context of each text and author. The seeming eclecticism of the different literary genres I examine in the chapters that follow therefore is methodological, as I seek to construct a well-rounded sense of James's response to, and influence on, distinct notions of women's writing.

I also emphasize cross-genre analysis as it better enables me to explore both differences and interpenetrations among versions of James's "private" and "public" authorial selves. Each chapter addresses the specific works by James that are most relevant. In the chapter on Annie Fields, I read fourteen letters, for the most part unpublished, that James sent Fields from 1882 to 1914; the "Boston" chapter of *The American Scene* (1907); the essay "Mr. and Mrs. James T. Fields" (1915); and his two known, published letters to Jewett, as well as some of her related correspondence. In the chapter on Emily Dickinson I focus on *The Europeans* (1878), as she does in two personal letters. For the same reason, in the chapters on Marguerite Duras I examine the short story "The Beast in the Jungle" (1903) and the novella *The Aspern Papers* (1888), alongside Duras's two plays based on these works.

Therefore, while Chap. 2 closes in 1915, Chap. 3 necessarily moves backwards chronologically to 1879, the year Emily Dickinson refers to James and *The Europeans* twice in letters (L 619, L 622). Writing her close friend Elizabeth Holland and her "Preceptor," the editor and social activist Thomas Wentworth Higginson, the poet uses allusions to James and his characters to negotiate the parameters of these important personal relationships. Scholars have known of Dickinson's engagement with this novel at least since Jack L. Capps compiled an authoritative index of her reading in 1966; yet as of this writing only two short essays suggest that the connection might warrant more than a passing acknowledgment

(Sumner, Horne "Where Are...?"). As I argue in this chapter, in addition to using James to reflect on her relationships with Elizabeth Holland and T. W. Higginson, Dickinson offers what was for the time a strikingly unconventional reading of *The Europeans*. Contemporary American critics regarded the novel as a follow-up to 1877's *The American*, and emphasized the ways that it describes differences between European and American cultural ideals.[10] Dickinson instead directs our attention to the novel's critical exploration of New England ideals of femininity, morality, and paternal authority. In contrast to other authors T. W. Higginson considers more worthwhile, James and his unconventional style offer Dickinson a model for her own interrogations of notions of gender-specific writing and the role of the author.

Chapters 4 and 5 move to post-World War II Paris, as Marguerite Duras embarks on two collaborative theatrical adaptations of James's work. Neither 1961's *Les Papiers d'Aspern*, based on *The Aspern Papers* (1888), nor 1962's *La Bête dans la jungle*, based on "The Beast in the Jungle" (1903), has been translated. Published together in a 1984 Gallimard volume of Duras's plays, they have received limited critical attention. Duras herself has given scholars little insight into her use of James; other than these two adaptations and a brief 1983 essay in which she discusses the set design in *La Bête dans la jungle*, he appears in her corpus only in a single line at the conclusion of 1987's *Emily L.* (Duras 1987, 138). Yet as I argue in Chap. 4, Duras finds in James's work a powerful expression of "*l'écriture féminine.*" In her view, the genre of the theater better expresses James's original intent—she arranges the play as an encounter between different bodies and constructions of meaning. I briefly examine Duras in context before moving to *La Bête dans la jungle*. Duras's reading offers a viably and unequivocally feminist—and, just as unequivocally, French—alternative to Anglo-American readings of this story, even into our own period. Chapter 5 focuses on *Les Papiers d'Aspern*; while also reflective of Duras's interest in "*écriture féminine*," this adaptation draws out James's examinations of cultural and linguistic paternalism, in the Venice encounter between the Bordereau women and the unnamed "American critic" who seeks, through them, the final remnants of his literary hero. The political environment of late 1950s and early 1960s Paris—the rise of Charles de Gaulle and the 1954–1962 Algerian Revolution, as well as leftist Paris's responses to these events—are palpable influences in *Les Papiers d'Aspern*, more than in the other adaptation. As an author born into the lower tiers of the colonial system in French Indochina (Vietnam) who identified strongly with colonized "others," Duras's ambivalent relationship to France's ongoing history of colonialism informs her use of emerging anticolonialist ideas of the period, in constructing her version of the cultural and linguistic encounter between James's Anglo-American male narrator and two unplaceably foreign women living in Italy. I've given each play its own chapter, for a couple of reasons. First among these is the fact that they remain unavailable to English-language scholars. A closer textual focus also seemed necessary because there is no systematic examination of Duras's readings of or relationship to James, in French or English, within long-standing discussions of either these particular works or James's engagements with gender, sexuality, and language more generally.

In recent years, investigations of James's critical writing, and a highly productive revisiting of his letters and memoirs, have invited a modified version of the "master" back in. Scholars focusing on James's interest in material culture remind us that both his writing and our ideas about him result from concrete historical realities; a recent examination of James's style in some of the later memorial and biographical essays provides a corrective balance to a long-standing emphasis on his fiction.[11] I am in alliance with what I hope remains a consistent turn in James studies, in exploring the complex interpenetration of public and private contexts in his writing. While queer theory, feminism, and gender studies are predominant in these chapters, historical materialism is an equally influential if less visibly present theoretical lens; I seek to frame James with attention to his own time and place while also emphasizing that Fields, Dickinson, and Duras interpret James's writing and his engagements with what we call gender and sexuality according to their own distinct understandings of those terms.

*Henry James's Feminist Afterlives* is a selective study of the ways that James occurs and recurs in the work of women writers whose obvious differences (of genre, of language, of nation, of period) enable them to embody a series of conflicts surrounding women's authorship in distinct times and places. Across separate languages and histories, disparate regional and class identities, two continents, and the span of nearly a century, the image of James that emerges in their interpretations of him and his work serves as a clear, consistent provocation to both twentieth-century and contemporary scholarly versions of James himself. Emily Dickinson and Marguerite Duras both will come to be regarded as paragons of their respective national literatures; both also will be read by twentieth-century feminist scholars as epitomizing "feminine" forms of writing. Each, ambiguously and obliquely, sees Henry James as a predecessor, and understands him as an ally, as she critically examines gender and authorship. This must be significant. In what follows I investigate Fields, Dickinson, and Duras on their own terms, as readers who point us towards new ways of understanding James himself.

## NOTES

1. "If we are to look for a 'class consciousness' in Henry James...perhaps we should look first to women, lesbian and straight, children, and gays as contributors to such a class consciousness...[T]he victimization of these groups is...an essential part of James's social critique of bourgeois values" (Rowe, *Other* 19).
2. See Chap. 2, note 6.
3. See Linda Simon, and the final section of *Henry James in Context* (edited by David McWhirter), for summaries of the history of James studies to 2007 and 2010, respectively. In 1984 Elizabeth Allen famously presents a feminist alternative to existing scholarly models by tracing the ways that James's women characters develop from "simply...sign(s)" to fully-developed figures with agency (10). In the 1990s, Vivian R. Pollak proposes that James identifies with his female characters, and voices an "intelligent empathy with the situation of women who seek to outwit their cultural fates" ("Introduction" 11). Other feminist readings of James's project, understood generally—many although not all predominantly focusing on *The Portrait of a Lady*—include Louise K. Barnett, Heike Fahrenberg, Susan Griffin, Juliet Mitchell, Peggy McCormack, Nancy Roberts, Kaja Silverman, and William Veeder ("The Portrait"). Chris Foss, writing in 1995, is critical of feminist analyses of James from the 1980s and 1990s, arguing that "many of the recent feminist recuperations...ultimately, if unwittingly, serve to repress the persistency of the texts' masculinist vision" (254). See similar objections by Alfred Habegger (*Henry James*) and Martha Banta. More directly relevant feminist discussions will be addressed in-text where appropriate.
4. On James and masculinity, see Kelly Cannon as well as Eric Haralson (*Henry James*), Leland Person, Hugh Stevens (*Henry James*), and Veeder ("The Portrait"). Kimberly Lamm uses Bersani as the basis for one of the few recent queer feminist readings of James; see also Benjamin Bateman and Gert Buelens.
5. The term "homosexual" does not emerge until 1892 (Foucault 42–44). See Elizabeth Reis, Introduction and Chapter 3; Alice Domurat Dreger, Prologue; Anne Fausto-Sterling, Chapters 1 and 9. For context, Gary Williams's introduction to Julia Ward Howe's *The Hermaphrodite* (written in the 1840s, published 2005) is helpful.

INTRODUCTION: ON JAMES, MASTERY, AND TRANSGRESSION    13

6. Alfred Habegger, in 1989's *Henry James and the 'Woman Business'*, views James as appropriating American women's writing; he rejects readings that, in his view, "underestimate James's condescending view of women" and attempt to "rehabilitate James for feminism" (4–5). In a similar vein, see Banta, Foss. Most useful of these "critical" feminist readings is Lyndall Gordon, who presents a nuanced analysis of the ways that, in her view, James sympathetically uses intelligent women, specifically Constance Fenimore Woolson and his cousin Minnie Temple.
7. See *Complete Letters*, of which ten volumes are extant at the date of this writing. Four volumes of selected letters relevant for my purposes were produced by Susan E. Gunter (2000), by Gunter and Stephen H. Jobe (2001), by Philip Horne (1999), and by Michael Anesko (1997).
8. "By light of the misrecollection James is not just reading the words. He is also being represented by them: 'After long exile and martyrdom, [he/she] came to this peace'." Cameron provides both Dante's original Italian as well as her translation of James's version. From the *Paradiso* (10:128–129) the relevant lines are "*ed essa da martiro/ e da essilio venne a questa pace*," which James transcribes as "*Dopo lungo esilio e martiro/ [Venne] a questa pace*" (14–15). See also Victoria Coulson, Chapter 1.
9. There have been many studies of Alice James that touch on her intimacy with Katharine Loring, her literary and intellectual abilities, and her relationship to her second-oldest (and clearly favorite) brother. In addition to Coulson, see Jean Strouse and Ruth Bernard Yeazell. I also rely here on various biographical studies of the James family, including those by Paul Fisher, Gunter (*Alice*), Habegger (*The Father*), R. W. B. Lewis, and Jane Maher.
10. Hayes 49–64.
11. For material culture readings, see Hazel Hutchison, Kendal Johnson, and Thomas Otten. On James's personal writing, see Oliver Herford.

CHAPTER 2

# "Those Who Know": Henry James and Annie Adams Fields

In 1914, near the end of both of their lives, Henry James wrote a brief note to his friend Annie Adams Fields. Although an author in her own right, Fields was best known as the widow of James T. Fields, editor of the *Atlantic Monthly* from 1861 to 1871, and as the center of an American cultural and literary world that revolved around her home, on Charles Street in Boston.[1] Following her husband's death, Fields developed an intimate relationship with Sarah Orne Jewett, which lasted until Jewett died in 1909. In the 1914 note, James refers to "Mrs. Fields," as he nearly always termed her, as one of a small number "of 'those who know,' as Dante says" (July 25, 1914). The phrase suggests his nostalgia for the past, an expatriate's longing for old friends and literary figures from his American youth, which he later will evoke more fully in "Mr. and Mrs. James T. Fields," an essay published shortly after her death in 1915 and primarily focused on his relationship with Annie Fields and their shared social circle, during what he describes as "the golden age" of American letters, in the 1860s and 1870s (*American Essays* 270). James's elegy for writers who felt what he terms "the Puritan whip" (*American Scene* 172)—the moral force of a specifically New England version of secularized, American Calvinist approaches to cultural production and community involvement—is both a lament for that lost sense of purpose and a clear demarcation of his present from their literary past.

Dante had specific personal meaning for both Fields and James. Although she had read his work in Italian, as several members of the group

© The Author(s) 2018
K. Wichelns, *Henry James's Feminist Afterlives*,
American Literature Readings in the 21st Century,
https://doi.org/10.1007/978-3-319-71800-2_2

had not, as a woman Annie Fields had not been part of the "Dante Club," a gathering of literary men including her husband and William Dean Howells that met weekly in the mid-1860s to review Henry Wadsworth Longfellow's 1867 translation of the *Divina Commedia* prior to its publication. She used a line from the *Purgatorio* as the epigraph for her poorly-received, anonymous novel *Asphodel* (1866) in the same period. Rita K. Gollin, a biographer, suggests that the epigraph reveals Annie Fields's sense that she belonged in the club, if only by proxy (13, 47, 52). James's references to Dante imply both transatlantic cultural exchange and also, in his letters and critical writing, a particular individual's emotional and artistic sensitivity. In his essay on the central figure of the period that he elsewhere terms "the Age of Emerson," James cites Emerson's dislike of Dante as proof of his "insensibility"; he hypothesizes that Emerson may have disapproved of Dante's interest in "human perversity" (*American Scene* 179; *American Essays* 73–74, 75).[2] In Chap. 1, I briefly examined Sharon Cameron's analysis of another of James's simultaneously public and private deployments of Dante: in writing of the death of his sister Alice, James makes Dante a vehicle for and means of displacing personal feeling as well as gender specificity.

James's descriptions of Alice suggest his own self-recognition in a woman who is non-heterosexual but otherwise relatively gender-conventional, and who is evoked predominantly through memory. A similar dynamic is clear in a number of James's fourteen extant letters to Annie Fields, and particularly in the note that he writes in response to Jewett's 1909 death. Readers of James have long known of the correspondence, but the bulk of the letters has never been published; therefore, they remain only incompletely and sporadically incorporated into scholarship.[3] In what follows I explore the manuscripts of his letters to Fields, as well as his two known letters to Jewett and relevant selections from her other correspondence. These letters help illuminate the vexing question of James's relationships to women, gender ideals, non-marital and particularly non-heterosexual intimacy, and the period- and class-specific notions of privacy those mores represent. For James, Annie Fields is a literary woman of his own privileged, Anglo-American background—central to the artistic and literary culture of what he terms "old," "disappearing Boston," her two intimate relationships both embodied and functioned outside of the boundaries of marital partnership (*American Scene* 169, 171). Fields becomes, therefore, more than simply an early supporter and old friend—both she and Jewett are fellow-travelers in many senses. In the 1909 letter of condolence,

James evokes what scholars since the 1990s (see Graham; Haralson, *Henry James*; Looby, "John"; Moon; Ohi; Rowe, *Other*; Savoy; Sedgwick; Stevens) have variously explored as the "queerness" that he shares with Fields and Jewett—it is synonymous for him with exile, cultural liminality, and a status as an observer of society. The complex form of personal exile and public observation that we might understand as resulting from a biographical status as a non-marital or non-heterosexual adult, a status that he shares with the older Fields, is built upon upholding and practicing nineteenth-century gender-specific notions of privacy; these are practices that Annie Fields embodies, and that Henry James lauds in the correspondence, in "Mr. and Mrs. James T. Fields," and in the "Boston" chapter of *The American Scene*. Therefore, among other uses, these letters enable us to understand James's descriptions of "queer" or unconventional feminine sexuality with a fuller sense of personal context.

It seems obvious but also important to emphasize that James's regard for the post-Civil War Boston literary milieu Fields represents for him is nostalgic—simultaneous with an ongoing choice to write, and live, as far away as possible. As Peter Fritzsche argues in his study of nostalgia in nineteenth-century Europe and America, "While nostalgia takes the past as its mournful subject, it holds it at arm's length. The virtues of the past are cherished and their passage is lamented, but there is no doubt that they are no longer retrievable. In other words, nostalgia constitutes what it cannot possess and defines itself by its inability to approach its subject, a paradox that is the essence of nostalgia's melancholia" (1595). In a related analysis that emphasizes the resistant possibilities of nostalgia, Elspeth Probyn calls for a critical engagement with narratives of personal history, emphasizing the affective and political value for non-heterosexual subjects of what she terms "queer nostalgia." Nostalgia deployed in this way functions "not as a guarantee of memory but precisely as an errant logic that always goes astray," thereby "unsettling generational and heterosexual orderings" (462, 454, 446).[4]

Using these later ideas with attention to James's historical setting helps to shed light on his correspondence with Annie Fields. His first letter, in 1882, follows Fields's travels in Europe with Jewett, the year after her husband's death. Jewett's epistolary tone to Fields changes from one of friendship, in early 1882, to passionate romantic exchange after their return later in the year. It seems likely that their friendship transformed during this voyage. As Christopher Looby suggests, in the 1880s the same interpersonal dynamics that would have been read as evidence of a non-sexual romantic friendship between two women in the U.S. readily would be understood, in French society, as distinctively lesbian; their time in France together may have made it possible for the women to reconsider their earlier friendship through this lens. Regardless, Henry James saw Fields, and was first introduced to the woman writer whom he later would call the "new center" of her life, in London near the end of this important trip (Looby, "Sexuality" 429–431; James, "Mr. and Mrs. Fields" 278). The shift in their relationship probably was clear to him; if so, it would have reordered his views on Annie Fields and the regard in which he held her and the Boston past that she represented for him. The nostalgia apparent throughout James's correspondence to Fields, which begins in late 1882 (alongside her partnership with Jewett) and lasts until her 1915 death, is "queer" not just because both he and Fields occupy positions outside of heterosexual, marital paradigms: in these letters he strikingly and recurrently uses nostalgia to disrupt clear notions of his own beginnings. James's nostalgia in his letters to Fields is not a form of conscious critical practice by a self-identified queer adult, in the manner Probyn proposes: instead, he performs the profound ambivalence of his decisively expatriate longing for his own origins, as represented by the (pre-new immigrant) Boston of the 1860s as well as by the *Atlantic Monthly* of that period, its authors and editors. His critical relationship to Annie Fields's Boston, as suggested in this correspondence at least, seems both obvious to us (as outside readers), and probably not entirely conscious.

James's lament for the Anglo-American Boston past also announces, and performs, its irretrievability. The form of nostalgia he evinces, while potentially "queer," also is race- and class-specific—and ambivalent on all of these counts. His complex longing for the private, domestic post-Civil War Boston literary and artistic atmosphere that Annie Fields embodies renders her a living representation of the past. James's regard for Fields is enriched by her relationship with Jewett, with whom he shares a mutually critical and supportive artistic kinship: as I will argue, although he is the more authorized interlocutor in his exchanges with Jewett, he is by no means a dominating or even dominant presence, as scholarship that focuses on only one of his two known letters to her tends to imply. Annie Fields's status in James's view as holding stakes in equally but differently significant communities (non-heterosexual or non-marital, Anglo-American, upper-class, Boston, literary) further is informed by James's expectations of her femininity. He assumes that "Mrs. Fields"—although the formal salutation is conventional, James never includes her first name, as he does elsewhere when addressing Jewett and other women writers—values privacy above all else. But she is the widow of a publisher, and she edits and publishes Jewett's letters after her partner's early death in 1909.

James's responses to public expressions of non-heterosexual desire and/or gender-transgressive behavior inform my reading of these letters. Others have discussed thoroughly and at length how Oscar Wilde's 1895 libel trials are a source of simultaneous interest and disgust for James. Although in epistolary writing from that year he speaks sympathetically of the disgraced author, after an 1882 meeting he infamously describes Wilde himself as "an unclean beast" (Horne, *Henry James* 279–280, 133–134). Although years later he would co-sponsor Wilde for membership in London's exclusive Savile Club, he nevertheless insisted that he was "not Wilde's friend" (Salamensky 276; Richard Ellman 179). Yet Wilde has been suggested as a potential source for characters in works as diverse as "The Turn of the Screw," *The Tragic Muse*, "In the Cage," and *The Awkward Age*.[5] Similarly well-traversed scholarly ground covers James's fascination and discomfort with George Sand, as a writer, a woman, and a public figure.[6] He published four extended essays on Sand, more than on any other author. However, throughout he emphasizes a gendered disparity between her "character" and literary talent, which he frames as male, and her romanticism, which he sees as proof of her femininity. In 1877, he states "there is something very liberal and universal in George Sand's genius, as well as very masculine, but our final impression of her always is that she is a woman and a Frenchwoman."[7] He is both intrigued by the interpenetration of Sand's life and art, and appalled by her failure to keep her personal relations private: indeed, in the 1897 essay, James chastises her for not having been "a gentleman" (*European Writers* 712, 749) after she publishes thinly-disguised accounts of her extramarital liaisons. Verena Tarrant, the passive, pretty spiritualist of *The Bostonians* (1886), may have been modeled on Sand's standard romantic heroine—Verena will be drawn into an intimacy with the magnetic, forceful Olive Chancellor. In *The Bostonians*, potential lesbianism—through Olive—is presented in largely negative terms, but the correspondence with Fields suggests that James in fact felt a personal sympathy with a woman (in addition to his sister Alice), of his own class and nationality, whom he at least privately acknowledged to be in a "marriage" with another woman. Significantly, Annie Fields and Alice James shared other characteristics that differentiate them from Oscar Wilde and George Sand, or the fictional character of Olive Chancellor: both women embodied normative gender ideals and practiced a separation between public life and private relationships. In short, these letters may allow us to examine James's depictions of women more generally, homosexuality, and queer or heteronormatively unconventional women in particular as predominantly reflecting class- and racially-specific, nineteenth-century ideas about privacy rather than internalized homophobia or misogyny as conventionally understood. Indeed, he equates privacy with femininity: for James the class- and period-specific femininity Fields practices is structurally central to "a time so much less strident" (*American Essays* 277). Distinct from the modern, 1915 version of womanhood, the nineteenth-century femininity that Annie Fields represents becomes, like Alice James's gravestone, an ambivalently sympathetic other self, simultaneously recognized, eulogized, and displaced.

Annie Fields was born in 1834 and married at age 19 to James T. Fields, seventeen years her senior and a partner in the successful Boston publishing firm of Ticknor and Fields. She would come primarily to influence American cultural life through her letters and personal relationships, and through organizing and managing social events at her home. Rita K. Collin, a biographer, examines what she describes as Annie Fields's "conservative feminism," which emphasized women's individual fulfillment through (heterosexual) marital love, a commitment to service, and the attainment of social authority "without violating cultural norms that required womanly self-subordination" (45–54, ix). As this description suggests, James T. Fields and his young wife were partners who worked closely together from their separate gender-specific sites of authority. Ticknor and Fields purchased the *Atlantic Monthly* in 1859, and Fields took over editorship from James Russell Lowell in 1861; his charming, literary wife was a necessary asset for the editor of an increasingly important New England literary journal. Susan Goodman, in her analysis of the influence of the *Atlantic Monthly* of this early period on notions of American letters, states "if Boston was the hub of the universe, then Fields's house was the hub of the hub…Apart from advising her husband, she created an oasis of civility and fellowship. Her veneration of the arts and artists lent an air of glamour and higher purpose to the commercial aspects of authorship" (56–57). James Fields often deferred to his wife's opinions in seeking out new authors, as well as relying on her social skills as hostess in the important domestic aspects of his business.

For Susan K. Harris, author of *The Cultural Work of the Late Nineteenth-Century Hostess*, Fields was one of a small number of privileged American and British women who served as what she terms cultural "facilitators," a role determined by their gender, class, and racial positions and dependent on their very lack of a "public" presence. As roles for women gradually changed in the closing decades of the nineteenth century, these women would come to occupy more public—although still acceptably gendered— roles. Harris writes that after James Fields's death, "Annie Fields took the skills she learned while entertaining her husband's literary friends and acquaintances into her 'second career' in social welfare in late nineteenth-century Boston." She advocated for women's and children's rights, labor laws, and temperance. However, instead of making speeches or breaking windows, she organized charity fundraising events, opened a string of coffee houses as non-alcoholic public gathering places for working-class Bostonians, helped found Boston University as the first co-educational university in the state, and published extensively on the need for pragmatic social welfare reform (Harris 2–3; Gollin 163–168, 171–188; Roman 75–88).

While I primarily address Fields as James's correspondent, the role she played in her letters to him is of a piece with her larger position as a genteel activist and "community coordinator." This was more than social duty: Annie Fields's position as the private center of the predominantly male world of the *Atlantic Monthly* was based on her own commitment to the project of promoting American letters. She had an abiding belief in the importance of strengthening transatlantic cultural ties, particularly between American and British writers (Harris 13–14).[8] Later, as Jewett's partner, Fields continued this work; she was the organizing figure in a network of relationships, conducted through letters and visits, increasingly made up of women writers, many of whom also were suffrage activists. Both in the first and second halves of her career, as James Fields's and then as Sarah Orne Jewett's partner, Fields "considered it part of her business to record and disseminate information about other people, especially when they were people she considered culturally significant. This is gossip of a high order," serving ideological and cultural rather than strictly personal ends (Harris 115–116, 108). Annie Fields's correspondence with Henry James is an extension of this social role—as a promoter of a specific version of American literary culture, she is writing an increasingly famous author who also is ideally situated for the transatlantic, progressive cultural project that she saw as her life's work.

Henry James moved to Boston in 1864, at age 21, with his parents. His first signed work, "The Story of a Year," appeared in the *Atlantic Monthly* the next year. As James later recounts, James Fields considered him "precociously dismal," and evidently accepted "The Story of a Year" only reluctantly (James, "Mr. and Mrs." 273; Horne, *Henry James* 2). Later, James Fields agreed to publish 1870's "*Compagnons de Voyage*," retitled "Traveling Companions," because Annie thought he should do so (Goodman 58).[9] James Fields hired William Dean Howells as assistant editor at the magazine in 1866. With Annie Fields, Howells would come to champion the young Henry James's writing. Goodman describes Howells's resistance to James Fields's emphasis on publishing work based on its ideological or moral content. When Howells took over the editorship in 1871, he inherited a "Boston magazine"; as editor, he set out to make it truly national, in part by fostering realist and regional writing (Goodman 88–89, 91–93). Even many years later, in "Mr. and Mrs. James T. Fields," Henry James remembers a criticism James Fields—as a member of his father's social circle, Fields was speaking from a position of paternal as well as literary authority—made of his early work. The comment, relayed long ago by Howells, still rankles: "I doubt whether I wince at this hour any less than I winced on the spot at hearing it quoted [from James Fields] that such a strain of pessimism in the would-be picture of life had an odd, even a ridiculous air, on the part of an author with his mother's milk scarce yet dry on his lips" (*American Essays* 272–273). In the context of James's essay, this inclusion seems like, and is, self-deprecation. At the same time, both the original comment and the fact that James returns to it, nearly fifty years later, suggest that he understood his own early writing to have served as a lightning rod for the generational conflict between ideas of American literature that characterized the *Atlantic Monthly* in the late 1860s and 1870s. Particularly when reading the later correspondence with Annie Fields, it seems clear that the younger James felt a connection with her that he did not necessarily have with her older husband, regardless of James Fields's greater importance. Henry James, writing in 1915, knows that James Fields merely "suffered him" (*American Essays* 273); by contrast, Annie Fields, and William Dean Howells, got him published.

Although he would return for sporadic visits, James left Massachusetts, and the U.S., permanently in 1875. The chapter of 1907's *The American Scene* devoted to the city was first published separately in March 1906; Henry James, then in his sixties, eulogizes "the disappearing Boston" of his youth, represented by Annie Fields's home at 148 Charles Street. Visiting again after many years in Europe, the older James feels the presence of the "Charles Street ghosts": the authors and artists whom he had met in the Fields's drawing room. He laments the lost greatness of these figures, arguing that "The Age of Emerson," with its moral and activist principles, was produced by the Puritan legacy of New England and centered in the "temple" of the Fields's home. In 1915, in "Mr. and Mrs. James T. Fields," he again evokes the lost (Anglo-American) spiritual and artistic energy of the city he knew as a young man. Still, at 148 Charles Street, Annie Fields serves as a respite and a reminder. Her house is "the little ark of the modern deluge," the "waterside museum" (*American Scene* 176–178; *American Essays* 267). James is himself, of course, at the vanguard of the generation of writers, including and championed by his friend Howells, who helped make "The Age of Emerson" part of the past—his nostalgia is simultaneously public performance ("Mr. and Mrs. James T. Fields" is elegiac) and private ambivalence for the changes in ideas of domesticity, privacy, womanhood, manhood, literature, and "Americanness" that he foregrounds throughout his literary corpus.

In 1965, Helen Howe—the daughter of Fields's literary executor, M. A. De Wolfe Howe—recalls her father presenting the Fields/Jewett union as James's model for the Verena Tarrant/Olive Chancellor relationship in *The Bostonians* (83). Christoph Irmscher, in 2007, concurs: James was intimately acquainted with two "Boston marriages," that of Alice James and Katharine Loring, and Fields and Jewett's. Generally understood as one of James's two most "political" novels, a categorization that it shares with *The Princess Casamassima* (published the same year), *The Bostonians* both caricatures and sympathizes with the turn-of-the-century suffrage campaigners represented by Olive Chancellor and her circle. In her classic provocation *The Resisting Reader*, Judith Fetterley opens her analysis of the novel with a series of reviews from important male scholars. Although she still sees James effectively as one of them—for her, he engages in the "more subtle sexism" of romanticizing the pain of unrequited desire—she also acknowledges that "in the character of Olive, James has grasped, regardless of whether he knew it or not and regardless of what he felt about it, the central elements of a radical feminism" (108, 152). Terry Castle, in *The Apparitional Lesbian*, goes further, taking on a long tradition of earlier readers who assert that the story isn't about lesbianism. Olive is "English and American literature's first tragic lesbian heroine," but "James, the master of multivalence, does nothing to suppress" misogynist and homophobic readings of the story (171, 177).[10] More recently, a number of scholars have either criticized James for his caricatures of presumed lesbians and women's rights activists, or overemphasized his sympathy for non-normative women, in an attempt to clearly define the novel's—and therefore, it seems, James's own—views on these topics. In the wake of Castle and others, we no longer question Olive's lesbianism. Nevertheless, analysis of James's fictional depiction of a "Boston marriage" roughly presents two contradictory possibilities: either James dislikes lesbians and opposes women's rights; or, alternately, he offers a potentially revolutionary analysis of "queer," late nineteenth-century women's lives. As one example of the latter trend, Kathleen McColley argues that *The Bostonians* inscribes feminine "homoerotic empowerment" (151). I think McColley goes too far here—but seeing James's ambivalence towards Olive as evidence that he is anti-lesbian also requires us to ignore important elements of the text.

Some of the readings that break roughly along one of the two lines I've traced are nuanced and insightful. For example, Valerie Fulton argues that in *The Bostonians* James presents marriage as the only realistic option for feminine security and fulfillment; his privileged position in the canon means that his preoccupation with the question of marriage has disproportionately influenced our views of nineteenth-century womanhood, when other writers (including Jewett) depict single women finding fulfillment on their own terms. Fulton also emphasizes that we should not universalize James's critique, as he limits his analysis to predominant Boston-area groups rather than to women's rights activism more broadly. As a counter to this perspective, Stephanie P. Browner explores women doctors in both *The Bostonians* and Jewett's *A Country Doctor* (1884), and suggests that Dr. Mary Prance, in James's novel, is intended as a feminist alternative to the blinkered provincialism evinced by Olive Chancellor and Miss Birdseye. In his depiction of Dr. Prance, "James refuses to assuage fears that medicine will masculinize women...[A]s the only stern realist in the novel [Prance] is a substantial presence, and James valorizes her judgments as the no-nonsense opinion of a practical-minded medical scientist" (166). Again, although both Fulton and Browner present compelling arguments, the choice between two antithetical readings of the novel lurks in the background. Either James is progressively sympathetic to non-normative/feminist women, or he is a reactionary, opposed to their ideas and behavior in principle.

I'd like to acknowledge but sidestep this ongoing debate about characters in *The Bostonians* and their implications for James's views, because a focus on defining the author's opinions distracts us from the textual work done in the novel itself. The unresolved ambivalence towards nonnormative women expressed in *The Bostonians* seems to me the source of its potentially feminist politics: women like Olive Chancellor and Dr. Prance serve as consistent lynchpins, around which conventional readerly expectations (of genre, of character, of gender, of morality, and so on) are relentlessly turned on their head. Alongside David Van Leer, who suggests that the story stages the linguistic and emotional missed encounters resulting from a confrontation between nineteenth-century sexual mores and an emerging, modern set of rules ("A World" 108), I argue that *The Bostonians* offers a structural analysis more all-encompassing than many recent readers allow. There are no clear feminist heroes in the novel, as each female character is actively complicit in the society in which she lives: Miss Birdseye is out-of-touch, Olive Chancellor is single-minded and controlling, and Verena Tarrant can't or won't think for herself. The Boston feminists James examines suffer from ideological blind spots as profound, tragic, and destructive as the opposing position represented by Basil Ransom, the novel's Southern phallocrat—who succeeds in stealing Verena from Olive's arms in order to lock her forever behind the doors of a traditional marriage. Neither Basil nor Olive is the right choice, but Verena can't see a way out of choosing one or the other. In both Verena and Olive, the novel stages an irreducible conflict between late nineteenth-century (women's) subjectivity and the pre-Industrial, class-specific gender expectations that continue to determine their, and their society's, ideas of what women can expect from life. James consistently portrays women as subjects whose impossibly contradictory imperatives—in a capitalist society that expects them to conform to outdated gender mores while valorizing individual self-determination—render them uniquely capable of engaging critically with the dynamics of *fin-de-siècle* culture, if only they are willing to risk everything of worth to them by doing so. This, rather than the author's personal views, renders *The Bostonians* open to feminist analysis.

Moreover, our understanding of the ambivalence towards non-normative, feminist, and/or lesbian women that is apparent in *The Bostonians* is assisted by an examination of James's relationships with "queer" feminists of his transatlantic circle of friends and acquaintances, including Annie Adams Fields and Sarah Orne Jewett. Conventional wisdom on the novel has colored the limited scholarship on his correspondences with both women. Put another way, the lack of attention to his friendships with non-heteronormative women has distorted our understandings of his work, and *The Bostonians* in particular. Simultaneously fascinated with the struggles of women caught within the snares of their impossible positions; and uncomfortable with those who defy the imperative of feminine selflessness (Olive Chancellor, George Sand, Emmeline Pankhurst), James often seems most sympathetic to a nineteenth-century version of womanhood consistent with Annie Fields's particular incarnation of feminism, in which a belief in women's essential difference from men—their greater spirituality, their closer ties to domestic life, their removal from the grubby public stages of politics and commerce—is seen as the foundation for their critically necessary role, as society's conscience. At the same time, as Browner argues, James consistently portrays alternative versions of womanhood, through peripheral figures such as Dr. Prance in *The Bostonians* (or Madame Prest from *The Aspern Papers*, see Chap. 5), who refuse the terms of this dynamic. In short, in his work he simultaneously points to the crux of late nineteenth-century conflicts surrounding appropriate womanhood, and also occasionally ruptures the terms of that conversation.

The arc of the later letters to Fields suggests that she becomes for James a keystone and representative of the Boston, Anglo-American literary milieu he'd left behind, one centrally determined by a specific incarnation of upper middle-class, white feminine privacy. If James's regard for Annie Fields indeed helps us to read *The Bostonians*, Olive Chancellor may be tragic not because of her women's rights activism or probable lesbianism, but because there is no clear separation between her public and private personas—and she lives in a society that destroys women who fail to conceal their true selves. By the conclusion of the novel James upends the conventional marriage plot he's constructed for his readers, in all of its heteronormative monstrosity. The climactic final scene, in which Verena gets her Ransom, occurs in an important Boston auditorium of the era, the Music Hall. Although Olive has arranged for her to speak, Verena instead will leave with Ransom, disappear from public life, and, effectively, never speak again. James's transgression of genre expectations is a perversion of form that reveals the deeper perversity of the marriage imperative itself, for young women like Verena. As Ransom hides Verena under her own cloak to escort her out "with muscular force," the passive young woman unexpectedly shrieks Olive's name—but her potential lesbian savior (whom she's just betrayed) now is standing in front of "the great public" in the sudden silence of the hall. James leaves it open to us to decide whether the formerly unruly crowd has become quiet because it realizes what is happening, or because it perceives Olive's move towards the stage as a signal that the event finally is underway. Many readers focus on Verena's obvious tragedy—once outside with Ransom, she declares "Ah, now I am glad!" but then is in tears, and James closes with the damning aside that "these were not the last she was destined to shed." But Olive's private heartbreak is marked in the text only by the public embarrassment caused by Verena's failure to appear as promised. Criticized by the acerbic Mrs. Farrinder for the delay ("'Well, Miss Chancellor,' said that more successful woman, 'If this is the way you're going to reinstate our sex!'"), Olive responds "as if Mrs. Farrinder's words had been a lash," and rushes to take the stage in Verena's place. Her sole comment, in this final section, is about public shame; the crowd expects Verena, so "I will be hissed and hooted and insulted!" It seems that only her romantic adversary recognizes Olive's lonely heroism at this moment. "Ransom, palpitating with his victory, felt now a little sorry for her, and was relieved to know that, even when exasperated, a Boston audience is not ungenerous" (431–433). This uncharacteristic concern for Olive is the means by which Ranson displaces his own guilt; it takes a form that both expresses and destabilizes his retrograde (for James, "Southern") views about gender. A gentleman like Ransom is chivalrous towards ladies, and gracious in victory; here, he's chivalrous in the wrong way, rather too late, and towards the wrong lady. Instead of recognizing his own responsibility for Olive's pain, he projects it onto the overdetermined signifier of the Boston audience, and then leaves it behind as the doors close. Olive is the only real "gentleman" here, in the fact that she faces the music in the famous hall—James emphasizes the roar of the impatient crowd, then its attentive hush as Olive takes the stage. At the end Boston, that pit of unruly radicals, is more chivalrous towards both women than Ransom, with his Southern manners, will ever be. Castle argues that James is telling us that we're used to the Verenas of the world being the heroines of novels, but in fact Olive is the protagonist of this one (170–179). Nevertheless, as Castle also acknowledges, Olive is "tragic"—and her tragedy is determined by her refusal of the private (heterosexual) life that Verena has "chosen." In a microcosmic reversal of the predominant drama of the American nineteenth century, Olive supports lost causes, and the representative of the South takes off with his human prize. The conflict that this final scene suggests about the period's brutal, contradictory imperatives for women is at the crux of James's simultaneous identification and discomfort with Fields and Jewett. James's later representations from *The American Scene* and "Mr. and Mrs. James T. Fields" of the ethnically homogenous, regional U.S. culture in which he had lived as a young man are a response both to Boston's Puritan, patriarchal literary past and—through Fields and the phenomenon of the "Boston marriage" specifically—its queer feminine (and first-wave feminist) present. In his letters to Fields, his feeling for both of these Bostons is simultaneously marked by identification and avoidance. Nevertheless, it is clear both from the letters and from his depiction in "Mr. and Mrs. James T. Fields" that Annie embodies an ideal of genteel, literate, private femininity that he associates with the Boston of his youth. That version of femininity, in this case, also happens to be queer and feminist—unlike Olive Chancellor, though, Annie Fields avoided putting herself at center stage, even in her "private" writing.[11]

Although she was only eleven years older than James, Fields's marriage had effectively rendered her of his parents' generation, and his early letters to her—although written during the first years of her "Boston marriage" with Jewett—still reflect a sense of disparate authority. Grateful for her advocacy and also fond of her personally, James's tone is that of an emerging male author, conscious of his reliance on family connections as he addresses the influential widow of an important man. She seems still to figure as a private extension of the public house of Ticknor and Fields, the role in which James had presented her in earlier postscripts tacked on to business letters written to James Fields on July 25 and November 15, 1870 (*Complete* 1855–1872 Vol. 2 368, 381–382). Years later, when he is much more famous, James still evokes this sense of a generational and authoritative disparity in writing "Mrs. Fields"; this seems one means by which he constructs and manages his nostalgic regard for the Bostonian past that she represents.

James began writing Annie Fields, as far as we know, on September 3, 1882.[12] Again, her husband had died in late April, 1881; Fields returned from a long trip to Europe with Jewett, and probably found this first extant note from James awaiting her in Boston. In it, James apologizes for not having had time to see her and "Miss Jewett" a second time, as evidently he'd promised to do, before their voyage home; he closes with a discussion of the weather. In another expression of regret dated June 15 of the following year, this time at declining an invitation sent during one of his rare trips to the U.S., James pleads overwork and family illness as an excuse. These brief notes are not intimate; they are comprised of twenty-one (two pages of notepaper) and thirty-nine (four pages) handwritten lines respectively. The third extant note, written nearly a decade later in 1892, is longer (fifty lines), and marked by an increase in personal content. Instead of discussing the weather in London, as he had in 1882, he uses affective descriptors to situate himself both geographically and historically, in "this hurrying age and roaring place." James expresses his sense of inadequacy when faced with the task of memorializing the recently-deceased James Russell Lowell; he shares his concerns about a mutual friend, from whom he's not heard in some time. Word choices surrounding feelings and impressions are more expressive, less polite and standard ("embarrassed," "stammering," "affectionate," "meagre," "dreadfully," "tragic," and so on; as opposed to "grateful," "regrets," "thanks"). A greater degree of closeness also is suggested in the closing, which for the first time is scribbled vertically at the margins of prior pages—this device, implying both a comfortable informality and a desire to say more, will mark five of the ten remaining letters for which we have complete manuscripts.[13] "Are not you and Miss Jewett coming once more to England? I should be delighted to see you, and I am dear Mrs. Fields yours and hers most faithfully..." (3, 1). This note evokes a conversation between friends, but the change in tone from the first letters also likely reflects the fact that in the decade between James has published some of his best-received mid-period fiction, including *The Portrait of a Lady* (serialized 1880–81) and *The Aspern Papers* (1888); he was establishing himself as a formidable literary critic by following *Hawthorne* (1879) with *The Art of Fiction* (1884). A celebrity in London, he writes to Annie Fields, the Boston promoter of transatlantic literary and artistic exchange, with a greater sense of his own authority.

A series of four letters surrounds Fields's September 1898 visit, with Jewett, to Lamb House, James's home in Rye, Sussex. James had moved there from London the previous year, and the women were taking their second trip to England together. While these notes mainly discuss practical details of the trip, his responses suggest the particular form of nostalgic regard in which James holds Fields. The personal meeting, far from the crowds of London and the buffer of other friends, was her idea. James's first two responses are full of apologies; he regrets that he cannot travel to London to see them. Yet he writes, "couldn't you, couldn't you both, come down here and spend the afternoon and the night? There is a lovely train at 11 from Charing C. which brings you to luncheon at 1.30—and a perfect one to take you back at 9.38 the next a.m.—and I am but 5 minutes from the station" (August 20, 1898; 3, 4). On September 5, he reminds her: "the 11 a.m. from Charing C. to Rye is a super-excellent train in spite of your having to change at <u>Ashford</u> at about 12.30, and have a wait there of 25 minutes...The <u>4.53</u> back returns you to Charing C. at 7.39" (5, 6, 7).[14] The third 1898 letter, sent on the day before their arrival, begins "Only a word to remind you with what pride and joy I expect you tomorrow"; again, he provides the specifics of the train schedule (September 12, 1898; 1–4). The detailed reminders seem excessive, even in light of late nineteenth-century gender expectations. James knows that Fields is an experienced international traveler, quite capable of finding her way in unfamiliar circumstances by train.[15] Harris suggests that shifts in stylistic mores for personal correspondence during the late Victorian era result from technological developments—the introduction of fast, reliable postal services and train systems shortened both the real and imagined distances between friends (54–55). As the sections from the 1898 letters quoted above reveal, James deploys informal constructions; words are shortened or indicated by the use of an initial letter or a symbol. Notes are sent the day before a visit, with full expectation that they will arrive before Fields has departed. Although James's style in the 1898 letters reflects the changes Harris indicates, the content evokes an earlier era: the two-hour train ride from London to Sussex becomes a monumental journey. James's anxious tone jars with the fact that he is hosting a well-traveled American woman, stopping by with her female partner for a visit, on their way back from another trip around the continent.[16] While it is possible that the period's, and his own, conservative notions of male hospitality towards women leads James to emphasize the burden she and Jewett are undertaking, these letters suggest that any social fiction is overladen with a corresponding affective truth. While James seems genuinely pleased to see her, Annie Fields's presence in Rye also represents a profound form of cognitive, temporal, and emotional dissonance.

Another development in the 1898 letters is that James now sends regards to Jewett as well, even when she has not directly been referenced in a letter's content. James was introduced to Jewett through Fields, but as he repeatedly expresses, he greatly admires her work. Writing friend Mary Ward, also in 1898, James urges her to "Read, if you haven't, Miss Jewett's *Country of the Pointed Firs* (I will send it you if you possess it not) for the pleasure of something truly exquisite" (Horne, *Henry James* 308). His allusions to Jewett in the 1898 letters to Fields suggest that his personal acknowledgment of Jewett's status in her life is separate from this form of professional or artistic respect—his expressed regards for Jewett, in these letters, are those for the spouse of a friend.[17] It seems clear that he sees the women's relationship as a marital union.

In these early notes, his references to Jewett are formal. "It is here beautifully fine—after these last wicked days—and I send you, on your way, a Godspeed from your and Miss Jewett's very truly, Henry James" (September 3, 1882; 1). However, on August 20, 1898, he writes "You and Miss Jewett are delightful to hear from" (1). It is quite unlikely that James received a dually-authored note from both women, as the rest of the correspondence is exclusively with Annie Fields; both women were prolific letter-writers with rich and independent epistolary relationships. Jewett, when corresponding with James, did so on her own. By 1898, James seems to regard the women as a permanent unit: he addresses Jewett primarily through Fields, assuming that she speaks for them both and that their lives are intertwined.

James's recognition is specific to the relationship itself. Even quite passionate feminine intimacies would not have been understood as *prima facie* sexual during the period—at least in Anglo-American circles, as Looby reminds us. To open the section devoted to the nineteenth century in *Surpassing the Love of Men*, her classic study of women's "romantic friendships," Lillian Faderman turns to an 1811 libel case brought by two mistresses of a girls' boarding school against the grandmother of one of their students. The case resembles the Oscar Wilde trials late in the century, in that the court was asked to determine whether or not Marianne Woods and Jane Pirie indeed were in a sexual relationship, as alleged. Despite evidence of the women's romantic and probably sexual attachment, the case demonstrates the period's investment in pseudoscientific proofs of (white) women's asexuality. The justices found for Woods and Pirie, against the student and her grandmother, in large part because they were unable to comprehend the possibility that upper-class British women had sexual impulses, much less actual lesbian sex. Without men present, the court concluded, sexual intercourse could not happen, and indeed even desire itself was absent. One result of the doctrine of women's asexuality was a comparative freedom granted to their romantic lives, as long as no men were involved.[18] As twenty-first century readers encountering Fields and Jewett—and, indeed, Emily Dickinson's relationships with women, which I will discuss in Chap. 3—we need to recognize that even quite passionate "romantic friendship" is not in itself evidence of a sexual relationship. Faced with unreliable forms of birth control, comparatively primitive practices of obstetrics and gynecology, and high maternal mortality rates as well as their own internalized shame, many would have repressed any form of sexual desire, considered unnatural in (white) women in any case. Even if they recognized the potentially erotic nature of their passionate intimacies with other women—a big "if"—an entire hegemonic apparatus was geared towards keeping them from acting on those desires.

At the same time, as Susan Koppelman suggests, we seem to have no difficulty in seeing heterosexuality everywhere, in nineteenth-century writing: we assume that it is a factor in nearly every encounter between men and women. Why then are we so hesitant to see what often were more obviously romantic, passionate relationships between women for what they are?[19] Representations of the relationship between Fields and Jewett indicate that its libidinal nature was recognized as such, by those around them. Henry James is certainly not the only one of their contemporaries to acknowledge the women's union—others were more obviously ambivalent. In her published edition of Jewett's letters, Fields edited out approximately "four-fifths" of the couple's pet names for each other, partly due to advice from her friend and literary executor, M. A. De Wolfe Howe, who feared people "reading them wrong." Yet after Fields's death, in *Memories of a Hostess*, De Wolfe Howe terms the women's relationship a "union— there was no truer word for it" (Helen Howe 84; Gollin 274–277; M. A. De Wolfe Howe 282). Fields's own conservative relationship to ideals of domesticity and privacy is well-documented, so she may have engaged in these sorts of edits regardless of De Wolfe Howe's advice. The unpublished manuscripts of Jewett's letters to Fields provide a different account of the relationship. Particularly during the first flush of their romance, in 1882–83, Jewett's unedited notes are full of pet names, child-like wordplay, and a regular pose of erotic naughtiness. In a December 1882 letter, Jewett writes, "Good night my darling my darling. I wish I could get hold of you, but Pin [Jewett's own pet name, in the couple's correspondence] to be very good." A June 5, 1883 note rejoices, "I will be with you tomorrow—your dear birthday. How I am looking forward to Thursday evening!...I am tired of writing things. I want now to paint things and drive things. And *kiss* things!" (1, 1).[20] However fully conscious we may be of the alienness of nineteenth-century ideas about women's desire, it would take a very determined reader indeed to interpret these and other notes as evidence of a non-sexual friendship.

James had insider's access to the dynamics of this particular "Boston marriage" both because of his friendship with Annie Fields, and because Sarah Orne Jewett was close with Katharine Loring, his sister Alice's partner. Loring and Jewett corresponded, and saw each other regularly; Jewett left Loring several meaningful items in her will, to be delivered by Fields. Moreover, William Dean Howells had a house on Kittery Point, Maine, less than fifteen miles away from Jewett's home in South Berwick; he visited often when she was there. In 1919, a decade after Jewett's death, Howells terms her "my dear friend"—he tells her sister Mary that he was brought to both laughter and tears, rereading a box of Jewett's manuscripts. James visited Jewett in South Berwick himself in 1905, during his last visit to the U.S.; he would have made a significant detour to see the ailing Jewett, alone, before Howells arrived to join him (Howells, *Selected* Vol. 6 146–147).

Scholarship on James's relationship to Jewett and her work has been disproportionately influenced by one letter, long the only published part of their correspondence: his much-discussed criticism of *The Tory Lover* (1901). Taken out of context as it necessarily has been, this letter does not allow us to see James's and Jewett's shared respect for each other—and this lamentable limitation on our scholarly resources has further been complicated by a lack of general access to the Fields letters. In the 1901 letter, appalled by Jewett's turn to the newly-fashionable genre of "historic fiction," James famously urges her to "go back to the dear *Country of the Pointed Firs*, *come* back to the palpable present *intimate* that throbs responsive, & that wants, misses, needs you, God knows, & that suffers woefully in your absence" (1). Framing his response to Jewett's work solely through this letter, we understandably have missed James's emphasis: he objects to Jewett's choice of genre, not her writing as a whole. Recurrent elements in this 1901 critique reflect a shared sympathy and respect established in personal visits in 1882, 1898, and 1905—as well as an earlier known letter in 1899. As James writes in 1901, "it would take me some time to disembroil the tangle of saying to you at once how I appreciate the charming touch, tact & taste of this ingenious exercise, and how little I am in sympathy with experiments of its general (to my sense) misguided stamp." Later: "the 'historic' novel is, for me, condemned, even in cases of labour as delicate as yours" (Horne 359–360). The various qualifiers would seem simply polite, if this were the only letter we had. Fortunately, however, we do have more to go on. In addition to the other extant letter to Jewett, from 1899, and his references to Jewett in the unpublished Fields correspondence, in a 1909 letter to Howells James describes writing to Jewett "with great benevolence not long before her death"—that letter and at least one other for which strong secondary evidence exists have not been located.[21] Armed with evidence of a more extensive correspondence, we grasp not only how passionately James disliked *The Tory Lover*, but also why: appreciative of *The Country of the Pointed Firs* and the related volume *The Queen's Twin and Other Stories*, and an advocate of realism, James saw Jewett's "historic novel" as a betrayal of her voice. Epistolary context suggests that one of James's favorite American authors was following what was, in his view, the very worst of commercial trends.

Although James was the more established and celebrated author, his age difference with Jewett was slight. The power differential we might initially expect is complicated by Jewett's "marriage" to an influential figure in Boston (and therefore American) publishing circles. Following the women's 1898 visit to Lamb House, James seems to regard Jewett as a friend in her own right, although not one as close as Fields or, say, Howells. In 1901, sharing his objections to *The Tory Lover*, James tells her that, as a fellow "craftsman and woman of genius," he owes her honesty, not "the mere twaddle of graciousness" (Horne, *Henry James* 36). Indeed he *was* merely polite, or rather simply silent, about Fields's own fiction. His 1899 letter to Jewett evinces an entirely different kind of regard. Opening, he reminds her of her visit to him a year before: "I sit in one of the little rooms you wot of, on Christmas eve, & I thank you very kindly indeed, very rejoicingly, for the precious 'Queen's Twin'," a collection published earlier that year. After an evocative and intimate description of his surroundings—one wordsmith writing another—he praises the stories themselves. "I feel too much about them. *No one*, at any rate, I firmly believe, squeezes more of the whole fragrance out of your exquisite work than I do. The sense & the sound, the colour & the taste, the meaning of every stroke & the felicity of every—felicity: these things I am at home in as in the very lap of the Muse." After exploring the specific details of a couple of the stories (which, as every writer of fiction knows, marks someone who indeed has read the work carefully), he exhorts her to continue in the same vein. "Don't intermit—don't languish—don't *not* do anything that ever occurs to you: for I desire & require you with the revolving season. I wish I had something, myself, to send you," he writes, before describing his current projects (Horne 332–333; emphasis original). These and other lines suggest that James writes to Jewett as one author to another, whose work and opinions he values. Later, when she takes him up on the encouragement to "do anything that ever occurs to you" and sends him a copy of *The Tory Lover*, he does not hesitate to say that he thinks she is headed down the wrong artistic path. In keeping with the mutuality of this 1899 letter, while Jewett took his negative response to *The Tory Lover* to heart, she also pushed back against it.

Although we have no letters from Jewett to James himself surrounding his 1905 visit to Maine,[22] a note she sent Howells beforehand helps trace his itinerary. "My dear friend, please, please come! The miserable thought of your stopping at the Car Barn is not to be borne. You shall be driven to an express train, and then take the last trolley home from Kittery Junction if you must save time. To have you and Mr. James together will be such a delight and make me sure of the future of American Literature. (I speak as the author of *When Knighthood was in Flower* to the holder of many Degrees.)" (Jewett, Letter to Howells 1). This note makes it clear that at some point in his 1905 visit to the U.S., Jewett had James to herself; Howells then met them at her house in South Berwick to escort James to his own home in Kittery Point. The playful closing remark suggests the nature of her response to James's objections to *The Tory Lover*, which

Howells shared and presumably also had communicated to her. Jewett's reference is to an 1898 historical novel by Charles Major, another "historic fiction," but one that would inspire a play and several film adaptations. Here, she jokingly claims authorship of a commercially-successful work that Howells knows she did not write, and by that means expresses an implicit resistance to his judgment about her own work in the same genre. This is not the only indication in her letters that she stood by *The Tory Lover* despite the fact that two powerful (male) friends disliked it. In March, 1903, to Annie Fields, she wrote:

> What do you think I read yesterday but a good piece of *The Tory Lover*! You know how long it takes before you can sit down to a book of your own with any detachment—as if somebody else had written it? I have taken it up now and then and found that it only worried me but yesterday was different—it seemed quite new and whole! and I really was delighted with my piece of work. I have never succeeded in doing anything except the *Pointed Firs* that comes anywhere near it—my conscience upholds this happy belief, and whether it was a hundred years ago or not, is apart from the question altogether…The book of Ruth was…an historical novel in its day. (1)

The closing biblical reference is a direct allusion to James's primary objection in the 1901 letter, with which Fields must have been familiar. Drawing a parallel between *The Tory Lover* and the Book of Ruth, Jewett defends her novel as another in a long series of literary representations of women's bonds, perhaps evoking this "historic" tradition as a truer alternative to the "realist" fiction championed by James and Howells. The female writer from backwater Maine figures herself, consciously or no, as a misunderstood outsider. In this analogy, James becomes another Boaz, to whom her approach seems awkward and inexplicable. But the connection to Ruth implies that Jewett is willing to face humiliation in service to an important (feminine) cause: despite its title, the hero of *The Tory Lover* undeniably is Mary Hamilton, a fervent young American who saves the rather boring "Tory," Roger Wallingford, by traveling with his mother to the enemy territory of England to fight for his release. The bulk of the novel, like the Book of Ruth, focuses on the close and loving relationship between these two women, of different ages and political sympathies.

The final 1898 letter James wrote to Fields, sent to arrive with the women's return to the U.S., demonstrates that Jewett may have underestimated his ability to sympathize with a position so different from his own. James reflects "on the patience and courage (whereat I am still stupefied,) in which you emulated each other and in which my sympathy with your fatigue, when I surrendered you to the final Hastings horde, emulated you both" (September 23, 1898; 1–2). The description evokes an ongoing focus in James's writing, particularly from this period and afterwards, on public privacy, and the ability of anonymous, indifferent urban crowds unknowingly to witness and even participate in significant private events ("In the Cage," 1898; "The Beast in the Jungle," 1903; *The Ambassadors*, 1903; as well as *The Bostonians*). In addition to emphasizing the burden they've undertaken to see him, his allusion to the women's symbiotic "patience and courage" also paints Jewett and Fields as an intimate pair. He ends by saying, "I wave my hat again to Miss Jewett and I am hers and yours very constantly" (4, 1). This is the first time Jewett has preceded Fields, in James's closing formula; and the warmer, personal note suggests that a deeper level of friendship, which includes both women, has been reached.

The final 1898 letter also provides insights into the ways that James constructs Fields as a representation of the Boston past. "It was a delightful general reminder and re-consecration to see you. I am so glad this is going to Charles St., 'round which memory clings" (4). The phrasing reflects his expectations of her class-specific femininity, as Annie Fields becomes an extension of her domestic space. Yet an analysis of this letter prefaced on the assumption that James's notion of female privacy is uncritically conventional is undermined by the fact that here he renders domestic womanhood central, rather than peripheral, to the true work of a society. For James, in this note and later in "Mr. and Mrs. James T. Fields," Fields's home is the locus of a community of like-minded artists and writers whose public lives—and publications—serve predominantly as concrete evidence of the existence of the community itself. James regards that (lost) environment in near-religious terms: seeing her, and writing Charles Street, is a "re-consecration." At the same time, this particular line, in a letter that is much more relaxed and assured in tone than those that immediately preceded the women's visit, also suggests that James may be glad to send this note to Charles Street because that means Annie Fields is back in Boston. With her safe departure, his present-tense life in England no longer is forced into uncanny coexistence with his American past. As Probyn writes in her discussion of the temporal "disordering" of nostalgia: "Far from being reassuring, the retrieval of the past into the present is profoundly dislocating, disorienting. Bringing forth beginnings results in the loss of bearings" (456).

The period 1900–1909 sees four extant letters from James to Fields. The first, dated October 24, 1900, is longer than earlier notes (six pages of his larger, post-1898 stationery, with additional vertical writing on the final four), perhaps because a busy and increasingly well-known James feels guilty for allowing a lapse in the correspondence. This is another iteration of an emerging pattern, whereby Annie Fields makes efforts to extend the relationship; James responds with evidently heartfelt warmth and gratitude, and then retreats for a time until she reaches out to him again. His apologies in this particular case are effusive, even read in the context of turn-of-the-century epistolary conventions or James's letters in particular: he spends nearly half of the six-page October, 1900 note in detailed self-recrimination. In answer to Fields's inquiry about a rumor that he may be returning permanently to the U.S., James states that his tenure in England will be permanent. "It's embarrassing, ungracious, rude almost, to be saying it, but I am not returning to my native land to live or ceasing to live in this snug corner of this one...Such is the shy, the stammering truth—which didn't sound invidious when one simply took it for granted" (4). Fred Kaplan reads this letter for its insights into James's relationship to questions of nationality and publicity (471). I would like, alternately, to focus on its place within the arc of the correspondence with Fields: the combination of assertion and apology which so marks this letter, and the correspondence more generally, suggests the particular form of complex nostalgia in which James holds both Fields and the Boston literary and cultural past that she embodies for him.

Another element of the October, 1900 letter helps us to understand James's particular response to Jewett and her work, further illuminating the 1899 and 1901 letters sent to Jewett herself. Most of an extended closing greeting to Jewett, who otherwise is unmentioned, is scrawled vertically over the last four pages of the letter, in reverse order. "If Miss Jewett is with you kindly commend me to her most productive consciousness. She helps me much to live, but I require stoking. I wish I could see her approach with a fresh armload of fuel. I send her my love, in short, as, if I were writing to her, I shld. send it to you, and I am, dear Mrs. Fields, yours very constantly (6, 5, 4, 3). This is the third time James has requested more work from Jewett; and this time he is, more assertively, doing so via Fields. The postscript seems to support my reading that James sees Jewett as a close artistic ally. Of course, it also is evidence of his recognition that the two women are a marital couple—"love" can, and should, be sent to one via the other. Indeed, as revealed in later letters, particularly the 1909 note sent after Jewett's death (as well as in 1915's "Mr. and Mrs. James T. Fields") James repeatedly uses his own appreciation of Jewett's writing—a gift that they share but which in his view, it seems, also serves to differentiate them both from Annie Fields herself—as a means of expressing private recognition of the women's romantic intimacy. The first form of recognition is public, or in the epistolary instances could be made public without violating Fields and Jewett's privacy, but that does not render it less important to him than the second. James here engages in a typical gesture, whereby he intimately uses his public persona—the writer expressing regards to another, whose work he values—to convey a private acknowledgment, in this case of the two women's coupled status. Framing his letters to Jewett in light of the romantic partnership they validate—not just the fellow (female) author they acknowledge—provides a more complete perspective on James's responses to Jewett and her work.

James sends two brief notes, focused on the practical details of a reunion, to Annie Fields during an extended visit to the U.S. in 1904–1905, his first return in twenty years. As far as we know he does not write again until 1909, but a long letter, dated August 25, is the most revelatory of the correspondence. It was sent from Lamb House, in response to a letter from Fields, to convey James's sympathy: Jewett had died two months earlier, on June 24, 1909. For modern readers, this missive seems delayed, arriving well after Jewett's death and only after Fields had written him herself. However, in his analysis of epistolary writing of the period, William Merrill Decker presents the delayed letter of condolence as conforming to the particular conventions of nineteenth-century Anglo-American epistolary writing. Discussing similarly "late" responses to a death, penned by Emily Dickinson and Ralph Waldo Emerson, Decker notes that waiting was considered respectful: "That the newly bereaved were subject to an impenetrable solitude and silence seems to have been a prevalent Anglo-American assumption" (168). Both in its form and its content, as well as in the fact that it arrives two months after Jewett's death, James's response to Fields's grief reflects the conventions of an earlier generation of Anglo-American writers, those of "the golden age" that he describes in "Mr. and Mrs. James T. Fields." Simultaneously, this letter also erases geographic and personal distance, enabling us insights into the rest of the correspondence, and his characterizations of Fields and the Boston past that she represents for him.

It opens intimately. Terming her, for the only time that we know of, "My very dear old Friend," James continues as follows:

How beautiful, how exquisite of you to write to me about our admirable, our quite unspeakable Sara Jewett, and how deeply I am touched and interested by it! It is I who should have written to you, as I at once and all tenderly thought of you; and all the more as I felt the need to express, and felt it strongly, that sense of the all too lamentable with which the news of her death filled me. I did express it, poorly enough, to two or three of my correspondents on your side of the world who would know what I meant—and I then spoke to them of you—and they will have known what I meant by that too. (1)

Limiting his usually lengthy apologies to the brief line that "I should have written to you," James marks this letter as distinct; this reflects its unique context, but it also may suggest that because of Fields's mourning James forgoes the distancing gesture of his usual expressions of guilty ambivalence, and instead writes "from the heart." As Decker and others suggest, this intimate tone itself reflects the conventions of the nineteenth-century condolence letter.

The non-specific "two or three of my correspondents on your side of the world," evoked twice in the final line of the August 1909 letter quoted above, allow James both to express deep understanding and displace it onto these others, potentially strangers to Fields but geographically closer to her. The nature of their understanding, like the sentence itself, is doubled through repetition. These other American correspondents "would know what I meant" by James's own grief at Jewett's death: an important American writer, one whom James admired, had been lost to him, and to the country at large. The nature of their more private and "unspeakable" understanding is joined to the first by one of James's eloquent long dashes. "I then spoke to them of you—and they will have known what I meant by that too." The unnamed others know, as the rest of the world may not, that Annie Fields is twice widowed: a community of other queer or non-heterosexual Americans recognizes the nature of her mourning. They are close; they surround and support her, although they remain anonymous. Importantly, the second, secret form of understanding does not undermine the significance of the first. Through this sentence, James suggests that Sarah Orne Jewett was both a great writer and a woman in an intimate relationship with another woman. With all other literate Americans, Annie Fields, Henry James, and these "others" have lost an important and unique national voice. But James—and the "others"—uniquely know that Fields's sense of a larger cultural loss coexists with the exclusive grief she feels as Jewett's partner.

As the letter continues, James speaks of Fields as "a constant near witness of the beauty of [Jewett's] life—and the constant gentle heroism of her whole long sacrifice" (1–2). For a reader aware of his sister Alice's long invalidism and his great love for her, as Fields of course would have been, this depiction of Jewett seems particularly poignant.

> She was, for so long, so cruelly and tormentedly stricken, and stricken in her charming conscious genius—which she was allowed, by her hard ironic fate, just helplessly to see, and to feel, blighted and baffled within her; and with the only appeal or redress left her to take her tribulation with an unsurpassable grace and sweetness. I have never known a harsher visitation, and to a spirit admirably and utterly exempt from harshness, and have never known a more native and touching dignity of patience and fortitude, given the fact of her exquisite sensibility. (2)[23]

This also could be a portrait of, and eulogy for, Alice James, another "brilliant" queer female invalid. Nevertheless, "I have never known," stated twice to a correspondent who knows James's family, suggests a comparison between Alice and Sarah Orne Jewett in which James's sister is found lacking. The sentence that contains the repeated phrase mirrors itself across the hinge of the second comma ("I have never known a harsher visitation…, and have never known a more native and touching dignity"). The repetition serves as emphasis; additionally, the structure of the sentence echoes its meaning, establishing two parallel subjects and also indicating that the second surpasses the first. Jewett's "native and touching dignity," described in the second half of the sentence, is a victory over her "harsher visitation." Moreover, her "spirit admirably exempt from harshness," "her exquisite sensibility," and her published record of literary "genius," distinguish her from the similarly intelligent and artistic but unpublished Alice James.[24] Evoking his own grief at his beloved sister's death, James simultaneously emphasizes that Annie Fields's loss of her spouse is more devastating.

The admiration for Jewett's ability to conquer the adversities of chronic illness grows out of this comparison. Of Jewett, James states "she had been a charming and impeccable genius and artist, and has left her little monument of beautifully squared and fitted and polished block which speaks for her now, through all the frustration and the dreariness" (2, 1). Jewett published a huge body of work, including poems and essays as well as short stories and novels. Her "polished block" refers to her literary output as well as her gravestone, but the fact that it is rendered decidedly singular—James suggests one perfect "little monument," not a series of them—refers to his long-expressed preference for *The Country of the Pointed Firs*. This is not ungenerous—as he wrote in the October 1901 note to Jewett, as a fellow artist he owes her honesty. Even in death, even in a letter of condolence to her grieving widow, James shows Jewett the respect to avoid what he had described to her as "the mere twaddle of graciousness" (Horne, *Henry James* 360).

James closes the letter by again bearing witness to the marital intimacy that Fields shared with Jewett. "Fresh and bright enough to bring tears to my eyes that gallant visit of yours and hers to me long ago here. My quiet little old house is always conscious of you together, and I am all faithfully and gratefully yours and hers" (1). The specifically domestic nature of Jewett and Fields's intimacy is here indicated by the physical space of "my quiet little old house." The phrase recalls the 1899 note to Jewett, in which he writes of "the little rooms you wot of." The collapsing of temporal and geographic distance—importantly, through a depiction of a domestic space—is a declaration of his more-than-sympathetic identification with the two women. In the home of their unconventional, nonheterosexual literary friend, Annie Adams Fields and Sarah Orne Jewett were truly "together," and they were recognized as such. More to the point, this letter suggests that in James's view the women's marriage is most clearly expressed through domesticity. This could mean that it cannot be acknowledged openly in the outside world, but James's tone also may suggest that private, and perhaps even publicly concealed, intimacy is the only genuine sort. "I am all faithfully and gratefully yours and hers," he reminds her, conveying the truth of their relationship even after Jewett's death, and helping the bereaved Fields to keep it alive.

After this intimate note, the next, sent less than five months later on January 2, 1910, seems an abrupt return to greater distance; the shift cannot be explained entirely through the fact that this is not a condolence letter. The 1910 letter has been extensively integrated into scholarship on James's epistolary writing.[25] The "bonfire" James describes has been used as a means of understanding his relationship to future literary biographers; as evidence of the depression that would continue to plague him in the years to follow; or as a means of framing his fictional representations of letter-burning, such as in the 1888 novella *The Aspern Papers* (see Chap. 4).[26] While several generations of readers explore this letter as a general indication of James's views on privacy and legacy, the relationship with its actual recipient has been ignored. We risk misreading any single letter when we separate it from its place within a long correspondence—and perhaps particularly this one. Rosenberg is not atypical in his analysis of this letter when he describes Fields, with startling inaccuracy, as "an editor chasing after the remains of [James's] correspondence with Sarah Orne Jewett" (258). Moreover, framing the January 1910 note within the arc of the writing to Fields can offer us new insights into both James's probable depression and the "gigantic bonfire" to which he alludes; we should consider this note both on its own terms and as a performance for a specific, well-known addressee, with whom James had been exchanging letters and transatlantic visits for twenty-eight years by this point. Annie Fields is in the process of editing Jewett's letters, and in response to this project James unequivocally asserts the sanctity of his own privacy—and that of his other correspondents, including, by implication, Jewett herself. But it cannot be a coincidence that this note so closely follows the 1909 letter of condolence, in which James describes a transatlantic, queer literary community that includes himself, Fields, and Jewett.

The letter begins with another lengthy series of apologetic explanations, comprising two pages of the larger stationery. James refers to a request from Fields for copies of any letters from Jewett; he has no manuscripts to provide, and he describes why he has been delayed in letting her know. The apologies close, at the beginning of the third page, with the famous confession.[27]

> I find our admirable friends occasional communications have submitted to the law that I have made tolerably absolute in these last years as I grow older and think more of my latter end: the law of not leaving personal and private documents at the mercy of any accidents, or even of my executors! I kept almost all letters for years, till my receptacles will would no longer hold them; then I made a gigantic bonfire and have been easier in mind since— save as to a certain residuum that had to survive. (January 2, 1910; 3)

Again, while the context of this letter is quite different, nevertheless the change in feeling between these two notes seems marked. In August 1909, Fields is a "constant near witness" of Jewett's life, and James is "conscious of the two of you together." Now, a few months later, Jewett has become "our admirable friend." The phrase supports the very fiction that he seemed to combat in August: now Fields's grief, rather than being incommunicably unique, could be shared by Jewett's other "friends," including

James himself. His description of his "gigantic bonfire" suggests his horror at Fields's plan to publish the private letters of an author who also, and more significantly, was her own marital intimate and a fellow non-heterosexual. James's disapproval of the project may inspire his more formal tone in this note. As he writes, "I will with the greatest joy in any other way—if any memorial to her is in course of taking shape to which I might contribute a few pages" (4). In a postscript, James further elaborates upon this offer; the greater warmth of this addition may reflect his reconsideration of the remonstration contained in the letter's body. His offer now is concrete, and indeed he even sounds enthusiastic about the proposed contribution: "P.S. I would for instance with pleasure address you a letter, as editor—a letter of reminiscence and appreciation and making 25 pages of print or so, which would serve, if you cared, as Introduction to your volume: a thing very frank, familiar, as a thorough friend, etc.; and oh so tender and so admiring—as I do admire her work!" (1).[28] Although he can or will not assist in the publication of Jewett's private letters, James assures Fields that his official recognition of the author of *The Country of the Pointed Firs* will be deeply personal—nevertheless, it will be written for public consumption, and to Fields as an editor, not as Jewett's partner. As it turns out, the postscript to the January 1910 letter will be his only contribution to Fields's memorialization of Jewett. In 1922 M. A. De Wolfe Howe publishes an edited version of Annie Fields's diaries and other papers, which includes a copy of James's postscript, along with the caption "Reduced facsimile of a postscript of a letter from Henry James, expressing the intention, which he could not fulfill, to provide an Introduction to the 'Letters of Sarah Orne Jewett'" (299). In her diary entry for March 7, 1911, Fields herself indicates that James remains in the grips of depression, "still unfit to write" (qtd. in Roman 161). Whether or not the two events are directly related, the fact that James announces his "gigantic bonfire" in the more carefully conventional letter that follows his intimate note of August 25, 1909 indicates some anxiety that Annie Fields has proven herself a not entirely confidential correspondent. The deletion at the line in which James states that "I kept almost all letters for years, till my receptacles will would no longer hold them" could reveal that James deliberately underestimated, for Fields's benefit, the number of letters that he still had in his possession at this date. Unwilling to make any letters from Jewett, or other correspondents, available for public consumption, James might have found it easier to pretend, to his publishing "dear old Friend," that they no longer existed.

As it turns out, he needn't have worried: Fields's *Letters of Sarah Orne Jewett* (1911) offers a heavily-redacted version of Jewett's relationships with other women, including Fields herself. The final extant letter from James to the then 80-year-old Fields is dated July 25, 1914: she died less than six months later, on January 5, 1915.[29] Perhaps he has seen *Letters of Sarah Orne Jewett* in the interim, but in any case this note again demonstrates intimacy and warmth. He writes in response to a "so beautiful and touching letter prompted by your generous appreciation of my volume of Notes" (*Notes of a Son and Brother*, published 1914). "It is meanwhile the sympathy of old friends from far back like yourself, of 'those who know,' as Dante says, that is the reward of my attempts to reach back a little to the unspeakable past" (1–2). The knowledge that Annie Fields shares with James has multiple meanings: here, she primarily is evoked as a representative of a lost time and place, late nineteenth-century Boston. But personal, familial, and affective memory is laden onto that more public past. *Notes of a Son and Brother* is an autobiographical volume focused on the 1860s that included selected and revised letters by William James and their father. As James states, "I really like to think of those who know which I am talking about—and such readers are now of the fewest" (1). Repetition in James usually is more than simple emphasis; here, the phrase "those who know" seems to have more than one meaning. Annie Fields "knows": a central figure in the place and period he recalls in *Notes of a Son and Brother*, she has been privy to his and his family's personal joys and sorrows. She is an adept literary reader and editor, as well as one of the earliest supporters of his work. She, too, has had an affective life that lay outside the publicly recognized, marital norm—as a widow, and then through her relationship with Jewett. This form of knowledge that James and Fields share echoes that of "the two or three others on your side of the Atlantic," from the August 1909 note. In addition, as a woman—one, moreover, of his own class, regional, national, and ethnic background—she "knows" in ways that are not available to heterosexual, normatively-gendered men. Arguably, Fields's embodiment of gender-specific ideals of femininity enables James's close sense of sympathy with her, as expressed in this letter. The use of the word "unspeakable" is another, probably unconscious, repetition—the only other time in the correspondence when he deploys that adjective is in the 1909 letter to a grieving Fields, in which he describes "our admirable, our quite unspeakable Sara Jewett" (June 24, 1909; 1). The word "unspeakable" was in transition during the nineteenth century. For Noah Webster, constructing the first edition of his *American Dictionary of the*

*English Language* in 1828, it meant solely "that which can not be uttered." In England, later in the century, it also meant, "indescribably or inexpressibly bad or objectionable." Although it is possible that he means to imply only the American, nineteenth-century definition of "unspeakable," James plays with doubled meanings throughout his writing, and it is unlikely that after nearly four decades spent living in England he was unaware of the other meaning.[30] Closing a few lines later, he returns to the tone of exile: "The only thing is, none the less, that almost nobody understands what we mean, do they?—we can say that to each other...even if we can't say it to them. I think of you very faithfully and gratefully and tenderly, and am yours affectionately always" (2). Whatever his ambivalence about the relationship itself, Annie Fields shares a common language with James—his regard for her is based on a sense of mutual belonging, in a series of interfolding, simultaneously public and private communities. In evoking and eulogizing the more general loss of the personal Boston history that he shares with Fields, the expatriate James longs for even as he distances himself from his own family and national origins; again, he also may obliquely be announcing his own citizenship in a transatlantic community of queer artists and intellectuals.

The particular nostalgia expressed here enables us better to understand what may be allusions to sexually or at least affectively queer experiences from James's young manhood, in the "Boston" chapter of *The American Scene*. Returning to the city in his sixties, James describes visiting "the haunted drawing room"—this is Fields's "museum" of American literary culture at 148 Charles Street, where "the concentrated Boston of history, the Boston of Emerson, Thoreau, Hawthorne, Longfellow, Lowell, Holmes, Ticknor, Motley, Prescott, Parkman and the rest—...could be seen in as definite, and indeed now in almost as picturesquely mediæval, a concretion, appear to make as black and minute and 'composed' a little pyramidical image, as the finished background of a Dürer print" (182). The prior American generation of writers is part of a cataloged list of names, jumbled together into an anachronistic blur of definitively disappeared pasts. Whether ancient ("pyramidical") or medieval ("a Dürer print") their work is simultaneously "composed" (the word calls to mind its antonym, "decomposed") and "finished." In addition to rendering their subjects firmly dead, these references to specific periods may represent a form of queer coding. As Alan Bray and Will Fisher separately argue, writers in James's period used ahistorical idealizations of classical Greek and European Renaissance culture as a means of alluding to male homosexuality.

Bray points out that by James's era the Renaissance was understood as a time in which "the dark constraints of the monkish Middle Ages were past," where "sexual and artistic freedom went hand in hand" (1). In his trials, Oscar Wilde gave a public face to the figure of "the sodomite," in part by memorably framing the love of boys as the most noble form of Greek *eros*. Here, James also evokes the ancient Egyptians; this is his only non-European cultural reference, and in context it also suggests associations with death and alternative sexual mores. Victorian society, then in the grips of Egyptomania, was duly fascinated by the details of Egyptian funerary and sexual practices, including various forms of erotic art and stories from Egyptian mythology that addressed sexuality frankly.[31] All of these distinctively alien cultural pasts form the foundation for modern Anglo-American "civilization" as James understands it, in the same way that "the Age of Emerson" preceded James and his own generation of American writers.

In this piece, James opens his portrait of the modern city of Boston, uncannily haunted by a palpably present past that only he and Fields seem to remember, with an account of visiting the street where he had lived with his parents in the late 1860s and early 1870s, "the Ashburton Place that I anciently knew." He describes their former house as one of only two still standing on the street; and indeed, he will be shaken to discover that both have been demolished, when he returns a month later at the conclusion of his visit. "Their shuttered, lidded eyes had closed, their brick complexions had paled, above the good granite basements, to a fainter red—all as with the cold consciousness of a possible doom." Standing in front of the faded pair of houses, James finds himself

> reading into one of them a short page of history that I had my own reasons for finding of supreme interest, the history of two years of far-away youth spent there at a period—the closing-time of the War—full both of public and of intimate vibrations. The two years had been those of a young man's… and the effect of actual attention was to recover on the spot some echo of ghostly footsteps—the sound as of taps on the window-pane heard in the dim dawn. (*American Scene* 170)

In one of the piece's more personal evocations, memory arrives as a secret lover, keeping an illicit dawn tryst. The reader is left to imagine that the "ghostly footsteps" and "taps" are themselves memories, of real events in a "young man's" life. Although the emphasis on his youth may be a means of dismissing these experiences as indiscretion or experimentation, this period is placed consciously in an historical context that renders it deeply significant. To describe "the closing-time of the War" as one of "public... vibrations" seems like vast, and intentional, understatement. Like the (other) Civil War, this period of "vibrations"—the term throughout his writing has specifically sexual or at least sensual connotations—profoundly reordered James's sense of himself.[32] It is remembered ambivalently, but there is no going back to the period "before" the South broke away from the North, and a young Henry James began to vibrate to the sound of "taps on the window-pane heard in the dim dawn."

Like his analysis of Boston itself, James's published memorial of Annie Fields simultaneously seems to render her both uncannily still present and thoroughly relegated to an emphatically "ancient" past. "Mr. and Mrs. James T. Fields" first appears simultaneously in the July, 1915 issues of the *Atlantic Monthly* and the *Cornhill Magazine*, a British journal that also had published a number of his works (including *Daisy Miller* in 1878 and *Washington Square* in 1880). The choice of British publication seems telling. *Cornhill Magazine*, popular in the middle of the nineteenth century, had experienced a decline by the time "Mr. and Mrs. James T. Fields" was published; while it continued publishing into the 1970s, by 1915 it already was synonymous in the public mind with nostalgic content.[33] James's choice of venue necessarily frames "Mr. and Mrs. James T. Fields," for British readers at least, as both temporally and geographically distant.

As suggested by the fact that the essay is published one year after James's final letter to Annie Fields, and seven months after her death, the essay titled to include James Fields focuses primarily on his widow. It represents her as an embodiment of normative, nineteenth-century femininity—and it eulogizes both her and the Boston past for which she becomes an emblem. As Gollin might suggest, James's essay is entirely consistent with Annie Fields's sense of herself—as evinced by the "feminism" of self-sacrifice and service to others that she embodied in her personal and social lives, her published and unpublished writing, and her philanthropy and activism. At the same time, and particularly when read in light of their correspondence, James's final word on Annie Fields represents a complex form of nostalgia. Like the city of Boston and her Charles Street drawing room, Annie Fields herself is displaced, coming to symbolize, in the swirl of too-present memory, James's youth and America itself. In part, again, this regard relies on James's recognition of both Fields's traditional femininity and her non-heterosexuality. This piece also has clear resonances with the "Boston" chapter of *The American Scene*. However, in "Mr. and

James T. Fields" the present-tense conflict of World War I, rather than the Civil War evoked as past, becomes the public conflict that echoes private disruption. James's sense of betrayal at Woodrow Wilson's declaration of American neutrality, on August 19, 1914 (just a few weeks after the U.K. declared war on Germany) is palpable here—for him, the Anglo-American U.S. had abandoned its English kin, and the larger cultural project their shared language and sympathies represented.[34]

"Mr. and Mrs. James T. Fields" therefore is a eulogy, not just for its individual subjects, nor even simply for the Boston past that they represent, but for the "innocent confidence" of an American citizenry that believed itself still to be linguistically and culturally tied to Britain. The essay begins, "If at such a time as this a man of my generation finds himself on occasion revert to our ancient peace in some soreness of confusion between envy and pity, I know well how best to clear up the matter for myself at least and to recover a workable relation with the blessing in eclipse. I recover it in some degree with pity, as I say, by reason of the deep illusions and fallacies in which the great glare of the present seems to show us as then steeped" (*American Essays* 261). It is not only Annie Fields who has just died; in the brutal present of World War I, as Britain struggles to survive without American support, James also mourns the loss of the conservative Anglo-American cultural project Fields represented.[35] His conflicted response to living in what he terms "the end of our civilization" becomes a form of envious condescension—the performatively world-weary gaze of an elderly, more modern writer—towards the "complacency" of the American past. Jarringly, he describes the wake of the bloody Civil War as "our ancient peace," the period of his own as well as his country's "innocence": the naiveté of "the Boston constellation" lay in "being able to measure with some closeness the good purpose to which they glittered" (266). Far from the battlefields of both the Civil War and World War I, made parallel repeatedly in James's writing, Boston's sense of itself as a national moral compass—the "Puritan whip" that drove abolitionism and other nineteenth-century progressive causes, including, perhaps, women's suffrage—has been revealed at last to be a delusion, lovingly championed by Annie Fields (*American Essays* 172). "I have but to recall the dawn of those associations that seemed then to promise everything, and the last declining ray of which rests, just long enough to be caught, on the benign figure of Mrs. Fields...she was so intrinsically charming a link with the past and abounded so in the pleasure of reference and the grace of felicity" (263). The anachronistic sense of extreme historical distance displayed in this essay allows James an emotional alternative to "envy," as he declares—arguably, however, it also suggests the particularly "queer" form that his nostalgia takes. Eulogizing Annie Fields, he enacts the death of his Boston, and of his sense of fealty to America. At the same time, the Annie Fields portrayed in this essay threatens to dissolve the historical distance that James establishes.

Elsewhere evoked as a representative of a lost Boston past, Annie Fields nevertheless also is "insistently modern" and "consentingly modern." Among other aspects of her philanthropic work, this suggests her efforts as a women's rights activist. For readers familiar with the representations of Boston-area feminists in *The Bostonians* and the 1912 letters to Edith Wharton and William Dean Howells, the phrasing may seem puzzling. However, James's objection is not to women's rights activism *per se*, but rather to the "unfeminine" form that he regards it as taking in some instances: Fields's conformity to nineteenth-century notions of femininity, based in privacy, seems the important distinction here.[36] While her ideas themselves are "modern," her class-specific, gender-normative relationship to social activism stands in marked contrast to the "modern" feminist type suggested by Olive Chancellor or Emmeline Pankhurst. As he emphasizes, "the very sound of the consent [to modernity] was as the voice of a time so much less strident" (277). Here, he describes both the timbre of Annie Fields's voice as well as her approach to social issues—she organized teas, rather than breaking windows. It is just after drawing this distinction, between Fields's "less strident" modernity and that of Pankhurst and her peers, that he writes of the 1898 visit to Rye. "Mrs. Fields, revisiting England, as she continued to embrace every opportunity of doing, kindly traveled down to see me in the country, bringing with her a young friend of great talent whose prevailing presence in her life had come little by little to give it something like a new center" (*American Essays* 278). The final phrase, in a description of a widow, seems a deliberate allusion to a second marital relationship—although this is James's only gesture towards rendering Annie Fields and Sarah Orne Jewett a couple, it seems a remarkably clear one, particularly when juxtaposed with the Fields correspondence. "Mrs. Fields," defined through her intimate relationships, lived a life with two centers. At the end of this paragraph, he carefully states that Jewett "had come to Mrs. Fields as an adopted daughter, both a sharer and a sustainer," but in the light of the first description this seems either a nod to propriety or a defense of Annie Fields's chastity—indeed, her intimacy with Jewett seems to have developed quite soon after James Fields's death.

Doubling references throughout the essay emphasize that Sarah Orne Jewett was as significant a figure as James Fields had been, and occupied a similar role. In detailing her early widowhood: "Mrs. Fields was to survive her husband for many years and was to flourish as a copious second volume—the connection licenses the free figure—of the work anciently issued" (276). This "second volume" has both public and private meanings: it is of her own writing, and it describes her efforts on behalf of women's rights. It also refers to her second intimate relationship, which here is seen to continue her "work" with James Fields. It is just after this point that James emphasizes her "modernity," as distinctly opposed to the "ancient" past represented by her husband.

The structural doubling that marks the piece extends to his description of Jewett, who functions as a replacement for James Fields. James emphasizes Jewett's regional difference when he states that her "brave ghost" might "resent my too roughly Bostonizing her," reminding himself and his readers of her "right setting" in Maine; however, he then turns again to "Mrs. Fields' happy alternative home" on Charles Street, where Jewett spent approximately half of each year throughout the nearly three decades of their relationship. Annie Fields also made two homes, in the same house, with two different partners (*American Essays* 279). James recounts the couple's "emphasized susceptibility" to each other, which also marks his own response to their visit to their "confessingly a bit disoriented countryman" in 1898 (278). James, Jewett, and Fields share multiple forms of citizenship, in privately queer as well as publicly and culturally Anglo-American, transatlantic, upper-class literary communities. The term "countryman" evokes this specific version of Americanness, but also their shared queerness; again, the public meaning is not less meaningful to James than the private.

When read as a public coda to the long correspondence with Annie Fields, "Mr. and Mrs. James T. Fields" presents a version of female same-sex intimacy that enables us to historicize and contextualize his representations of lesbians, non-normatively gendered women, and/or turn-of-the-century women's suffrage activists. He engages in a complex, ethnically-tinged gender essentialism that is simultaneously idiosyncratic and also period- and class-specific. Privacy and containment—not wifehood, motherhood, or even heterosexuality—are the necessary attributes of womanhood for James. Fields's own activism suggests that he sees no contradiction between social progressivism *per se* and ideal womanhood, as long as women's activism takes appropriately "feminine" forms. James himself, throughout his responses to Fields, expresses an ambivalent identification with the version of femininity he defines through her example. In the next three chapters, I will explore the ways that other writers reading his work—women who, like Annie Fields, simultaneously embody and resist period-specific notions of femininity—resonate with James's relationship to and descriptions of womanhood.

NOTES

1. In addition to writing a number of essays on literary figures, Annie Fields was the editor of *Life and Letters of Harriet Beecher Stowe* (1897) and *Letters of Sarah Orne Jewett* (1911); her other works include *Asphodel* (1866), *How to Help the Poor* (1883), *Authors and Friends* (1896), and *A Shelf of Old Books* (1894).
2. James's essays on James Russell Lowell and Charles Eliot Norton separately describe both authors as both transatlantic and sensitive—these seem closely related to him—in part because of their work on Dante (*American Essays* 81, 110, 114, 123–124). Elsewhere, in his preface to Rupert Brooke's 1916 *Letters from America*, James uses "Dante in harassed exile" as the first in a list of examples (followed by Shakespeare, Milton, Keats, and others) of genius surviving under duress (x–xi). In his letters, James uses references to Dante facetiously, as gentle self-mockery to male friends, or as an example of poetic greatness (Horne; *Henry James* 3, 395, 503).
3. All transcriptions are my own, from manuscripts, unless otherwise noted. As of this writing, published volumes of *The Complete Letters of Henry James* cover periods predating the correspondence with Annie Fields. Three letters (January 26, 1892; September 5, 1898; and January 2, 1910) were included in Leon Edel's four-volume edition *Henry James: Letters*, published 1974. In his explanatory comments following the first two inclusions, Edel misleadingly describes Jewett and Fields simply as "close friends" (III 371–372; IV 77–78, 541–542).
4. Both Linda Anderson and Gilad Padva describe the influence of Probyn's 1995 essay on twenty-first century versions of queer theory.
5. See Neill Matheson, Nicola Nixon, Shelley Salamensky, and Paula Smith.
6. Diana Bellonby suggests that the character of Madame Merle, in 1881's *The Portrait of a Lady* is both a "surrogate author" and a Sand figure. "As James's implicit analysis of Sand's literature and lifestyle, Madame Merle becomes a rhetorical proxy through which he works out his fascination with Sand and his evolving definition of literary mastery" (204). Earlier, Sarah Daugherty criticizes James's "condescension" and "sexism" in his writing on Sand, but also argues that *The Bostonians* is "a more truly feminist novel than any of [Sand's] romances" (42–43, 46).

7. "What was feminine in her was the quality of her genius; the *quantity* of it—its force, and mass, and energy—was masculine, and masculine were her temperament and character. All this masculinity needed to set itself free..." (*European Writers* 716). *Notes on Novelists*, published in 1914, contained the 1897, 1899, and 1914 essays. The 1877 essay on Sand was included in 1878's *French Poets and Novelists*.
8. Harris emphasizes that Fields's letters were "an extension of her social role," which again had ideological and cultural implications (116, 5). She wryly notes that Fields and her Anglo-American New England contemporaries "had not yet divested themselves of the sense that the English and Scots (if not the Irish) were culturally superior" (104).
9. In a diary entry dated July 16, 1870, Annie Fields describes the story as "good (though the handwriting was execrable)" (qtd. in M. A. De Wolfe Howe 119). For more on her advocacy of James's early writing, see Gollin (37–38).
10. For earlier interpretations of the novel and the character of Olive Chancellor in the vein that Fetterley and Castle criticize, see Louis Auchincloss (42), F. W. Dupee (131), and Tony Tanner (153).
11. Fields's diaries, which she may have written with an eye towards eventual publication, are informal in tone but reveal little about their author's feelings. In her account of the September 1898 visit to Lamb House, for example, Fields describes the travel details and recounts memorable *bon mots* by both Jewett and James, but says almost nothing about herself ("Diary" 14–21). My thanks to the Massachusetts Historical Society for access to this material.
12. As Horne reminds us, "Many of James's letters are *not* in libraries: they are in the hands of private collectors, or in the hands of the descendants or heirs of the recipients," and editors have no way of knowing precisely how many may exist (*Henry James* xviii). Some may simply be lost.
13. Two final pages, noted by the Huntington Library as part of the August 20, 1898 letter, have gone missing. At some point between September 1898 and October 1900, James obtained larger notepaper, which he used for the remainder of the correspondence.
14. This is the second of three letters in the correspondence that Edel published, in *Letters*, Vol. III (77–78).
15. This was Fields's fourth trip to England; on this particular voyage, she and Jewett already had spent the spring and summer traveling France by train, alone. Years earlier, with her husband, Fields had traversed the Midwest, by bus and train, with what she describes in her diary of this period as "the unwashed." She also kept a diary of an 1896 trip with Jewett around the Caribbean, during which the two regularly ventured off the regular tourist routes. My thanks to the Massachusetts Historical Society.

16. On September 5, "the journey can be is performed in rather exceptionally easy conditions" (3–4). Yet a week later, on the day before she arrives, he reminds her yet again of the train schedule, and terms the trip an "ample... pilgrimage" (September 12, 1898; 2).
17. Compare with other notes from 1895 to 1898 in which James includes closing greetings to spouses or family members of his friends, including several written to William Dean Howells (Anesko 297–299, 299–301, 302) as well as Alphonse Daudet and Edward Warren (Horne; *A Life* 285–287, 322–323).
18. Co-determining this discussion, and perhaps the judgment in the women's favor, were intersecting nineteenth-century ideologies of race, as Faderman notes. The accusing student, the child of an extramarital union between a white Englishman and an Indian woman, was judged by the court to have concocted fantasies about Miss Woods and Miss Pirie's friendship out of her own perverse, racialized imagination.
19. In introducing her collection of nineteenth-century "lesbian" stories, Koppelman points out that "[w]e so take for granted these kinds of romantic love between men and women that we qualify nonromantic love between men and women by its own special term: Platonic love…The stories in this book are stories about non-Platonic love between women" (11).
20. All emphases original. Fields does not include the December 1882 letter in her edited volume of Jewett's correspondence. Although she prints a version of the June 5, 1883 note, she combines sentences and changes punctuation to shift Jewett's emphasis. For example, "And *kiss* things!" becomes "…and drive things, and *kiss* things, and yet I have been thinking all day what a lovely sketch it would be to tell the story of the day we went to Morwenstow…" (*Letters* 16–17). These small changes diminish the intensity of Jewett's romantic declaration, and subsume it into the bracketing discussion of her writing process, which it originally had interrupted—in Fields's edited version the literary discussion takes precedence. Richard Cary, a 1967 editor of Jewett's correspondence, includes neither letter. My thanks to the Maine Women Writers Collection at the University of New England.
21. In a 1909 note to Howells, James speaks of writing to Jewett just before her death that year (Anesko 435–436). Helen Howe transcribes an undated note to M. A. De Wolfe Howe from Jewett, probably dating from 1905 or 1906. In it, Jewett quotes fragments of another missing letter to her from James (93–94).
22. The time he spent with Jewett at her Maine home was memorable to James—he refers to it afterwards. Writing Elinor Mead Howells in August 1905, James recalls "those 2 wondrous days at Kittery Point and at Sara Jewett's place" (Anesko 417).

23. My thanks to Philip Horne and Oliver Herford for their help deciphering James's handwriting in this letter.
24. Alice James left behind her letters and a diary, which was published after her death in a private run of four copies by Katharine Loring. James was horrified to realize that his sister had written down so much of their conversations; later, Loring told her niece Mary James Vaux that he had torn up his own copy (Strouse 319–323). The diary has come to be regarded in the last few decades as a significant piece of work, of value to feminist and nineteenth-century literary scholars as well as readers of William or Henry James.
25. This is the only part of the correspondence with Fields that Leon Edel includes in both his longer, multi-volume edition of James's letters and his shorter *Selected Letters* (*Letters IV*, 541–542; *Selected Letters* 383–384).
26. Edel's interpretation of both the letter-burning and the depression is contained in the final volume of his four-volume biography of James, *The Master: 1901–1916* (140–144, 433–35, 438–444). Joseph Elkanah Rosenberg and Carol Holly both engage in similar readings.
27. On April 8, 1904, James sends a note to Mrs. Eveleen Myers, who similarly was writing to inquire about letters from her late husband, Frederic William Henry Myers, a poet and essayist. In it, James uses the same line ("I never had *many* letters from your husband") and also states "When…I broke up my London existence, I committed to the flames a good many documents, as one does on the occasion of the great changes & marked dates & new eras, closed chapters, of one's life" (Horne, *Henry James* 398–399).
28. The Huntington Library, which holds both the postscript and the letter itself, has filed them separately, but it seems clear that they are part of one letter, as the library notes.
29. Another very short note, dated February 16, 1911, is sent from Cambridge, Massachusetts on William James's letterhead, during Henry's final visit to the U.S. following his brother's death. The note refers to "Bill," elsewhere in letters of this period a nickname used for William James, Jr., so it is likely that his nephew joined James when he last saw Annie Fields in person (*Letters IV*, 449, 653, 672).
30. From Webster's 1828: "That cannot be uttered; that cannot be expressed; unutterable; as unspeakable grief or rage." The OED adds a second definition, "indescribably or inexpressibly bad or objectionable," supported by entirely British literary usages from 1831, 1843, 1876, 1896, and 1902. A number of scholars have addressed James's relationship to doubled meanings; for representative examples from a few theoretical approaches, see Wendy Graham, particularly Chapter 5, as well as Hugh Stevens ("Queer Henry"), Hutchinson, Sarah Campbell, and Adam Sonstegard.
31. See R. B. Parkinson and Greg Reeder for examinations of depictions of male homoeroticism in the literature and art of ancient Egypt, much of it

known during James's era. Steve Vinson suggests a Ptolemaic "*femme fatale*" story as one inspiration for the character of Ayesha ("She-Who-Must-Be-Obeyed") from H. Rider Haggard's 1887 novel *She: A History of Adventure*. Oscar Wilde's 1894 poem "The Sphinx" depicts the creature as immortal and sexually voracious.
32. For discussions of the homoerotic resonances of the word "vibrations" for James, see Ohi 101–102; Naomi Z. Sofer; and Stevens, *Henry James* 64–65, 86–87, 105–107. Andrew Taylor suggests that James uses the word to suggest the "delicacies and extremes of [artistic] sensibility" (19–20), but these two interpretations are not necessarily opposed.
33. For background on both the nineteenth-century heyday and long twentieth-century decline of *Cornhill*, see Katherine Malone, Barbara Quinn Schmidt, and J. Don Vann.
34. James took British citizenship on July 26, 1915, and made sure that this was publicized as "a good example." The day after his naturalization, he sent a declaration of his "Reasons for Naturalization" to James Brand Pinker, his friend and agent; Pinker published the statement in the next morning's *London Times*. Written in the third person, these reasons include "his desire to throw his moral weight and personal allegiance, for whatever they may be worth, into the scale of the contending Nation's present and future fortune." The day after the *Times* announcement, James experienced a return of the illness he would experience intermittently until his death in February 1916, more than a year before the U.S. declared war on Germany (Horne, *Henry James* 556–557).
35. See Toni Morrison. Walter Benn Michaels's response is in a 1995 special "Race Forum" issue of the *Henry James Review*. See Kenneth W. Warren for a substantive analysis of the recent history of scholarly readings of the specter of race in James, which largely grew out of the Morrison/Michaels discussion. Warren argues that James's relationship to race reflects his class-based, nineteenth-century expectations surrounding "good service" and, correspondingly, his own sense of *noblesse oblige*.
36. For an analysis of James's friendship with suffrage activist and playwright Elizabeth Robins, see Joanne E. Gates.

CHAPTER 3

# Emily Dickinson's Henry James

Henry James published *The Europeans* in serial form in the *Atlantic Monthly*, July through October 1878. The next year, Emily Dickinson refers to the novel or its author twice in personal letters (L 619, L 622). Writing her close friend Elizabeth Holland and her "Preceptor," the editor and social activist Thomas Wentworth Higginson, Dickinson uses James and his characters to supplement her own voice. Jack L. Capps compiled an index of the poet's reading in 1966, which included these allusions to James; yet only two short essays, published in 1971 and 2015, suggest that the connection might be meaningful (Sumner, Horne "Where Are…?").[1] This dearth of scholarly material likely reflects the fact that these are the only obvious references to James in the poet's large epistolary corpus. Nevertheless, Dickinson clearly read James's novel, and used his words in the important context of her personal letters. Agnieszka Salska reminds us that the poet "lived in a culture that persistently encouraged the fusion of literary and personal experience"; indeed, a close identification with literature is evident throughout her correspondence (166). Dickinson regularly relied on literary allusion, often as a form of writing in itself; Capps suggests that the frequency of her references is not in itself a reliable measure of a literary figure's importance to her life and writing, as "her true evaluation lies not in what she says about an author's work but in what she does with it" (24). As I will argue, Dickinson does a great deal with her two brief allusions to *The Europeans*.

Through James, she reflects on her relationships with Elizabeth Holland and T. W. Higginson—she also directs her reader's attention to James's engagements with questions of patriarchal authority and women's artistic self-determination. Dickinson's reading stands in marked contrast to contemporary reviews of *The Europeans*; rather than seeing the novel as simply a depiction of transatlantic cultural differences, she finds in James an interrogation of period-specific, New England ideations of gender and authorial voice. This is a project that resonates with her own.

Like Annie Adams Fields, another privileged white woman in nineteenth-century Massachusetts, Dickinson's letters are one of a limited number of acceptable means of communicating her experiences and ideas with those outside her household. Fields writes letters to build and sustain important relationships, as she works to promote both women's rights and an Anglo-American, transatlantic notion of cultural value. Dickinson, quite differently, uses her epistles to share her poetry with a select audience, effectively self-publishing even as she resists placing her work in journals. Marietta Messmer argues that the poet's correspondence is key to understanding her artistic approach. "[O]wing to their audience orientation, it is her letters and letter-poems—rather than her (fascicle) poems alone or in isolation—which seem to be most representative of Dickinson's fundamental choices about literary production" (3). Additionally, her letters allow the poet a controlled means of negotiating the space between private and public. Logan Esdale suggests that Dickinson's epistles reveal an adept "artificial naturalness," deployed in the context of a reading culture that understood "naturalness" to mark a private, more authentic voice (3, 5). This conscious performance of a private self, for an audience, is reflected in her approach to literary allusion. The poet employs the words of other writers in letters to augment or complicate her own statements, and she rarely provides a clear source; epistolary citations also intersect references to earlier letters or shared history, indicating that her personal relationships inform readings of the allusions contained in her correspondence. Messmer argues that Dickinson stages different versions of her own relationship to femininity in letters to her two closest female friends, Elizabeth Holland and Susan Gilbert Dickinson. "In contrast to her gender-transgressive fictionalized poses in her correspondence with Sue Gilbert, Dickinson presents herself in her letters and poems to Holland as inhabiting culturally sanctioned subject positions for women so completely...that possible gender-role ambivalences are largely erased from this epistolary exchange" (98). Although I disagree slightly with Messmer's reading of the relationship with Elizabeth Holland, at least as it pertains to this one letter, her analysis suggests that Dickinson offers each of these closest female friends a persona that conforms to each woman's notions of femininity—and her own. This negotiated expression of nineteenth-century gender ideals, which emphasized familial relationships, service to others, and marital pairing over (women's) individual identities, is at the heart of her reference to *The Europeans* in Letter 619.

Written in October, 1879 and addressed to "Mrs. J. G. Holland", the note begins as follows:

> Little Sister,
>     I was glad you wrote—I was just about addressing the Coroner of Alexandria—You spared me the melancholy research—
>     Are you pretty well—have you been happy—
>     Are your Eyes safe?
>     A thousand questions rise to my lips, and as suddenly ebb—for how little I know of you recently—An awkward loneliness smites me—I fear I must ask with Mr. Wentworth, "Where are our moral foundations?"[2]

In the corresponding notes, Johnson tells readers that "Mr. Wentworth" is the New England patriarch portrayed in *The Europeans*. The letter goes on briefly to relate family news, and then concludes with the following lines:

> I ask you to ask your Doctor will he be so kind as to write the name of my Philadelphia friend on the Note within, and your little Hand will take it to him—
> You were so long so faithful, Earth would not seem homelike without your little sunny Acts—
> Love for you each—
>             Emily.

The "Doctor" to whom the poet refers is Josiah Holland, Elizabeth's husband. In his biography of Dickinson, Alfred Habegger follows the lead of many others in speculating that "my Philadelphia friend" may be the Reverend Charles Wadsworth; similar requests trace the history of Dickinson's correspondence with the prominent orator, which remained a secret from most of her other intimates. Habegger tells us that Dickinson knew of Wadsworth's return in 1879 to Philadelphia after a long absence, and surmises that "the Note within" Letter 619 contains an invitation that results in Wadsworth visiting her in Amherst the following year. The poet seems to have been reluctant to send letters to Wadsworth from her own home, addressed in her own handwriting, and she often used the Hollands as couriers (Habegger, *My Wars* 594).

However, speculations about the "Philadelphia friend" have fueled decades of scholarly investigations, and indeed a number of figures have been presented as possible romantic interests for the famously unmarried poet. Georgiana Strickland notes that "much ink has been spilled" by readers attempting to ascertain the nature of Dickinson's relationship with Wadsworth on little evidence: she quotes David Higgins's poorly-documented 1967 account of an anecdote shared about the poet's niece, Martha Dickinson Bianchi. In 1936, Bianchi may have admitted that, when asked by a publisher to choose a love interest for her aunt in order to quiet readerly speculation, she somewhat randomly picked Wadsworth (105, 112 n. 29). We are right to hear in the long history of attempts by scholars and publishers to find a man—any man?—for Dickinson echoes of Eve Sedgwick's call for scholars to stop enforcing the "centuries-old code" of insistently asserting the presence of "(heterosexual) nothing" in an author's life and writing (204). Sedgwick's famous alternative is to point out the possibility of a "homosexual something"—yet long before Sedgwick, a consistent focus in analyses of Dickinson's life and writing has been her "romantic," and potentially erotic, intimacy with her eventual sister-in-law, Susan Gilbert Dickinson.[3] To provide one early example, Lillian Faderman—whose analysis of the freedom granted to "romantic" relationships between upper-class white women in the nineteenth century is detailed in Chap. 2—is one of a number of readers to describe how Martha Dickinson Bianchi went beyond just choosing a male lover for her aunt: she heavily edited the poet's correspondence with Susan Gilbert (Bianchi's mother) in order to eliminate any suggestion of homoeroticism (174–176). Paula Bennett's 1990 analysis, as ground-breaking for Dickinson studies as Sedgwick was for James scholarship, provides an extended reading of what she terms the "clitorocentrism" of Dickinson's work; she argues that the poet "experienced female sexuality (and female creativity) as a separate and autonomous power equal to, but different from, men's own: a 'little' but 'explosive' force." For Bennett, Dickinson's use of a childlike posture in early letters and poems indicates a refusal to conform to the expectations of women of her class and time—eventually, her adaptation of a negotiated adult persona ("Wife—without the sign") suggests that the poet has found a means of forging a livable position as both woman, according to the terms that both she and her society recognize, *and* poet (*Emily Dickinson* 173, 184, 154).[4] I follow Bennett and the others I've footnoted above in considering Dickinson's romantic love for her sister-in-law to be roughly synonymous with what today we would call lesbian or at least homoerotic inclinations; however, rather than representing that argument, I'd instead like to emphasize simply that Dickinson's relationship to "heterosexual orderings" was fundamentally resistant. Regardless of the specificity of her desires, for a woman of her class, race, and region during this period, remaining unmarried was a queer choice. Moreover, it is one she shares with James; in that historical context, both writers would have been marked as aberrant.

At the end of an article about one of Dickinson's many revisions of the work of other poets, Mary Loeffelholz notes in passing certain stylistic parallels with James. Briefly hypothesizing that this might reflect their shared status as outsiders according to private and public forms of social placement, Loeffelholz reminds her readers that both James and Dickinson "were in their different ways noncombatants in the Civil War as well as nonparticipants in consummated or publicly witnessed heterosexual bonds" ("Decoration" 681). A recognition of these biographical resonances is most productive for scholars when we use them to help illuminate the ways that both writers adeptly deploy gender, and gender transgression, in their work while simultaneously espousing and/or embodying what were relatively conventional ideas about womanhood. Dickinson's poetic and epistolary voices are critical performances—she works both within and counter to the parameters of the gender-traditional concepts of womanhood, privacy, and authorship that entirely formed her own notion of herself. Her voice is, to deploy Sharon Cameron's helpful phrase, evidence of a practice of "choosing not choosing."[5]

Along these lines, Letter 619 suggests the ways that Dickinson expressed intimacy with Elizabeth Holland while simultaneously acknowledging the two women's different engagements with the marital imperative. According to both Messmer and Habegger, Elizabeth Holland believed strongly in the necessity of marriage. This conviction, and the conventional nineteenth-century ideas about femininity upon which it relied, were foundational to her sense of women's outsized role in maintaining civil society. As editor of the *Springfield* (Mass.) *Republican*, Dr. Josiah Holland wrote essays denouncing the women's suffrage movement. Mrs. Holland seems also to have felt that women's proper occupation of the private sphere gave them access to a higher purpose. Women "voted" through their moral influence on their sons and husbands: suffrage would actually undermine the basis for that private authority (Messmer 97–105, 108; Habegger, *My Wars* 308–310, 383).

Whether or not the "Note within" Letter 619 itself was a violation of Mrs. Holland's notions of feminine chastity, in this one letter at least we should question Messmer's characterization of the women's friendship as unmarked by Dickinson's "possible gender-role ambivalences." If the enclosed note indeed was intended for Rev. Wadsworth, Dickinson's choice to quote James's Mr. Wentworth serves several purposes. First, she wryly acknowledges that she asks the Hollands to pass on a secret note to a preacher, one just like Mr. Brand, but for the all-important difference that he is married. Perhaps Dickinson also is indicating that, unlike James's Gertrude Wentworth, she *does* seek spiritual guidance from sanctioned religious authorities. By extension, her letter to the married Wadsworth is perfectly innocent—and who would think otherwise?

That potential message points towards what I suggest is her primary goal in quoting James. Through situating herself as conformant to Mrs. Holland's traditional views of womanhood, Dickinson also communicates her resistance to those views. This suggests a tactic along the lines of those employed by first-wave (white, non-working-class) feminists of the late nineteenth-century period: as the moral "mothers of the nation," their comparatively conservative ideas about femininity justified greater public roles, including but not limited to voting rights.[6] Dickinson presents her ideal, privately-oriented femininity as giving her the clarity to realize a higher purpose, one that requires her to disobey petty social rules (i.e. that a single woman should avoid writing secret letters to a married man) in pursuit of the more important law of spiritual self-actualization. Her position as a poet, and as a nineteenth-century spiritual seeker (like Emerson, or Thoreau, or indeed Henry James's Gertrude Wentworth) trumps her role as an unmarried woman. If perhaps not unambiguously "transgressive," to return to Marietta Messmer's characterization of her self-depiction in letters to Elizabeth Holland, her voice here in fact does seem to express "possible gender-role ambivalences." In both this note and Letter 622, Dickinson's relationship to nineteenth-century imperatives about women's writing suggests a simultaneously resistant and obedient engagement with (heteronormative) gender roles.

Elements leading up to Dickinson's request to Mrs. Holland in Letter 619 reveal a doubled, non-exclusionary deployment of distinct versions of normative femininity. The poet portrays her friend as a representation of perfect womanliness, both physically and affectively. Mrs. Holland's "little hand" helps make the world "homelike." Elsewhere Dickinson describes the smallness of her own body and features. Again, as Bennett argues, the poet's emphasis on feminine smallness is a means of articulating sexual difference, and often has erotic overtones that render her, and potentially all women, united in their resistance to heterosexual desire (understood as exclusively male, phallic, and overwhelming). Yet in describing her own "littleness," the poet uses terms that suggest nature, animal life, or a compressed volatility rather than a safe, comforting domesticity—this is an alternate (erotic) physicality, not the absence of one. "I...am small, like the Wren, and my Hair is bold, like the Chestnut Bur—and my eyes, like the Sherry in the Glass, that the Guest leaves" (L 268).[7] In Letter 619, Dickinson evokes the vows of marriage to suggest an ideal of sisterly friendship: "You were so long so faithful." Elizabeth Holland will demonstrate her continued fidelity and ideal femininity if, despite her possible disapproval, she succeeds in getting Dickinson's enclosed letter to its intended recipient. The poet carefully presents her own voice in order to reflect a compelling version of Elizabeth Holland back to her friend. Mrs. Holland's perfect feminine fidelity is, of course, thrown into question in the opening line, as Dickinson gently complains about too long a lapse in the correspondence. In part, this beginning seems to imply the importance, both to the friendship and to Mrs. Holland's sense of self, of the request that will follow. This theme continues, as she writes: "A thousand questions rise to my lips, and as suddenly ebb—for how little I know of you recently—An awkward loneliness smites me—I fear I must ask with Mr. Wentworth, 'Where are our moral foundations?'"

This reference to James's *The Europeans* is notable in part because Dickinson makes her source unusually clear. Here, she differentiates another's words from her own with quotation marks, and provides Mrs. Holland with enough information to identify the reference. She doesn't employ these niceties consistently in her correspondence; at times, in fact, she seems deliberately to disguise her sources.[8] Other exchanges with the Hollands reveal that the poet relied on a shared set of contemporary literary and cultural references in her letters, as gleaned from the periodical literature both households consumed (Capps 128–133). *The Europeans* is full of characters with the surname "Wentworth," and there is only one possible "Mr." among them. All this suggests that Dickinson seems to have taken special pains to ensure that Elizabeth Holland would recognize the source of "Mr. Wentworth's" question in Letter 619. Nevertheless, she then proceeds to misquote the character. In both the serialized version of *The Europeans* that Dickinson and Elizabeth Holland would have read the year prior in *The Atlantic Monthly*, and the book form first published in 1878, Mr. Wentworth twice speaks of "moral grounds," not "moral foundations" (*Europeans* 1027, 1030).[9] The care with which Dickinson approached literary references in her epistolary writing makes it unlikely that she would accidentally or casually have changed James's wording. The slight difference between James's original and Dickinson's revision may be part of her message, or perhaps a form of emphasis. At the very least, the misquotation, with its clear demarcation and broad clue, seem to beg the reader to recall the specific context of Mr. Wentworth's "moral foundations."

In another example of his ambivalent nostalgia for New England, James—having moved from Paris to London two years prior to the novel's publication—sets *The Europeans* in the countryside outside Boston in the 1830s. For his contemporaries, this place and time would immediately suggest the snap of "the Puritan whip" to which he refers year later, in *The American Scene*; his American readers in particular would recognize in his descriptions of the Wentworth family's home and surroundings the environment that fostered the Second Great Awakening as well as Transcendentalism, movements differently characterized by an emphasis on introspection and the questioning of accepted beliefs. For James, this setting also would have evoked his own vacillating, progressive father— "caring for our spiritual decency unspeakably more than for anything else, anything at all that might be or might become ours"—and the senior James's ever-shifting pedagogical philosophy that, as both Maher and Taylor separately argue, gave rise to both brilliance and a profound sense of insecurity and alienation in all five of his children.[10]

The novel examines the conflict, surrounding a young woman struggling for self-determination, between a traditional New England sense of patriarchal moral vision and the alternate values of a hybridized, French-American artistic secularism. Mr. Wentworth's daughter, Gertrude, is a source of great concern for the widower. We are introduced to the Wentworth family as Gertrude refuses to join their regular Sunday attendance at church; therefore, she is alone in the house when her French cousin, Felix, arrives unexpectedly. James describes Gertrude as "restless" several times in this early section, and he uses the whiff of sexualized scandal that this opening suggests as one means of examining tensions between

American and European relationships to gender-specific moral codes (888, 890, 891). Wentworth enlists Mr. Brand, a sober young clergyman, in his struggles with his daughter; as the novel progresses, Gertrude becomes increasingly irritated by Mr. Brand's awkward attempts to provide spiritual guidance. In the final chapter, Wentworth faces the culmination of his fears, as Gertrude finally stages a full rebellion. This climactic section is Dickinson's source in Letter 619. She quotes Mr. Wentworth's startled response to Gertrude's announcement that she has decided to marry Felix and depart permanently for Europe. Changing abruptly from absolute paternal authority to confused old man in this chapter, Wentworth conflates his own private feelings, his resistance to what he perceives to be the chaotic dissolution of his family, with "moral" law. Prior to this point, Wentworth's rule has been subtle; he presents himself as a loving and reasonable father concerned only for his children's well-being. In the scene Dickinson cites, this veil has been lifted, and we see that the law of this father is neither reasonable nor necessary. James has demonstrated repeatedly by this point in the story that, despite her "strange notions," Gertrude's behavior is decorous even by her society's high standards. Yet as she reveals her plans in this chapter, Wentworth strangely fears for her "moral" safety (915, 917, 933, 1020, 1027). Her actions are unassailable, but her free-thinking refusal of patriarchal religious ideology is heretical; Gertrude's movement towards self-determination threatens Wentworth's sense of both her place in the world and his own. His solution is an attempt to marry her off to the young minister, a substitute clerical father, despite the fact that by this point their incompatibility is obvious to everyone else, even Mr. Brand.

Gertrude's father refers to "morality" twice in the last chapter of *The Europeans*. "'It is difficult to explain,' he said. He wished, evidently, to be very just. 'It rests on moral grounds, as Mr. Brand says. It is the question whether it is the best thing for Gertrude'" (1027). The first appearance of the phrase "moral grounds" suggests that this particular version of ethics indeed is "difficult to explain," as it relies on a concatenation of culturally-specific abstractions: patriarchal rights, traditions of legal justice, and (masculine) religious authority. Felix counters, citing Gertrude's feelings. "It is usually a fairly good thing for a girl to marry the man she loves!" Yet James directs us to the realization that Felix's statement is a more benign version of Wentworth's paternalism: she is "a girl" to his "man." Significantly, Gertrude enters just as Felix finishes speaking. Crossing the threshold of her father's study, the site in the novel that most clearly demarcates hierarchies of gendered authority, she states that the right to "discuss" her "future" is hers alone. Wentworth's questioning, second use of the phrase, which Dickinson cites in her letter to Elizabeth Holland, follows this assertion, Gertrude's counter to her lover as well as her father: she doesn't need or want either of them to speak for her. Although directed to what suddenly has become a strong quorum of her supporters—Mr. Brand joins Felix and Gertrude's sister Charlotte to press Gertrude's right to choose her own fate—Wentworth's question is a response to his daughter's resistance. James writes, "Mr. Wentworth stood staring." Then, "'Where are our moral grounds?' demanded Mr. Wentworth, who had always thought Mr. Brand would be just the thing for a younger daughter with a peculiar temperament" (1028, 1029, 1030). Wentworth's "moral grounds" shift beneath him, as he faces his daughter's suddenly unapologetic independence and Mr. Brand's defection. He changes from declarative statement to interrogatory, and Gertrude wins the debate.

Wentworth's ideas about his French nephew also seem increasingly rigid and irrational as the novel progresses. Emerging as a reminder of the family's past, Felix and his sister Eugenia at first seem to embody lax, European ideas about sexuality and gender roles.[11] Felix is an open-hearted painter whose lack of respectable occupation inspires his uncle's initial distrust. However, as the story develops, Felix demonstrates moral qualities that James's audience would have recognized as ideally American. His love of nature and clear, if secular, code of interpersonal ethics recall both Emerson and the Enlightenment deism at the core of the nation's founding. The young man falls in love with Gertrude because he values her "strength" and "self-possession." Unlike her family and community, Felix recognizes that Gertrude has been "dormant...waiting for a touchstone" to begin life on her own terms. "But now she is beginning to awaken" (1007). Gertrude's "awakening" echoes the religious ones of her period, and would not have seemed strange to James's readers; early nineteenth-century spiritual movements emphasized self-examination as the path towards growth. By contrast, Wentworth increasingly seems to consider empty religious practice an acceptable substitute for genuine faith. By the novel's conclusion, James has blurred the boundaries between "European" and "American" sensibilities.

James's permanent emigration distinguishes him: a number of nineteenth-century, male American writers traveled to Europe and back, in an updated version of the "Grand Tour," and then wrote contrasted the stultification of monarchal Europe to the freedom of the "New

World."[12] Through Felix, James undermines the premises behind this project of literary nation-building. The New England that Wentworth represents is stunted by frigid winters and Puritan moral and religious traditions; Felix's Europe is a breath of free-thinking fresh air. Wentworth's approach to managing his family becomes a synecdochal representation of a paternalistic sense of national purpose that requires conformity and "self-control," particularly of its women (917). In this model, political independence from Europe has had the paradoxical effect of curtailing freedom and enforcing useless, suffocating social hierarchies. Gertrude's youthful, feminine vitality stands opposed to the Puritan code represented by both Mr. Brand and her father. Early in the novel, her eyes are described as both "dull and restless." Yet as she realizes she is in love with Felix, Gertrude begins to step "lightly." Throughout her poetry and letters, Emily Dickinson's self-descriptions emphasize her material body; similarly, as Gertrude "awakens," James uses increasingly specific imagery to indicate her physical presence. In a conversation with Felix, her "heart began to beat" (888, 968, 969). She comes alive through a desire that is physical, intellectual, and spiritual—it is a desire both for Felix and for freedom from the restrictions her community places most heavily on intelligent and expressive young women. In the final chapter, Wentworth and Mr. Brand come into direct conflict with the "new" world offered, in James's twist, by European culture. The reversal of Wentworth's logic becomes clear in Felix's Emersonian response to his uncle's question about "moral grounds": "It is sometimes very moral to change, you know" (1030). The "change" that Felix proposes is embodied by James's examination of a "strange," thoughtful young woman; her declaration of independence requires her to escape the paternalism of American "moral" consciousness. The conclusion makes it clear that Gertrude, like Henry James, will "not return" to her "native land to live" (October 24, 1900; 4). Indeed, in order to "live," both she and he must go elsewhere.

Gertrude's pending departure sets in motion the eventual marriage of Mr. Brand to the Wentworth daughter that suits him best, the sweet-tempered and domestic Charlotte. These rearrangements resolve the conflicts of the novel, but Wentworth experiences these changes as a loss of personal authority. In Letter 619, Dickinson in part seems to identify with Wentworth, impotent in the face of shifting relationships. The poet's attribution to James's character is prefaced by statements that suggest intimacies strained by distance: referring to her own "awkward loneliness,"

Dickinson declares "how little I know of you recently." Perhaps her slight change in Wentworth's wording, her "misquotation," indicates that the poet means to "tell it slant," or simultaneously endorse and critique Wentworth's relationship to family, his understanding of American moral purpose, or his ideas about the spiritual education of young women.[13] Speculations about the "Philadelphia friend" Dickinson refers to in Letter 619 offer us the possibility that the poet may be arguing, with Gertrude Wentworth, that she has the right to love or associate with whom she chooses, regardless of her family's (or Elizabeth Holland's) opinions. More interesting for my present purposes is the fact that Dickinson uses James as a means of expressing a cloaked but palpable resistance to Mrs. Holland's ideas about femininity. James makes it clear that Wentworth's need for order has blinded him to what is really "best for Gertrude." Her self-assertion at the threshold of the study—as she counters both her father and her future husband—marks her attainment of self-actualized womanhood, a process of personal maturation that the novel also carefully traces. Like Gertrude Wentworth, Dickinson is an unmarried daughter; although her father is dead by this point, she still lives in his house with her mother and sister. Writing to Mrs. Holland, she indicates that despite her seemingly dependent position, she is in charge of her own destiny. Gertrude, "strange" to her family members, chafes within the limitations of the roles available to her, as a young woman in 1830s Massachusetts. Unlike Charlotte, she finds it impossible to sit through long church services, and she cannot accept that she must accede to the will of her father and Mr. Brand instead of trusting her own judgment. Writing to her "Little Sister," the poet may be saying that she suffers from a similar affliction. Elizabeth Holland and Charlotte Wentworth are suited to the roles assigned to them by (heteronormative) gender conventions, but Emily Dickinson and Gertrude Wentworth are not. The quotation from James enables the poet to suggest that her own ambivalence about notions of womanly selflessness reflects a difference of character rather than a dangerous personality flaw. More to the point, her hard-won independence is critical to her sense of self, and it makes her poetry possible. As Martha Dickinson Bianchi reflects, despite the seeming narrowness of her life, "Aunt Emily" was the family member most "free to her chosen horizon" (57; qtd in Bennett, *My Life* 43).

Throughout *The Europeans*, Charlotte serves as Gertrude's gentle advocate. More than her father, Mr. Brand, and even Felix, Charlotte understands and sympathizes with her sister's internal struggles; eventually, she and Felix become unlikely allies through their shared appreciation of Gertrude's "beautiful nature" (1020). Messmer suggests that Dickinson's correspondence with Mrs. Holland was influenced by several painful early losses, of female friends who stopped writing back (71–81). Dickinson's letters reveal that several beloved schoolmates at Amherst Academy, "saved" in evangelical Christian revivals, began to distance themselves from the poet as she failed to undergo the same process. Dickinson's formal education, both at Amherst Academy and particularly later during her year at the newly-formed Mt. Holyoke Female Seminary, was marked by pressure from teachers and peers towards personal conversion, an important tenet in Mary Lyon's interpretation of Congregationalism. In discussing this period in the context of the poet's lifelong ambivalence towards religion, Jane Donahue Eberwein suggests that Dickinson's resistance may have resulted from her recognition of "the connection between submissive behavior fostered by religion and the docility that would soon be expected of these young women as wives in patriarchally ordered Christian homes" (76–77).[14] In Letter 619, Dickinson may be asking Elizabeth Holland for the sisterly trust and support that the devout and obedient Charlotte Wentworth demonstrates towards the doubting Gertrude. At the same time, she uses *The Europeans* to present an alternative to Mrs. Holland's, and Mr. Wentworth's, ideas about feminine submission.

In December, 1879, two months after her letter to Elizabeth Holland, Dickinson writes Thomas Wentworth Higginson. Part of a well-known correspondence that lasted more than twenty years, until her death in 1886, Letter 622 is a reply to Higginson's gift of a copy of his *Short Studies of American Authors*, published that month. *Short Studies* included essays on the work of Hawthorne, Poe, Thoreau, William Dean Howells, Helen Hunt Jackson, and James. Dickinson expresses disagreement with Higginson's analyses of several of these writers. This letter also continues the work, begun in earlier missives, of developing beyond her initial epistolary performance as Higginson's "pupil." Higginson spends some time on *The Europeans* in *Short Studies*; Dickinson must have had the novel, so recently read and quoted to Elizabeth Holland, in mind when composing her response. The figure of Henry James plays a complex role in this letter, serving both as a stand-in for the poet and as an admired author in his own right whose approach to literature she sees as productively opposed to Higginson's.

Today Thomas Wentworth Higginson[15] is remembered for his relationship with Dickinson and his editorship, with Mabel Loomis Todd, of the first edition of her poetry. However, for his contemporaries Higginson was a prominent figure in American literary culture, and a standard-bearing proponent of civil rights for women and African Americans. Higginson gained fame prior to the Civil War as a preacher whose skill made him a spokesman for Boston-area abolitionists. During the war, he commanded the First South Carolina Volunteers, a regiment of freed slaves that was the first African American unit in the Union Army. *Army Life in a Black Regiment*, in which Higginson wrote of the courage and integrity of his troops, was published in 1869. He used his later editorial positions at the *Atlantic Monthly* and *The Nation* to introduce women writers, including Helen Hunt Jackson, to the American public. Higginson's progressive editorial politics may have inspired the note from Dickinson that initiated their correspondence. Her first letter is most directly a response to "A Letter to a Young Contributor," which Higginson wrote for the April, 1862 issue of *The Atlantic Monthly*—but the Dickinson family would have known of Higginson's activism, much of which was documented in the pages of that periodical. As biographer and editor Howard N. Meyer indicates, between 1859 and 1862 Higginson published numerous essays in *The Atlantic Monthly*, defending John Brown and other "radical" abolitionists, proclaiming the inevitability of a war over slavery, and advocating for women's rights (17–20).

In "A Letter to a Young Contributor," Higginson both solicits material from women and expresses conventional beliefs about feminine authorship. In a tone of gentle humor, he urges his "young contributors" to use their own names rather than male pseudonyms, and submit clean copy (in Meyer 528–542). Dickinson encloses four poems in her first letter, in which she famously asks "Are you too deeply occupied to say if my Verse is alive?" (L 260). Higginson's reply is lost, but she wrote back immediately; she includes two additional poems, suggesting that his response had been positive. In this second note, Dickinson first asks Higginson to "be my Preceptor," and she will continue to address him by this deferential term even as she expresses greater skepticism of his criticism. Years later, although the tone of her letters has changed and she no longer requests his feedback, she twice declares to Higginson that he "saved my Life" (L 265, L 330, L 621). A male literary authority who believes women can and should publish, he provides crucial recognition and support. Upon this necessary foundation, Dickinson constructs the gradual resistance that marks her maturation as a poet.

Like her letters to women friends, Dickinson's correspondence with Higginson reflects both an adherence to and a tactical deployment of gender expectations. By her third letter, in June 1862, Dickinson's assumption of the role of a pupil is simultaneous with the emergence of an appropriately submissive critique of his suggestions. Considered in historical context, these two messages are not contradictory. For Dickinson, Higginson is a (paternal) literary authority. She seeks and values his input, even as she sees the limitations of his analysis. In this note, Letter 265, Dickinson equates Higginson to a doctor who has "bled" her; the obedient patient is dismayed by her "uncontrolled," feminized body of work. She both affirms and undermines this hierarchical relationship by suggesting that "The Sailor cannot see the North—but knows the Needle can—." Higginson becomes Dickinson's compass, as he knows where to direct the ship. Yet her work is her own: he is a nautical tool, not the ship's captain. The female poet who rarely left her father's home takes on the position of a male explorer. As a lowly "Sailor," Dickinson does not declare herself the authority of her own craft. However, while her "Preceptor" is a reliable guide to point the way, it is she who decides which direction to follow.

Higginson's ideas about women's writing rely on relatively conservative notions of both gender identity and literary style. After Dickinson's death Higginson and Mabel Loomis Todd edited her poetry into conformance with traditional form; they inserted rhyme, standard punctuation, and regular meter. Scholars debate which of the two was most responsible for these changes, which were corrected by subsequent editors. Yet Miller tells us that nineteenth-century poets were accustomed to having little control over the editing of their work. Although this could be one reason why Dickinson chose largely to avoid publishing her poetry, Miller hypothesizes that this seems unlikely in context. When late twentieth- and early twenty-first century readers emphasize the unconventionality of her style, we risk ignoring elements in a number of her poems that were quite standard for the period (180–190). At the same time, Higginson's advice to Dickinson, particularly in the first few months of their correspondence, seems to consist of repeated urgings towards traditional rhyme and meter. While his letters are lost, her responses quote him back to himself. She thanks him for serving as her "surgeon," and seems genuinely to value his feedback, but she also defends her poetic choices. "You think my gait 'spasmodic'—I am in danger—Sir—/You think me 'uncontrolled'—I have no Tribunal" (L 271, L 265). In Letter 268, she writes "You said 'Dark.' I know the Butterfly—and the Lizard—and the Orchis—/Are these not *your* Countrymen?," suggesting that she feels misread. Sending more poems with Letter 271, she asks humbly "Are these more orderly?...I think you called me 'Wayward.' Will you help me to improve?" Much later, in 1874, after she has sent him "The Wind begun to knead the Grass—," Higginson responds to the poem with a single disappointing line, contained in an otherwise chatty letter: "Your poem about the storm is fine—it gives the sudden transitions" (L 405a). It seems largely at Higginson's behest that Helen Hunt Jackson, Dickinson's former Mount Holyoke classmate and another of his female "pupils," takes an interest in the poet's work. Both then and now, Jackson is best known for her 1884 best-seller *Ramona*, an important activist novel that uses sentimental tropes in depicting the life of a mixed-race Native American woman experiencing racism and other hardships in Spanish-speaking California after the Mexican–American War. According to Johnson, Higginson indicates that Jackson "did not know of (Dickinson's) poems till I showed them to her...But she remembered her from school" (L 330). Higginson may hope that a renewed acquaintance with Jackson will provide Dickinson with an example of good (feminine) writing. Like Jackson, Dickinson seeks Higginson's editorial advice and regards him as an authority, but their relationships to form and style could not have been more dissimilar; clearly, Higginson misunderstood what model Dickinson needed and would be likely to follow, as she sought guidance for her poetic development.

The year prior to the publication of *Short Studies of American Authors*, Higginson attained the post of poetry editor for *The Nation*. He seems to have regarded this position in the light of a patriotic duty, to foster what biographer Brenda Wineapple terms "an art of open arms" (289). Although Higginson's activism indeed extended to his editorship, he promoted authors whose writing evinced clearly "American" values of accessibility, democracy, and optimism, as well as a notion of personal honor that was gender-specific and heteronormative. Higginson's editorial work and critical essays suggest that he considered adherence to traditional form to be essential to literary quality. Dickinson could not have missed the contrast between his analyses of her poetry and the effusive essay on Jackson's work in *Short Studies*. Again, as Messmer and Loeffelholz emphasize, in her correspondence Dickinson actively is negotiating a relationship to authorship in response to gendered social and literary traditions that are central to her sense of self (Messmer 71–105; Loeffelholz, *Dickinson and the Boundaries* 1–7, 47–81). In one letter, Dickinson asks Higginson if she can use his "disapproval" as an excuse for refusing to give copies of her poems to Jackson. The request echoes an earlier evocation of her father's resistance as the reason for her unwillingness to leave Amherst to meet

Higginson in Boston. These letters suggest that Dickinson selectively deploys patriarchal authority in order to justify her own choices (L 316; L 319; L 476). Arguably, her use of Henry James in Letter 622 in part represents a similar tactic. James is closer to Higginson in authority, but even early in his career—in *The Europeans,* for example—he departs from the prior generation's ideas about literary aesthetics in a way that echoes the divide between William Dean Howells's *Atlantic Monthly* and James T. Fields's. Moreover, Higginson's objections to James in *Short Studies of American Authors* strikingly echo his critical suggestions for Dickinson's poetry. Letter 622 suggests that she recognized the parallels.

William James was named after their paternal grandfather; Henry, the second son, shared a name with their father, a well-known religious philosopher. Many early reviewers (including Howells, at one point) differentiate Henry James from his famous progenitor by the designation "Jr." The title of "Henry James, Jr." is unremarkable, then; but the essay itself is marked by dismissive condescension. Higginson, the elder literary statesman, laments the low quality of recent American writing as an aberration in the nation's otherwise steady cultural development. A description of the dilettantism that increasingly marks the artistic education of young American authors builds to his first direct reference: "Mr. Henry James, Jr…may be said to have been trained in literature by literature itself, so early did he begin writing, and so incessantly has he written" (51). Couched as paternal advice to an overeager young author, boring the public with an excess of inexperienced prose, this criticism sets the tone for the rest of the essay. Even prior to discussing James's work, Higginson quickly sketches an image of an impulsive youth with questionable abilities and dangerously un-American commitments. Many contemporary American reviewers objected to James's complex sentences, as well as to his transatlantic settings, characters, and themes; indeed, he often was criticized for betraying European sensibilities or even simply for living in Europe.[16] While Higginson's essay hits these familiar notes, his analysis more specifically emphasizes the (gender-specific) moral and political values of what he terms "good writing." Higginson's complaints about James's style—"how prolix it is, what repetitions, what a want of condensation and method!"—provide grounds for an analysis of the author's lack of patriotism. James "does not quite appreciate the strong point of republicanism" and "one hardly knows whether he would wish to be accounted an American writer, after all" (52, 53). For Higginson, these ideological and artistic failings are synonymous with an inadequate masculinity.

Unlike William Dean Howells, James's fellow in "the international school" who lived in the United States, "Mr. James has kept a little too good company: we do not find in his books such refreshing types of hearty and robust manhood as Howells...[but] Then Mr. James's life has been so transatlantic..." (52). Here, both James and his characters are emasculated by the author's European influences and themes. Moreover, James's novels leave one "discontented." As Higginson elaborates, "if in this respect he seems behind Howells, it must be remembered that James habitually deals with profounder emotions, and is hence more liable to be overmastered" ("Howells" 32–39, 35; "James" 59). Voicing the emerging cultural nationalism that serves as a powerful, simultaneous counter during this period to the literary Anglophilia of Annie Adams Fields and others, Higginson describes Howells as "without an equal in America—and therefore without an equal among his English-speaking contemporaries." By contrast, he dismisses James, who "should employ someone else to write the last few pages" of his novels ("James" 56–57; "Howells" 33; "James" 58).[17]

In "Henry James, Jr.," Higginson equates conventional style with what today we might term normative gender expression—both are included in the moral qualities that are essential to good literature. This concatenation is, of course, standard for his period; it also is consistent throughout his critical corpus. In fact, compared with his writing on Walt Whitman, his response to James seems mild.[18] For Higginson, Whitman's refusal of standard rhyme and meter is symptomatic of a profound failure of masculinity. In "Women and Men: The Victory of the Weak," a brief 1887 essay published in *Harper's Bazar*, Higginson evokes the figure of a cheerful female invalid, and suggests that she represents "the manfulness of a true democrat." By contrast, Whitman lacks this necessary manliness, epitomized by self-control (214–215). This comparison seems remarkable to us for several reasons, including its indication that "republican" masculine courage is attainable by women. This ideal, shared by a number of his feminist contemporaries and later aptly termed "the Wollstonecraft dilemma," does little to unsettle a masculine model for (feminine) citizenship.[19] In this piece Higginson equates manhood and socially-responsible authorship exclusively with upper-class Anglo-American values that by necessity include the private practice of (hetero)sexuality, within the confines of marriage.

Nelson and Price provide a previously unpublished 1908 essay in which journalist and literary biographer William Sloane Kennedy addresses Higginson's dislike for *Leaves of Grass* and its author. Writing Kennedy in

1895, Higginson states that Whitman, whom he met once, "never seemed to me a thoroughly wholesome or manly man." He provides a list of arguments to support this claim, which includes the objection that the poet never expresses "any personal love for any individual women," but rather "the mere craving of sex for sex." Clearly, as Nelson and Price emphasize in their analysis of this essay, Higginson evinces homophobia in this piece and throughout his writing on Whitman. However, as they also note, Higginson's (homophobic) disgust for Whitman is based on what are for him other obvious indicators of the poet's inadequate masculinity (497–524, 504, 507–508). In calling attention to Whitman's lack of "love" for "any individual women," Higginson may object to the promiscuity of the narrative voice in *Leaves of Grass*—its failure in his view to rise above lust to the higher standard of "love" for an "individual" (woman)— as well as to its homoeroticism. The faults that he describes in his 1895 letter to Kennedy include Whitman's lack of "personal honesty" and the fact that he chose nursing over soldiery for the Union Army during the Civil War. For Higginson, these details are proof of cowardice, and an effeminacy that for him is not necessarily bound to physical sex. Whitman not only rejects the poetic conventions Higginson cherishes, he offers a very different view of maleness that celebrates the working classes and a non-heterosexual, gender-transgressive ideal of physical and cultural communion with the American others he catalogs throughout *Leaves of Grass*. For the poetry editor of *The Nation*, Whitman's "democratic" writing goes much too far: in sexualizing Higginson's "art of open arms," it represents a profound personal and national threat.

The upper-class Henry James may not have inspired quite this sense of danger, but the tone of "Henry James, Jr." suggests that Higginson's analysis in this essay is consistent with his responses to Whitman. Higginson would have known, for example, of the notoriously "obscure hurt" that kept James from serving in the Civil War.[20] "Henry James, Jr." echoes Higginson's message from the writing on Whitman that non-traditional form indicates an inferior masculinity, questionable morals, and probable homosexuality. Particularly following the glowing essay on Helen Hunt Jackson that precedes "Henry James, Jr." in *Short Studies*, the fact that Emily Dickinson's "Preceptor" attributes (gendered, heteronormative) moral and patriotic values to gender-specific conventions of style and clear activist commitments would not have escaped the poet's notice. Arguably, it is to this ideological conflation that she most objects in Letter 622.

The letter begins as follows:

> Dear friend—
> Brabantio's gift was not more fair than your's, though I trust without his pathetic inscription—'Which but thou hast already, with all my Heart I would keep from thee'—Of Poe, I know too little to think—Hawthorne appalls, entices—
> Mrs. Jackson soars to your estimate lawfully as a Bird, but of Howells and James, one hesitates—Your relentless Music dooms as it redeems—...

In another clear reference, the poet opens with Shakespeare's *Othello*; she quotes Brabantio's reaction to the discovery that his daughter has married the Moorish general without his permission. As a means of opening a letter of thanks for a small gift, Dickinson's choice of literary allusions seems odd. If we understand "Brabantio's gift" to be his daughter, Dickinson indicates that Desdemona is "not more fair" ("lovely," or "just"?) than Higginson's book. The perplexing simile may be an attempt to startle Higginson into closer attention, in preparation for the quotation that follows. In Shakespeare's play, Brabantio laments his own lost authority when he states to Othello, "I here do give thee that with all my heart / Which, but thou hast already, with all my heart / I would keep from thee" (I, iii, 193–195). Linking this "inscription" with Higginson's gift of a copy of *Short Studies*, the poet in part may present her "Preceptor" as another Brabantio, playing opposite her Desdemona. Written two months after Letter 619, and to a very different figure in her life, Letter 622 opens with another reference to a loving father whose outdated rules blind him to the needs of a self-directed daughter. This representation grounds Dickinson's examination of Higginson's analyses of Jackson, Howells, and James in the next section of the letter.

In the scene from *Othello* that Dickinson quotes, Desdemona undermines her father's authority by invoking the abstract concept of patriarchal rule. As she states, "I do perceive here a divided duty...I am hitherto your daughter: but here's my husband / And so much duty as my mother show'd / To you, preferring you before her father / So much I challenge that I may profess / Due to the Moor my lord" (I, iii, 181–189). Desdemona cites the law to justify her violation of it. Brabantio's bitterly ironic "Gift" to Othello, as he recognizes, is the daughter who already has given herself, against his wishes. Like Desdemona, Dickinson suggests that she is not a passive supplicant to her father-figure's authority; she has a degree of self-determination even within her adherence to the rules of the society in which she lives. Shakespeare sets this scene in a council chamber.

Brabantio's complaint, Desdemona's counter, and the discussion that follows is an ad hoc interruption of state business; regardless, this is a hearing before the Duke of Venice, who repeatedly uses legal terms throughout, and his counselors. The "case" ends when Brabantio accepts his daughter's argument. The Duke gives "a sentence," and returns to state affairs, dismissing Desdemona's trial as a private event (I, iii, 199–277). Her flagrant disobedience of patriarchal law occurs at the very center of civil power, yet it registers as an irrelevant distraction—and therein lies the success of her strategy.

Alongside Desdemona, Dickinson invokes the rule of a father as she begins a letter in which she presents her right to self-determination. At the same time, in her quotation from Shakespeare Dickinson seems also to present herself as Othello.[21] Early in Act I, Brabantio and his rage are awakened by Iago's appeal to what may be the most exploited of white racist paternal fears: "Even now, now, very now, an old black ram / is tupping your white ewe" (I, i, 88–89). Writing the famous abolitionist and author of *Army Life in a Black Regiment*, Dickinson in effect suggests that the Higginson of *Short Studies* is another father-figure blinded by personal prejudice. Like Othello, the poet "hast already" what Higginson "would keep from" her. Perhaps what Dickinson "hast already," with or without Higginson's approval, is certainty in her own poetic voice. In the first line of Letter 622, Dickinson prefaces her quotation of Shakespeare with the "trust" that Higginson's "gift" did not come with Brabantio's "pathetic inscription" attached: she manages to assert her artistic independence while also expressing the hope that she will not need to do so.

The single line that comprises the second paragraph of Letter 622 opposes Helen Hunt Jackson to those who receive the "doom" of Higginson's "relentless praise." "Mrs. Jackson soars to your estimate lawfully as a Bird, but of Howells and James, one hesitates—Your relentless Music dooms as it redeems—." "Mrs. Jackson" and the initial "your" connect Higginson with the sentimental novelist in the first section; the commas then establish a middle pair consisting of "Howells and James," followed by the hesitating "one," Dickinson herself. The dash disrupts the reader's expectation, implied by the sentence's structure, of a third literary partnership, perhaps with Dickinson in the place occupied by Jackson in the first clause ("Mrs. Jackson" and "your," "Howells and James," "one" and…). The second, capitalized "your" seems to follow this pattern by bringing the sentence back to Higginson, indicating the possibility of a neat completion via a final pair ("one" and "Your"). However, the capitalization also suggests that the dash between Dickinson's "one" and Higginson is a full stop;

"Your relentless Music" may in fact begin an entirely different sentence and thought. The last word, "redeems," is a metaphysical abstraction of the physical "soaring" of the "Bird"-like Mrs. Jackson. Therefore, the sentence reads like an interrupted chiasmus composed of disjointed, incomplete alliances. "Howells and James" share with "one" the fact that they are situated in the middle of the line's mirroring logic, between two active forces: "Mrs. Jackson" who "soars"; and "Your relentless music," which "dooms..." Dickinson refuses to sign herself, by name, into this uneasy structure. Simultaneously, she unsettles the notion that "one" might be allied with Jackson, or indeed even with Higginson himself, he of the "relentless music." The ambiguous punctuation hints that it may be with Howells and James that "one" shares closer artistic sympathies.

A comparison using the word "fair," and thereby mirroring the letter's opening line, begins the next section; Dickinson alludes to yet another source, a poem by James Russell Lowell that she calls "The Slipper Hymn." Johnson suggests that she may intend to "mystify" Higginson with this title. He identifies the original as "After the Burial," published in *The Atlantic Monthly* in 1868. Lowell's conventional relationship to rhyme, stanza, and meter regularly won Higginson's public praise. In fact, Higginson dedicated his own book of poetry, 1889's *The Afternoon Landscape: Poems and Translations*, to Lowell (47).[22] Dickinson devotes much of the latter half of Letter 622 to "The Slipper Hymn," a compression and revision of Lowell's poem. She would have known of Higginson's appreciation for Lowell from *The Atlantic Monthly*, and perhaps from his writing on American poetry for other periodicals. While Lowell's poem likely was familiar to Higginson, we cannot know if he got the disguised reference. In her distilled, burnished version of "After the Burial," Dickinson again emphasizes that her writing necessarily diverges from Higginson's ideal. She understands what he considers to be good poetry, and she demonstrates that she could write that way, if she wanted to. Loeffelholz argues that these revisions are "strategies of condensation and epigram" ("Dickinson's Decoration" 663–665). Dickinson's version of "After the Burial" in Letter 622 allows her to perform the growth of her voice in conversation with the rules of poetic convention that were so important to Higginson.

Dickinson's "Slipper Hymn" in Letter 622 immediately follows her objections to Higginson's analysis of Henry James, and comes two months after her tactical use of *The Europeans* in the letter to Elizabeth Holland. Both epistles suggest that Dickinson finds in the style and content of James's fiction a reflection of her own approach, and her own complexly adherent resistance, to gender-traditional notions of both feminine behavior and women's writing. We have no concrete evidence that Dickinson read any of his other fiction, but *The Europeans* is consistent with James's examination in later work of the specific consequences for women of the marital imperative, in the midst of shifting nineteenth-century concepts of gender, economics, and moral law.[23] Dickinson's revisions, of Lowell in Letter 622 and of Higginson in her 1877 version of "Decoration," read like demonstrations, virtuoso performances through which she claims equal footing with the acclaimed male poets of her period. By contrast, her use of Henry James is an elaboration on a shared theme. Loeffelholz reminds readers that Dickinson revised Higginson's "Decoration," a memorial poem for the Civil War dead; Higginson's original also appears in Henry James's *Notebooks*. James provides the entire poem near his account of visiting Alice James's grave, along with the gender-transgressive misquotation of the inscription from Dante that suggests his close identification with his (queer) sister.[24] For Loeffelholz, Higginson's poem provides both James and Dickinson with a means of situating her/his own unspeakable or publicly-invisible losses in relationship to a national mourning ("Dickinson's Decoration" 681). Indeed, Bennett reads the poet's work of the late 1850s and early 1860s as evidence of profound grief and anger, as she mourns Susan Gilbert's marriage to her brother, Austin Dickinson (*My Life* 33, 38–63). Alongside Alice and Henry James, Emily Dickinson shares a "queer" social status—outside of heteronormative pairings, and privately attuned to same-sex intimacy. In these letters, we see evidence of her ambivalence to the versions of femininity available to her—an ambivalence that parallels the relationship to normative womanhood that James articulates in his published corpus. Unlike Gertrude Wentworth or James himself, the poet found her own way forward by retreating inwards, rather than taking herself to Europe. But in her far-ranging poetic voice, as she identifies as "Malay" or "Circassian," and evokes "Naples" and "Van Dieman's Land," Dickinson claims the expatriate Henry James as a fellow-traveler.[25]

## Notes

1. Horne's 2015 essay responds to an earlier version of this chapter, while presenting a different reading.
2. Letter 619's first allusion, to "the Coroner of Alexandria," invites several interpretations. Dickinson could be alluding to Plutarch's depiction of the deaths of Antony and Cleopatra; alternately, she might be referencing the murder of Hypatia by a Christian mob, or Ptolemy's decision to steal Alexander's body and return it to Alexandria. Each of these possibilities

presents the reader with a different set of associative meanings, some of which are in keeping with my analysis of the letter as a whole.
3. Rebecca Patterson, in 1951's *The Riddle of Emily Dickinson*, first suggested that Dickinson's more sexually charged poetry was written for a woman; she proposed friend Kate Anthon as the intended recipient. Since then, a critical mass of work from various periods of scholarship on the poet has argued that Dickinson had a clearly romantic and probably erotic attachment to Susan Gilbert Dickinson. In addition to Faderman and Paula Bennett (*Emily Dickinson*), see also Kristin M. Comment, Judith Farr, Ellen Louise Hart and Martha Nell Smith, Sylvia Henneberg, Lena Koski, H. Jordan Landry, and Pollak (*Dickinson*).
4. By 2002, Bennett regrets her part in the "canonization of Dickinson" as a feminist poet because it has come at the expense of equal attention to other nineteenth-century women poets whose work is in her view, braver and more politically satisfying. "If my perception of Dickinson has so radically altered, it is because, after ten years spent studying other nineteenth-century American women poets, I now know much more clearly what she could have done and, therefore, what she did not do. Like other feminist Dickinson scholars, I believed when I wrote *Woman Poet* that there were strict limits to what nineteenth-century women could say in their verse and that part of the reason Dickinson chose not to publish was to give the radicality of her themes (not just her style) full play...I no longer believe this" (59).
5. Cameron devotes separate, equally foundational but unrelated books to Dickinson and James. She emphasizes the poet's sustained refusal to select one poetic word, version, or form over others, resulting in a consistent "heteroglossia or doubleness." As she suggests, in her poetry Dickinson "sets up a situation that seems exclusionary, and...she then refuses choices which seem inevitable"; or, in other words, "the presumption that choosing is necessary is contested by the representation of not choosing" (*Choosing* 29, 21, 23).
6. Although the quote references Anne K. Mellor's 2002 book on women's political writing in England, similar phrasing predominates in writing by American advocates for women's rights during the period. See, for example, Elizabeth Cady Stanton's "Speech at Lawrence, Kansas" and Susan B. Anthony's "Homes of Single Women" (in DuBois 114–118, 146–151). See also Jessica Berman, on James's ideas about women's roles in preserving Anglo-American culture.
7. Letter 268 was written in 1862 to Higginson, and again, audience is critical. Dickinson uses similar terms throughout her corpus, but as Messmer argues, all of the poet's self-presentations "both reveal and conceal the 'true' Dickinson" (13).

8. For one example, see Johnson's notes to Letter 622, discussed below.
9. Chapters X–XII of *The Europeans* were contained in the October, 1878 edition of *The Atlantic Monthly* (Volume 42, Issue 249). Mr. Wentworth's "moral grounds" are on pages 422 and 424 of that publication.
10. The quote is from *A Small Boy and Others* (*Autobiographies* 136). Maher traces the lives of the two James "failures," Bob (Robertson) and Wilkie (Garth Wilkerson) James, whose separate trajectories of bankruptcy and alcoholism are, in her view, as equally a product of Henry James, Sr.'s approaches to childhood education as William and Henry's successes. Alice, as a girl, was educated in only a limited way, and largely at home. See also Strouse and Habegger (*The Father*).
11. For James's contemporaries and many readers since, the "artful" Eugenia serves as a foil for the greater "naturalness" represented by her artist brother, as well as the American characters. See Judith Caesar for a counter to this reading that also discusses its predominance in twentieth-century scholarship.
12. Notable examples include Washington Irving's *The Sketchbook of Geoffrey Crayon, Gent.* (1820) and Mark Twain's *Innocents Abroad* (1869). See Jeffrey Alan Melton for an analysis of the ideological work of American travel-writing about Europe during the period.
13. "Tell all the truth but tell it slant" is 1263 in Franklin.
14. See also James McIntosh.
15. The name parallel may not be a coincidence. Edward A. Leary, in 1982, suggests that James's "Mr. Wentworth" might have been modeled on Higginson (34). Perhaps Higginson picked up on the parallel; this might help explain some of the vitriol of his essay on James in *Short Studies*. See also Alice James's comments on Higginson in her diaries (note 24, below).
16. Another early reviewer, in *Scribner's Monthly* 11 (February 1876) suggests that the majority of American characters in *Roderick Hudson* "are treated with a barren sneer." In a more positive review for the *Nation* from the same year, Grace Norton nevertheless suggests that the characters in *Roderick Hudson* "as if unconsciously to the author" become "a constant reminder that Americans lose much of their rightful charm and interest when transplanted from their own habitat and exhibited among the more cultivated growths of modern life." An English reviewer of *The Europeans*, writing for the *Pall Mall Gazette* in 1878, opens with the statement that "Mr. Henry James, although an American by birth, belongs by literary sympathies and antecedents essentially to Europe, and in Europe to France" (in Hayes 11, 13, 50). See Hayes 47–64 for other contemporary reviews of *The Europeans*.
17. Higginson attributes the criticism about James's conclusions to "a clever woman," a phrase biographer Anna Mary Wells indicates he often used to credit his wife (259–260). In a 1905 letter to Henry, William James expresses similar frustrations with his brother's style in *The Golden Bowl*.

"But why won't you, just to please Brother, sit down and write a new book, with no twilight or mustiness in the plot, with great vigor and decisiveness in the action, no fencing in the dialogue, no psychological commentaries, and absolute straightness in the style?" (Skrupskelis and Berkeley 301).

18. Higginson's better-known comments on Whitman include a few lines in "Literature as an Art": "It is no discredit to Walt Whitman that he wrote *Leaves of Grass*, only that he did not burn it afterwards" (753). In another piece, Higginson describes his single 1860 encounter with Whitman. "The personal impression made on me by the poet was not so much of manliness as of Boweriness, if I may coin the phrase; indeed, rather suggesting...'a dandy roustabout'" ("Cheerful Yesterdays" 676). As Robert K. Nelson and Kenneth M. Price suggest, the reference to New York's Bowery disdains Whitman as working-class while intimating homosexuality, as does the term "dandy" as well (499–500). In "Unmanly Manhood" Higginson uses Whitman and Oscar Wilde as examples of a rising tolerance for "immoral" literature. Again, insinuations of homosexuality are intermingled with judgments about each figure's failures "of action": Whitman's Civil War nursing service, and Wilde's refusal to follow the good example set by his mother, the Irish poet Jane Wilde, by writing about the exploitation of Ireland (1).

19. Carole Pateman is the first to use this phrase to describe the conflict inherent to struggles for women's rights within political systems that define citizenship according to implicitly or explicitly "masculine" criteria (14).

20. In *Notes of a Son and Brother*, James recounts being unable to enlist as the result of an 1861 back injury sustained while helping to fight a house fire, during a period in which the family was living in Newport, RI. A number of scholars have discussed the odd juxtapositions and perambulations of this account. James describes "the queer fusion or confusion established in my consciousness during the soft spring of '61 by the firing on Fort Sumter, Mr. Lincoln's instant call for volunteers and a physical mishap... having overtaken me at the same dark hour..." He continues by elaborately detailing the injurious event itself: "Jammed into the acute angle between two high fences, where the rhythmic play of my arms, in tune with that of several other pairs, but at a dire disadvantage of position, induced a rural, a rusty, a quasi-extemporised old engine to work and a saving stream to flow, I had done myself, in face of a shabby conflagration, a horrid even if an obscure hurt" (*Autobiographies* 437, 438).

21. See Páraic Finnerty, Chapter 8. According to Finnerty, Shakespeare's character enables Dickinson to explore questions of race. See also Bennett ("The Orient").

22. In this introduction, for schoolchildren, to one of Lowell's poems, Higginson relates his youthful impressions of and appreciation for the poet. Their personal relationship seems to have been friendly but not particularly close (Wineapple 94, 277).

23. See Robert Pippin for a detailed analysis of the ways that James presents nineteenth-century social convention and ideas about morality as inapplicable—indeed, even unethical—in the context of shifting economic and subjective realities.
24. Although we don't know if Henry James ever read Dickinson's posthumously published poetry, his sister Alice certainly did. "It is reassuring to hear the English pronouncement that Emily Dickinson is fifth-rate, they have such a capacity for missing quality; the robust evades them equally with the subtle. Her being sicklied o'er with T.W. Higginson makes one quake lest there be a latent flaw that escapes one's vision..." (227).
25. "The Malay—took the Pearl" (1862) is F451. "Some Rainbow coming from the Fair" (F162, 1860) and "Color, caste, denomination" (F836, 1864) both use the word "Circassian" to refer to the Eastern Caucasus region or its occupants. "The lonesome for they know not what" (1862) and "If you were coming in the Fall" (1862) are F326 and F356, respectively. "Van Dieman's Land" had become independent Tasmania in 1856, four years before "If you were coming in the Fall" probably was written. Dickinson references the city of Naples in "When Etna basks and purrs" (F1161, 1869). See Betsy Erkkila ("Dickinson and Class"), Pollak ("Dickinson and the Poetics"), and Bennett ("The Negro") for readings of representations of blackness in the first poem. See Miller's Chapter 5 for an alternate analysis, of the Orientalism in several of these poems, and its significance in the context of the Civil War.

CHAPTER 4

# Henry James, French Feminist: Marguerite Duras's *La Bête dans la jungle*

In September 1962, the Théâtre Athénée in Paris stages *La Bête dans la jungle*. Based on Henry James's 1903 short story, the play is billed as an "*Adaptation théâtrale de James Lord d'après la nouvelle* 'The Beast in the Jungle.' *Adaptation française de Marguerite Duras*" (7; "Theatrical adaptation by James Lord, after the original 'The Beast in the Jungle.' French adaptation by Marguerite Duras").[1] Focusing on May Bartram, the female character, Duras's version elaborates on James's examinations of gender-specific relationships to language and space, presenting the original story as an example of *l'écriture féminine*. James's lifelong interest in stagecraft is evident in "The Beast in the Jungle," and his pointed examination of the male narrator's limited viewpoint allows us to find, as Duras does, a great deal in what is not said. In 1984, the play is published by Gallimard within a volume that also includes *Les Papiers d'Aspern* (see Chap. 5) and *La danse de mort*, an adaptation of an August Strindberg work. Both of Duras's plays based on James's fiction have received little critical attention, and remain untranslated.[2]

With a few exceptions that I'll discuss below, for the most part scholarship on "The Beast in the Jungle" in the last several decades has taken place in the wake of Eve Sedgwick's ground-breaking essay "The Beast in the Closet," first published in 1986 and later included as a chapter in 1990's *Epistemology of the Closet*. For Sedgwick, Bartram is a tragically incomplete character who simply "consolidates and fortifies the closet for John Marcher" (206). In Duras's interpretation, by contrast, May Bartram's

© The Author(s) 2018
K. Wichelns, *Henry James's Feminist Afterlives*,
American Literature Readings in the 21st Century,
https://doi.org/10.1007/978-3-319-71800-2_4

85

gender-specific perspective is fully formed, but primarily through extralinguistic means, such as James's repeated references to music and art, as well as the story's use of non-linear time. Using tools specific to the theater, including set changes, lighting, and the fourth wall, Duras makes the female character's viewpoint central to the story. *La Bête dans la jungle* offers a particular feminist approach to James's story, and overall approach, that has remained largely unexamined in English language scholarship.[3] In what follows, I argue that both this play and Duras's 1961 adaptation of *The Aspern Papers* (see Chap. 5) deserve a prominent place on the short list of feminist readings of James's work.

Priscilla Walton's interpretation, in 1991's *The Disruption of the Feminine in Henry James*, bears the closest scholarly resemblance to Duras's approach. Walton does not discuss "The Beast in the Jungle," but she relies on Luce Irigaray, Hélène Cixous, and Julia Kristeva to argue more generally that James's texts repeatedly stage "the crumbling of the church" of Western logocentrism. Alongside Jacques Derrida and other more clearly feminist post-structuralists, Walton argues that gender is an ideological construct, determined by language, so "James's own masculinity does not restrict his writing" of this conflict (31–32). I have some objections to Walton: first, I see James as not so much managing to avoid the pitfall of his manhood as he is in fact succeeding—in ambivalent, vacillating, and contradictory ways—to transgress masculinity through his identification with and intimate exploration of a specifically Anglo-American version of nineteenth-century femininity. Duras's two adaptations influence my parsing of this distinction. In her view, James himself presents the versions of his work that she stages. Her interpretations roughly parallel the reading that Walton draws out via Cixous, Derrida, Irigaray, and Kristeva—significantly, though, Walton does *not* argue that her analysis is consistent with James's original intent. This distinction, of course, partially reflects the variation between an artistic and a scholarly project. Nevertheless, Duras offers readers of James a fully-realized French feminist analysis of his possible engagements with sexual difference in language—one that, as I argue, offers a compelling new perspective on his original project.

Additionally, although Walton uses post-structuralism in the service of a meaningful analysis of James (as will Coulson, in 2007), I fall among the numerous feminists and queer theorists of different stripes who argue that post-structural feminist uses of the originally Lacanian concept of "the Feminine" (including Walton's) consistently fail to incorporate meaningful analysis of cultural, ethnic, racial, and class difference.[4] As I will argue more fully in Chap. 5, Duras's representation of James also engages in a far-reaching and, in my view, distorting reliance on essentialist notions of femininity; in her *Les Papiers d'Aspern*, white womanhood becomes roughly synonymous with "colonized," ethnically-marked subjectivity. Ironically, this serves to whitewash and flatten out the provocative ambiguities of what she, Walton, I, and others regard as James's potentially feminist approach to sex and power. Based on the evidence presented in this chapter and the next, I will use the book's Conclusion to examine the fruitful implications for James scholars of a closer focus on the ways that his version of normative womanhood is itself situated—reflective of Anglo-American and upper middle-class ideals and conflicts—and therefore not universal in the way that Duras seems to suggest in these adaptations.

James first publishes "The Beast in the Jungle" in *The Better Sort*, a 1903 collection. In 1901, he sketches a detailed outline, which he suggests is "a very tiny *fantaisie* probably—in small notion that comes to me of a man haunted by the fear, more and more, throughout life, that *something will happen to him*: he doesn't know quite what." He foregrounds gender difference even at the inception of the story, indicating that another character is required: "Mustn't indeed the '2d consciousness' be some woman, and it must be she who *helps* him to see? She has always loved him—...and he, saving, protecting, exempting his life (always, really, with and *for* the fear), has never known it...She meanwhile, all the time, sees his life as it is. It is to her that he tells his fear—yes, she is the '2d consciousness'" (*Notebooks* 199). The plot chronicles John Marcher's relationship to his own sense that he has some purpose "to wait for—to have to meet, to face, to see suddenly break out in my life; possibly destroying all further consciousness, possibly annihilating me" (503, 504). He spends years having regular conversations about this great secret with May Bartram; she is the only other person who understands his experience, but then she dies. Returning from travel abroad, Marcher visits the cemetery where Bartram is buried, and suddenly realizes all that he has missed. "The fate he had been marked for he had met with a vengeance—he had emptied the cup to the lees; he had been the man of his time, *the* man, to whom nothing on earth was to have happened." The last two paragraphs are marked by temporal and narrative shifts, as Marcher realizes that "the escape would have been to love her; then, *then* he would have lived." It is with this epiphany that Marcher "saw the Jungle of his life and saw the lurking Beast; then, while he looked, perceived it, as by a stir of the air, rise, huge and hideous, for the leap that was to settle him" (540–541). Turning his back on it in horror, he collapses on Bartram's grave as the story ends.

Eve Sedgwick argues that Marcher's "beast" is "homosexual panic," an anxiety about his own relationship to the possibility of same-sex desire, realized in the confrontation with the male stranger in the cemetery. Therefore, at the story's conclusion Marcher manages not an epiphany but yet another defensive assertion of compulsory heterosexuality; he fails yet again to engage with his fear, and institutes another act of violence upon the dead Bartram. Established readings of "The Beast in the Jungle" at the time "The Beast in the Closet" was first published rendered May Bartram's absent presence reassuring evidence of Marcher's (heterosexual) normality—this reflects Marcher's own reading of their relationship, in the final paragraphs of the story. For Sedgwick, Bartram is significant to the narrative mainly because she allows Marcher to avoid recognizing his own homosexual potential (205, 204, 206). Only very briefly, Sedgwick examines textual evidence of May Bartram's alternate perspective on the relationship, which she reads as founded in heterosexual feminine masochism; interestingly, in the course of this analysis she also equates James with his narrator. Many before her saw James's relationships with women, and particularly Constance Fenimore Woolson, as proof of the author's unfulfilled romantic inclination towards women. Yet the anti-homophobic counterargument of "The Beast in the Closet" is equally unsatisfying in this regard, as Sedgwick cites James's relationship with Woolson to suggest that he had personal knowledge of Marcher's "homosexual panic."[5] Reading May Bartram as suffering from a clichéd version of feminine masochism, Sedgwick's vision for what she terms Bartram's potentially "gender-political resilience" is grounded exclusively in the male narrator and his struggle. "Whoever May Bartram is and whatever she wants, clearly at least the story has the negative Jamesian virtue of not pretending to present her rounded and whole" (199). By contrast, Duras sees the female character as entirely "whole"—indeed, in her reading Bartram is the story's focus, serving as James's vehicle for an analysis of sexual difference in language.

There are a few feminist readings of this story, each of which presents the text differently than Duras does.[6] Donatella Izzo views Bartram as an extreme practitioner of the injunction that women should wait for men to speak; Bartram's intensification of female propriety makes her "silence" a "counter-narrative" that effectively enables her "power-knowledge" over Marcher (Carolyn Tate 18–19; Izzo 226–243). In 2010's *Intimacies*, co-authored with Adam Phillips, Bersani reads "The Beast in the Jungle" in the course of his examination of possible approaches to a more "democratic" analyst–analysand relationship, providing a novel perspective on

May Bartram's reticence along the way. Bartram becomes Bersani's model for the analyst that, unlike the traditional figure represented by Jacques Lacan's "subject supposed to know," nevertheless also is vulnerable, invested, and open to her interlocutor through acknowledging her own counter-transference (12–30). Benjamin Bateman, writing in 2014, reminds us that "most frequently cited articles on 'The Beast in the Jungle' miss or undervalue...Bartram's primary role in instigating and motoring the important events of the story." However, Bateman regards Bartram's "transmutation into a beast" through the lens of animality studies rather than feminisms, and sees it as a "radical suspension of conventional womanhood" (467). These explorations of May Bartram's narrative silence do suggest alternatives to both Sedgwick's understanding of the character and earlier, heteronormative readings that similarly rendered her a helpless, gender-traditional victim of Marcher's selfishness. However, none of these scholars questions the idea that Bartram *is* silent. The mid-twentieth-century French context in which Duras interprets the story provides another option. For Duras, James provides abundant textual evidence that Bartram communicates in gender-specific ways that Marcher cannot understand. The anti-climax of the final scene becomes James's authorial declaration that this was never actually John Marcher's story.

In her influential 1975 essay, "The Laugh of the Medusa," Hélène Cixous cites Duras as one of three French authors, with Colette and Jean Genet, who epitomize "*écriture féminine*" (878–879, n.2). By the time *La Bête dans la jungle* is staged, Duras has developed a reputation as an avant-garde writer who explores "feminine" language—it is a key element in *Le marin de Gibraltar* (1952), *Un barrage contre la Pacifique* (1957), *Moderato cantabile* (1958), and the film *Hiroshima mon amour* (1959). For Duras, James provides abundant textual evidence that Bartram communicates in gender-specific ways that Marcher is unable to understand; theater, as a visual and aural medium, enables her to reveal what she sees as James's intent more clearly than is possible with the written page. The precise elements that she regards as evidence of James's focus on "feminine" forms of expression, in a relationship between a man and a woman, later will be understood by queer theoretical readers, in the wake of Sedgwick, as James's "queerness of style" or, alternately, his exploration of "queer temporality."[7] Each of these scholars nuances Sedgwick's reading, finding stylistic evocations of queer or non-heterosexual relationships to language, time, and narration, rather than the specifically homoerotic content that she discovers in the plot of the story. Nevertheless, the categorical emphasis remains: in none of these discussions does stylistic or temporal queerness in Henry James's work have any relationship to the feminist notions of gendered time, language, or writing that are so central to Duras's reading, as well as to twentieth-century French feminist approaches more generally. Duras seems to be one of only a few readers to have noted that the story's strange temporal shifts, like its representations of music and art, are associated with May Bartram, not the potentially queer Marcher—therefore, for her, the story not just invites but requires a feminist interpretation.

Duras's reading of "The Beast in the Jungle" is inextricable from her specific personal, political, and cultural surroundings. The development during the postwar period of what would come to be understood as French feminism (represented most prominently by Monique Wittig, Cixous, Irigaray, and Kristeva) is one factor, as also is Duras's independent artistic interest in these questions. Scholars have thoroughly dissected the influence on her work of this period of her father's death, her early life in French Indochina (Vietnam), her experiences as a member of the French Resistance, and her husband Robert Antelme's imprisonment; I will not reiterate their work here.[8] Considering Duras's method—a conscious blurring of her artistic output with her private life, as a highly public writer and filmmaker—we might initially find it strange that she chose to adapt Henry James. As I discussed in Chap. 1, James is not generally understood in English-language circles as the sort of author who would provide inspiration for the self-reflective, politically-conscious work that we associate with Duras. Yet only partly as a result of his fluent and frequent use of French,[9] his brief residency in Paris in 1875–76, and his transatlantic themes, by Duras's period James's work has gained a considerable set of French-language interpretations that, while not entirely inconsistent with Anglo-American readings, have a distinct emphasis. As Bessière and Symington emphasize, this reflects translation history; two separate generations of twentieth-century French readers, with different sets of translations, have distinct views of the author. Earlier dismissed in turn-of-the-century France as remote and inaccessible, James becomes increasingly popular among postwar intellectuals focused on the interplay between ethics and aesthetics in his work, and preoccupied with writing (like James's) that engages in self-reflexive examinations of the role of the author. An established signifier of Anglo-American high literary culture, James also represents—for Duras and her contemporaries—a simultaneously experimental and readerly writer, whose interests are allied with their own. Correspondingly, during the postwar period French intellectuals engage in "intense translation work," introducing French audiences to previously-unavailable works by James and producing revised translations of familiar texts (16–17).[10] While her choice to adapt James may surprise English-language scholars, readers of Duras will recognize the close parallels between French understandings of James and her own artistic ambitions.

Although *La Bête dans la jungle* shares with scholarly critiques of Sedgwick's portrayal of May Bartram a fuller examination of what Izzo terms the character's "counter-narrative" (236), Duras differs from these analyses by suggesting that Bartram's (heterosexual) subjectivity, her engagement with signification outside of the terms of the narrative, always was James's main focus. In her reading, "The Beast in the Jungle" is an example of *écriture féminine*. Her theatrical adaptation seems based on the assumption that James actively is presenting a resistant alternative throughout "The Beast in the Jungle," telling a different story that simultaneously coexists with and undermines John Marcher's narrative. Rather than emphasizing the final scene, Duras expands upon an earlier shift in authorial voice. The action of the story exclusively follows Marcher's perspective, rendered unreliable from the first page through his inability to recall the details of his first meeting with May Bartram years earlier, with one exception. This brief change occurs in the section surrounding a trip to the opera, an element in the story that both James and Duras associate with Bartram. At this point, James writes that Bartram gives the world a "false account of herself. There was but one account of her that would have been true all the while, and that she could give, directly, to nobody, least of all to John Marcher. Her whole attitude was a virtual statement, but the perception of that only seemed destined to take its place for him as one of the many things necessarily crowded out of his consciousness" (511). The description occurs just prior to the pair's final meeting before Bartram's death, the scene that Duras regards as the story's real climax. Primed by dialogical indicators to know that May Bartram is the more perceptive character, readers are ready to identify even more fully with her at this moment. James here is allowing us to speculate about the nature of "the beast." At this moment we know (or think we do), in large part because we also understand that May Bartram knows, but John Marcher is still ignorant. The reader's reliance on Marcher is ruptured, as James gives us access to a viewpoint and information that only May Bartram could provide.[11]

After this moment, the final scene at the cemetery that follows indeed is anti-climactic, but for Duras, that final anti-climax is an authorial proclamation. Throughout the story, James invites his readers to construct a tragic version of a conventional marriage plot: the final paragraphs announce our complicity in privileging Marcher's point of view. Duras emphasizes the feminist possibilities inherent in James's description of Bartram as "sibyl"-like, "inscrutable," a "sphinx" (529, 521)—and, unlike James, she explicitly identifies "the beast" as May Bartram, and the fear of (heterosexual) intimacy that she represents for Marcher. The unsatisfactory, anti-climactic feeling of the cemetery scene results from the fact that the real story (Bartram's) already has finished. Duras (like Walton, later) brings to the fore what she considers to be James's depiction of an irresolvable conflict surrounding language and sexual difference. Marcher, a writer, is represented by the language of the text and May Bartram communicates by other means (predominantly music and art). Her story becomes not one of silenced victimization, nor of masochism: throughout the story, if we know how to listen, Bartram speaks her own experience independent of Marcher's, outside of the narrative he constructs.

In a brief 1983 synopsis of *La Bête dans la jungle* published in a special issue of *L'Arc* focused on James, Duras describes her decision to set the play entirely at Weatherend, the English country estate where the original story opens, as only the most noticeable in a series of artistic choices that she made in order to ensure that her theatrical version emphasized what she regards as James's primary goal. "*Pour tout dire j'ai toujours cru que Henry James avait gardé ce deuxième temps à Londres pour confronter l'histoire d'amour avec un extérieur dangereux pour elle, la grande ville, pour en éprouver la fidélité, la profondeur... J'ai choisi de ne pas faire migrer l'histoire à Londres, mais au contraire de la garder là où elle avait commencé, enfermée dans le château de Weatherend*" ("*Le Château*" 100; "I have always believed that Henry James [moved the action] to London to confront the love story with a setting that threatened it, the big city, to prove its fidelity and depth...I chose not to move the story to London, but to keep it where it started, concealed in the house at Weatherend"). This is one of several means by which Duras shifts the focus away from what she regards as the deliberate distraction of John Marcher's narrative. She changes Bartram's name to "Catherine Bertram," which could be either French or English, and is spelled the same way in both languages. Playing on the dual linguistic identity of the text she has inherited from James Lord, Duras renders Catherine the only character that fluently occupies Henry James's English text, the "English" setting of the play, and the French "subtext" that the audience will see performed.

In James's story, May Bartram's divergent perspective on the relationship with Marcher exists dialogically only by implication, except in the one important moment that Bersani discusses. Duras develops this alternate, unspoken story in part by describing the spaces between the bodies of the male and female characters, and their different relationships to the passage of time. Her acts are "*tableaux*": playing on the dual meaning of the word, she renders her play a series of both "scenes" and "paintings," sharing space with the art housed at the "museum-like" estate.[12] Catherine Bertram is a "poor relation" who "paid for" her occupancy at Weatherend by showing its extensive collection of fine art to visitors, including Marcher. She plays the piano, and in his interest in "not being selfish" in their relationship, Marcher takes her often to the opera (497, 516). Art and music are both associated with Bartram in James's story, but Duras extends this metaphor by making non-linguistic forms of expression incomprehensible to John.

In James's story May Bartram's ongoing "ironic" engagement with John Marcher's story is a potent unsaid that haunts the narrative; it is expressed through questions left unanswered, gaps in conversation, pauses, hyphens, and elisions.[13] For Duras, aural and visual elements (music, paintings, set design, actor movements) subtly counter the spoken narrative; in addition, the story no longer is told in the third-person limited omniscient voice that mainly presented John Marcher's account in James's version. As the play opens, this new perspective is announced by the set. "*Le décor ce seraient des salons en enfilade, courbes, je vois la scène partagée en deux comme ça d'une façon que les gens apparaissent et disparaissent encore, comme dans une sorte de labyrinthe*" (13; "The set consists of rooms in a suite, curved; I see the stage divided in two in some way so that the actors appear and disappear, like in a sort of labyrinth"). Her set design recalls Duras's interest in Jean Racine's 1677 play *Phèdre*; she claimed Racine as an influence, and writes about him in 1987's *La vie matérielle*.[14] *Phèdre* is dominated by another labyrinth: Minos's puzzle is both a physical structure and a representation of a complex network of power relations. In staging her adaptation through the figure of a labyrinth, for a literate French audience that would have been familiar with Racine's depiction, Duras announces that both her work and James's will take place within the context of French literary history. Effectively, she is claiming James for France. Racine's complicated engagement with questions of gender and meaning becomes, in Duras's analysis, a French precedent for James's project (and her own). Writing James through reference to Racine's play about a woman who loved tragically and died, she portrays his work as participating in a conversation between men about women. At the same time, she inserts herself as an intermediary, a bridge between Racine and James that also interrupts the narrative she sees them both as constructing.

An important element of Racine's play is his adherence to formal conventions of seventeenth-century French poetry, which provide structure in the midst of the chaotic relationships among characters. Yet when confronted by Thésée, Aricie cannot speak of Phèdre's love for Hippolyte; unregulated feminine desire becomes a potent unsaid that ruptures Racine's rigid meter. "*Prenez garde, Seigneur: vos invincibles mains / Ont de monstres sans nombre affranchi les humains, / Mais tout n'est pas détruit, et vous en laissez vivre / Un...Votre fils, Seigneur, me défend de poursuivre* (V, iii, 1443–1446).[15] The broken line that ends with "*Un...*" is the only site in the text in which Racine violates the rules of his own literary format. Rupturing the reflective balance of the A-A-B-B rhyme scheme and perfect meter, the ellipses reveal the tenuous, constructed nature of both Racine's verse and, arguably, the notions of gender it describes: Phèdre's desire breaks the rules, in multiple ways. Walton doesn't offer a reading of *Phèdre*, of course; but the particularly feminist post-structuralist analysis of "the Feminine" as a form of absolute alterity is an obvious interpretation here. More interesting for our purposes is Racine's stylistic experimentation in the service of an analysis of sex and power—he provides a French precedent for what Duras understands as James's feminist literary project. Making her update of Racine's labyrinth the dominant feature of the set of *La Bête dans la jungle*, Duras also calls attention to her own role in connecting Racine and James. The visual cue of the set design would have asked a French audience to reinterpret both male writers through her viewpoint.

As Scene I opens, the curtain rises on a sinuous, curving set, composed of two sides ("*partagée en deux*") that return to each other to complete a single form. The figure recalls Irigaray's famous invocation of the doubled "two lips" of female embodiment: Irigaray refers to the mouth as well as the inner and outer labia in her discussion of what is for her the different way that women relate to language.[16] Initially, the two actors are framed as binary opposites: John and Catherine enter and exit from opposing sides of the stage, meeting at the center to regard a Van Dyck portrait of "the fourth *marquis* of Weatherend," invisible to us, but revealed, through dialogue, to hang on the fourth wall of stage front. The audience stands in for both the art and its subject: Catherine and John look out at us, describing the painting as an accurate psychological portrait of the *marquis* himself. John wonders why he is fascinated by the painting. Catherine suggests, "*Peut-être parce que le quatrième marquis était justement la sorte d'homme que vous auriez aimé être...Rien ne l'a jamais détourné de ce qu'il disait être son destin*" (16; "Perhaps because the fourth *marquis* is just the sort of man you would like to be...nothing ever turned him from what he said was his destiny").[17] In this first conversation John does not remember having met Catherine once already, years ago. She seems almost clairvoyant as he tells him his own life story, with the same assurance that she describes the history of the dead aristocrat in the painting. In the play's prologue, Duras describes "*le tableau du quatrième marquis de Weatherend...il serait emblématique de l'histoire. Sorte de double de John Marcher*" (15; "the portrait of the fourth marquis of Weatherend...it is emblematic of the story. A sort of double for John Marcher").

As a playwright, Duras tends to sketch open-ended suggestions for directors, preferring them to interpret as they see fit. The set instructions she provides for Scene II are unusually detailed.

> *Le même jour que le tableau I. Noir. Et puis lumière. La nuit est venue. C'est le même décor. Mais les fenêtres sont éteintes. Le décor est vide, et silencieux. Mais quelque chose a changé. Par exemple on pourrait avoir détourné un praticable de telle façon que le méandre central ait pivoté, et qu'en plein milieu de la cloison il y ait le portrait du quatrième marquis de Weatherend...Il y a des fauteuils là. (22)*
>
> The same day as in Scene I. Darkness. And then light. Night has fallen. It's the same set. But the windows are in shadow. The set is empty and silent. But something has changed. For example one could turn everything on a platform, so that the central twist [of the labyrinth] is made to pivot, and now the portrait of the fourth marquis of Weatherend hangs right at the middle of the partition...There are some armchairs there.

Whereas Act I took place on a set composed of two separated halves of equal size, the stage now indeed is revealed to be a "labyrinth," as we see a complex honeycomb of rooms that was invisible from the audience's earlier viewpoint, in Scene I. For a disorienting moment we think that we have moved; the "fourth wall" suddenly appears, drawing our attention to our own perspective, and making it part of the story. This is Duras's visual representation of the textual moment in which James gives his readers a momentary glimpse into May Bartram's viewpoint, in the original story; she will make this disjointed awareness of the differences between the perspectives of the male and female character central to the audience's relationship to the play. Our view shifts, and we see all that we "had missed" (James, "Beast" 540), as John Marcher will only at the end of the story. We reorient ourselves via the visual anchor of the portrait, and thereby are confronted with the fact that we were stand-ins for the doubled figure of John and the painted marquis.

The implied physical shift is that of one gender-specific perspective to another. In Scene I, we are limited to John's version of their encounter in front of the painting: Catherine looks familiar but he is unable to place her. Her account will dominate Scene II; like the new set, her story is both "the same" and significantly more complex. She reminds John of their first meeting years ago in Naples, and of an archaeological dig that they observed there together. The play itself will represent a series of interdependent but distinct conversations, all happening in the same place over a lifetime, like the folded layers of the set or the accumulated strata gradually unearthed by the archaeologists.

Indeed, as we regard the changed perspective of the turned set, an alternate "language" emerges: "*On entend complètement une musique lointaine, je veux dire que ce n'est pas un accompagnement mais que la musique est totalement jouée. Catherine et John arrivent séparément, donc en silence. Lui de son côté et elle du sien. On entend ses pas à lui à travers le château et puis ensuite les siens à elle et ensuite les pas se mélangent*" (22; "One hears, completely, far-off music; I mean to say that this music isn't mere accompaniment, it is played, totally. Catherine and John arrive separately and in silence. He from his side and she from hers. One hears his footsteps crossing the house and then hers, and then their footsteps blend together"). For readers of Duras, this scene recalls *India Song* (1975), or the opening of *Moderato cantabile* (1958). As in those other works, here the music, "played, totally," becomes another voice that counters or complicates spoken language. Throughout the play, Duras reminds us of this off-stage musical presence at odd moments; it is intended to nuance, and occasionally to counter, John's verbal narrative. Center stage becomes the third space where clear distinctions of past and present "*se mélangent*." As Catherine corrects and supplements John's memory in Scene II, the temporal setting of the story shifts fluidly, changing from Weatherend to London to Naples—the Italian city remains a constant presence through remembered place names (as in James's original). In the changed aural and visual space of Scene II, there is a different sense of time—simultaneously Italian, feminine, and musical—that renders the past sensibly present.

Duras's stage directions indicate that changes in season and time of day should be made apparent through lighting or other means; however, the effect unsettles rather than anchors a chronological sense of the play's development, as each scene traces a different point along a shifting, non-sequential timeline.[18] Scenes I and II take place on the same day; Scene III occurs during "daytime." Dialogic echoes link the third scene to the first two: these moments are proximate only by association, and we have no idea how much time has passed between them. At the close of Scene II, Catherine twice asks and once declares that John is "afraid"; Scene III opens with John's statement that *"Je me souviens, nous avions aussi parlé de la peur"* (33; "I remember that we have talked about the fear before").[19] Minor shifts at the beginning of each scene betray the passage of time, as we visit Catherine and John, over a lifetime of interrelated conversations, sometimes evidently with years in between. Occasionally only the set design—the same objects are moved around, becoming increasingly dilapidated as the decades pass—reveals that a particular exchange is happening at a different time than we might expect.

Scene IV describes a celebration: John takes Catherine to the opera for her birthday. Here, Duras offers another expansion of one of James's brief references, to Mozart's *Don Giovanni*, which she treats as a textual clue in support of her particular interpretation of "The Beast in the Jungle."[20] For Duras, *Don Giovanni* serves as another non-English, cross-genre precedent for James's own violations of form, which trace a resistant (feminine) counter-story within the dominant narrative. As Stanley Sadie notes, *Don Giovanni* dramatizes "the tensions of class and sex" (145)—moreover, Mozart engages in a stylistic twist that Duras sees as evidence of his critique of systematic oppression, in keeping with her readings of both Racine and James. Don Giovanni's lower-class victims violate the musical conventions that composers during Mozart's period used for characters of their social position. Zerlina, the young woman upon whom Don Giovanni asserts his *droit de seigneur*, is one prominent example.[21] Duras recognizes the echoes between these distinctive moments in Mozart, Racine, and James—Catherine mis-titles *Don Giovanni* as *"Don Juan,"* even though she knows the opera well enough to sing a famous section from memory. Drawing the attention of opera-savvy audience members to the error, Duras makes explicit her own connection of "John" with Mozart's villain. As Catherine quietly sings the first line of the Donna Anna's aria, John notes her use of Italian.

JOHN: Je ne savais pas que vous parliez l'italien, Catherine.
CATHERINE: Oh je n'en sais que quelques mots. Juste assez pour déchiffrer les livrets d'opéra.
JOHN: Je ne connais pas un traître mot, une seule langue étrangère. C'est honteux... (43)
JOHN: I didn't know that you spoke Italian, Catherine.
CATHERINE: Oh, I don't know more than a few words. Just enough to make sense of the operettas.
JOHN: I don't know a single word in any foreign language. It's haunting...

The passage suggests a reading of music and the Italian language in James that parallels Duras's analysis in *Les Papiers d'Aspern* (see Chap. 5). Opera and Italian become forms of communication that haunt (English, narrative) meaning—they provide a counter-reading that functions within the text. The fact that this play is written in French that is referred to as English by the "English" characters itself disrupts linguistic sense. Duras also employs this tactic in *Les Papiers d'Aspern*; she alerts the audience members to the fact that translation is a central focus of the play, and reminds them that their own linguistic perspective is just one possibility among many. The adaptation makes fleeting references to the fact that the dialogue is purportedly in English. The coding of English as French (and, by implication, French as English) concretizes the missed encounter between the two characters who have differently-sexed relationships to meaning. Moreover, it suggests an uncanny sense of alien familiarity: both characters speak a foreign language that is immediately comprehensible to the audience because it is not in fact foreign at all. John speaks "*pas un traître mot, une seule langue étrangère.*" Translated in context, the first phrase means "not a single foreign word," but read literally, "*traître*" also evokes "treacherous." Again, Duras makes the female character a simultaneously linguistic and sexual threat to the narrative authority of the male character. It is unclear what is most "haunting": Catherine's voice, Mozart's music, or John's monoglottism.

Unlike James, Duras provides the audience with little room for an alternative to her interpretation. She quotes from the aria, as James does not: "*Non mi dir, bell 'idol mio, che son io crudel con te: tu ben sai quant'io t'amai.*" In discussing the opera's departures from the formal conventions of the eighteenth century, Laurel Elizabeth Zeiss translates this section as "Do not say to me, my beloved, / That I am cruel to you; / You well know how much I love you" (Duras 1962, 43; Zeiss 122). This serves as another of Catherine Bertram's many confessions to the clueless John Marcher. It also references the critique of sexual power inherent to Mozart's opera—effectively, Duras presents both *Don Giovanni* and "The Beast in the Jungle" as proto-Marxist feminist readings of the particular ways that non-aristocratic women (like Donna Anna and Catherine Bertram) are used and destroyed by upper-class men, without consequences. Donna Anna unknowingly falls in love with the man who assaulted her and murdered her father in the opening scene. For Zeiss, this aria directs us towards Don Giovanni's eventual doom—his betrayal of Donna Anna ensures his destruction, via her father's ghost. The aria does not close, and it repeats words and musical elements of Don Giovanni's part, earlier in the scene (121–126).[22] Duras emphasizes the parallel she perceives between Don Giovanni and John Marcher with almost heavy-handed clarity: presenting him as "haunted," and as "Don Juan," she counters his spoken narrative with the musical foreshadowing of his own end, as sung by the woman whose emotional labor he exploits throughout both of their lives. In addition, the unsettling chronological shifts of Donna Anna's *rondò* echo the temporal disorderings of Duras's play.

Unlike the play's musical references, dialogue in the first two scenes suggests the possibility of productive collaboration between different constructions of meaning. The story develops through its repetitions, as Catherine repeats John's words, shifting them slightly to change emphasis. In Scene I, as John recalls the day of their first meeting, his account is marked by ellipses, question marks, and repetition. "*Mais je me souviens d'une excursion, d'une voiture—vous ne vous souvenez pas? Je me souviens d'un store blanc, d'une chaleur étouffante, terrible, et d'un store blanc...*" (21; "But I remember an outing, in a car—don't you remember? I remember a white awning, stifling heat, terrible, and a white awning..."). His narration dreamily turns back on itself, and then is repeated again when Catherine offers her version of the story in the next scene. "*C'est vrai. Si vous voulez nous pouvons nous souvenir de ce jour-là, de ce store blanc, des cette chaleur, des lieux où ces choses se sont passées*" (21, 23; "It's true. If you like we can remember that day, that white awning, that heat, places and things that are in the past"). Through her reference to "places and things that are in the past" Catherine reminds John that they are sharing an experience in the present. Her emphasis suggests a different relationship to both time and memory, which will be developed throughout the play; John avoids the present through his preoccupation with the past and fear of the future. The placement of the two actors, as they move together or in opposition throughout Scene II, traces the developing cooperation of the dialogue. The tension between Catherine and John, between their accounts, is irresolvable; however, at center stage they form a disunited whole through their constant movement towards and away from each other.

In constructing the narrative format of the adaptation, Duras significantly departs from James. Catherine speaks half of the dialogue, so John's perspective no longer dominates. Yet the play begins and ends with the limited omniscient third-person narration of the original story. A prologue is spoken by an anonymous off-stage voice, which never reappears in the play itself. In another temporal disorientation, this narrative voice recounts a version of the concluding scene of James's story, in which John throws himself upon Catherine's grave to escape from "the beast." In the play's epilogue, the same event is described, but the disembodied narrator of the prologue is replaced by John's own voice; he suddenly is describing his own actions in the third person. As the play is not translated and this section encapsulates Duras's elaborate, highly-selective revision of James, it seems worthwhile to quote it fully.

> JOHN: *La différence qui résulta de ce nouvel état de choses, la fin de l'attente, provoqua chez John Marcher un étonnement très grand, très vif, comparable à celui que l'on éprouve quelquefois lorsque la musique s'arrête—...*
>
> *Cet étonnement dura des années, des années pendant lesquelles John Marcher voyagea—toujours seul—sans jamais concevoir pour son avenir ni crainte ni espoir, tellement s'était retiré de lui tout souci du futur.*
>
> *Mais voici qu'un jour, un jour d'automne, alors qu'il rendait visite à la tombe de son amie Catherine Bertram, dans le grand cimetière de Londres John Marcher reçut en plein cœur, avec l'irrévérence, la vulgarité, l'insolence du hasard, l'une des réponses plausibles à tout son passé. Un autre homme que lui était parmi les tombes. C'était son analogue inoubliable. La douleur de cet homme était si forte, si terrible, que John se demanda quoi, quelle blessure, quelle injustice, quelle perte irréparable en était la cause. Et c'est alors—tandis que John Marcher voyait avec envie comment une femme, comment un amour pouvait être pleuré par un autre que lui—que la souffrance de John Marcher jusque-là comme endormie l'illumina, cela jusqu'à ce qu'il aperçût la bête surgir de la jungle et venir vers lui—cela donc jusqu'au zénith de sa vie au-delà de quoi il ne pouvait pas penser.*
>
> *Il crut voir la bête de la jungle se dresser devant lui. Elle était énorme, elle était hideuse. Il crut que c'en était fait de lui. Alors d'instinct, il essaya d'éviter le bond de la bête sur lui, ce bond qui allait l'achever et c'est ainsi qu'il se jeta*

*tête baisée sur la tombe de Catherine Bertram, afin d'éviter le bond sur lui de la bête de la jungle.* (59–60)
JOHN: The difference that results from this new state of things, the end of the wait, will provoke in John Marcher a very great, very sharp shock, comparable to that one experiences sometimes when music stops—...
This shock lasts for years, years during which John Marcher will travel—always alone—without ever conceiving for his life any fear or hope, so that he loses any concern for the future.
But it was one day, one day in autumn, while he was visiting the grave of his friend Catherine Bertram in the large cemetery in London, that John Marcher was struck right in the heart (with the irreverence, the vulgarity, the insolence of chance) with a plausible solution to his entire past. Another man was amongst the tombstones. This man was his unforgettable double. The sadness of this man was so strong, so terrible, that John asked him what, what injury, what injustice, what irreparable loss had been the cause. And it was then, as John Marcher stared with envy, like a woman, like a love that would be able to weep for another than itself—it was then that the suffering of John Marcher, who until then had always been like one asleep, dawned upon him. It was then that it appeared that the beast surged from the jungle and came towards him—finally, that zenith of his life, the aftermath of which he had never considered.
He believed he saw the beast in the jungle rise in front of him. It was enormous, it was hideous. He believed that it was made for him. Out of instinct, he tried to avoid the beast's pounce upon him, the pounce it would certainly have completed—and that was when he threw his head down on the grave of Catherine Bertram, in order to avoid the pounce of the beast in the jungle.

John's monologue begins with an evocation of "*la différence*" and ends with a reference to "*la bête de la jungle.*" The structure of this section circles back on itself, as much in this play does, and we encounter another iteration of what Duras has been telling us visually since the curtain first rose. "*La différence*" is the change in John's sense of himself, through grief and its aftermath; it also is sexual difference, understood more broadly. At the beginning of Scene VI, she is "*Allongée, très pâle, très blanche, quasiment morte. Comme si elle avait été 'la bête', comme si la bête avait été tuée en quelque sorte. Par le narcissisme de John Marcher*" (54) (*La Bête* 54; "thin, very pale, very white, almost dead. As if she had been 'the beast,' as if the beast had been killed somehow. By the narcissism of John Marcher"). Although the description of Catherine's final illness parallels a scene in James's novella, Duras again eliminates the possibility of alternate, or ambiguous, readings: Catherine is "the beast," a desiring feminine other whom John could never face, and whose death is wholly his responsibility.

As the scene closes, Catherine declares, "*Si je le pouvais je vivrais encore pour vous, mais je ne le peux plus*" (58; "I would go on living for you if I could, but I can't any more"). Darkness falls, and the play seems to be over, but after a moment the light returns. Duras indicates "*John Marcher a disparu de la scène. Il revient. Il dit l'épilogue de sa propre histoire. Il faudrait que le passage du vécu à la épilogue soit très marquée, soit très différent, que ça ne soit plus tout à fait le même homme qui parle*" (58 ; "John Marcher has disappeared from the stage. He returns. He speaks the epilogue of his own story. The passage to the experiences recounted in the epilogue should be very marked, very different, for this is not the same man who is speaking"). During that strange darkness, which Duras describes in another disorienting shift as "*un noir très court*" ("a very short night"), John's experience of his own life moves from first to third person, present to past tense. Duras condenses the climax of James's story into a brief afterword; like the disembodied prologue, the epilogue is separated from the rest of the text by page breaks. Yet she provides the stage directions for this section at the end of Scene VI, rather than on the next page, which indeed bears the title *Épilogue*, thereby emphasizing the significance of the final scene in which Catherine actively participates. Catherine announces her pending death, and both of their lives, as self-referencing subjects, are over. Everything changes to the past tense, and John Marcher no longer recognizes himself as "I." Duras parallels John's bodily shock at this development with that of a sleeper suddenly awakened, or the physical experience of an abrupt cessation of music. She elaborates on the bodily metaphors within James's original text: for James, John's loss, not simply the moment in which he casts himself upon the grave, is a deeply physical experience. The reference to the moment when *la musique s'arrête* and the temporal repetition (the prologue places the first scene in *un jour d'automne*) remind us of Scene I; the play has turned back on itself, again. However, John's experience of himself transforms in the blank space after the end of Scene VI, a textual representation of the audience's experience of the "*noir très court.*" When "*la lumière revient*" ("the light returns"), "*John Marcher a disparu de la scène*" ("John Marcher has disappeared from the stage"). It is at this point that he returns to recite the brief epilogue quoted above.

James also engages in odd temporal shifts in his story's final scene, as John Marcher discovers in the cemetery that the event he awaited has occurred at some point in the past, without his knowledge. James's

Marcher realizes "what he had missed" in an unsettling form of the present tense: in hindsight, and only when it is irretrievably over, Marcher sees his long relationship with Bartram differently. As in Duras's version, May Bartram hints that someday he will understand that she had watched "the beast" pass him by. "You were to suffer your fate. That was not necessarily to know it" (James, "Beast" 531). Near the opening of the final paragraph of "The Beast in the Jungle," Marcher, at Bartram's grave, recalls this final meeting. "Her spoken words came back to him, and the chain stretched and stretched. The beast had lurked indeed, and the beast, at its hour, had sprung; it had sprung in that twilight of the cold April when, pale, ill, wasted, but all beautiful, and perhaps even then recoverable, she had risen from her chair to stand before him and let him unimaginably guess" (540). The narratological present-tense "leap" of the beast, years after this final parting, is the inevitable completion of an already-accomplished act.

For Duras, this temporal unbalancing renders Marcher's experience feminine, and expressly, stereotypically heterosexual—he stares at the male stranger not with fear or avoidance, but "with envy, like a woman." Importantly, however, this also serves as his "awakening," the disruption of his lifelong self-regard: for Duras, it seems that femininity is equivalent with a capacity for empathy (or, as the epilogue indicates, being "able to weep for someone other than oneself"). "It is no longer the same man who speaks" because for Duras it is no longer a man, in the conventional sense. This line, of course, is not found in James's original. But it emphasizes that John now sees precisely as Catherine Bertram always has, and as the audience has since the set shift at the beginning of Scene II. For Duras, that viewpoint is decisively feminine.

Her use of a third-person voice in the epilogue, as John tells us of "John Marcher's" experience in the cemetery, is another departure from James. Micéala Symington argues that the profusion of visual metaphors in these last few paragraphs represent James's "suspension of action in favour of image," a stylistic development that made him particularly appealing to the French writers of *le nouveau roman*, with whom Duras is associated.[23] Symington suggests that James visually "'closes in' on John Marcher at the end of the story," whereas in her play "Marguerite Duras... create(s) a distance between the dramatic framework and the character who becomes narrator." She argues that this is James's attempt to make Marcher's experience seem more realistic; Duras reverses his approach, in Symington's view, primarily because it makes the ending easier to stage (15, 19–22). However, Symington misses an important dimension of

Duras's project. *La Bête dans la jungle* is an interpretation—but it also is a critical intervention into accepted French scholarly views of James, and a demonstration of the feminist possibilities of the theater.

Shortly before her allusion to Duras in "The Laugh of the Medusa," Cixous refers to women as "we the labyrinths" (878).[24] Cixous would not have been thinking of the set of *La Bête dans la jungle*, but Duras's play stages and realizes *écriture féminine* as Cixous presents it. Following Cixous's contemporary Irigaray, and previewing the examination of gender and language that Duras will use a few years later in 1964's *Le ravissement of Lol V. Stein*, the play visually and aurally performs the concept of the feminine "hole-word" (Duras, *Ravishing* 38), a self-referential disordering of phallogocentric sense that reveals the instability of meaning itself.[25] Duras's simultaneously bifurcated and labyrinthine set design evokes Irigaray's well-known concrete metaphor of the doubled "two lips" of women's language: Irigaray refers to the mouth as well as the inner and outer labia of the vagina in her discussion of the distinctive, embodied way that women, in her view, relate to both language and desire. Like Irigaray's "woman," Duras's set "is neither one nor two," and it contains a multitude of "self-touching," intricate possibilities (Irigaray 22–23, 26). Additionally, Duras's development of James's temporal shifts, as well as his use of Italian or French-coded-as-English, suggests obvious parallels with Julia Kristeva's work. For Duras, James's story stages both "women's time" and the related concept of a fundamental untranslatability of linguistic difference, along the lines that Kristeva explores in *Revolution in Poetic Language* (*Révolution du langage poétique*, 1974) and *Strangers to Ourselves* (*Étrangers à nous-mêmes*, 1988).[26]

For Duras, it seems, James himself presents this analysis: by means of her intervention, we finally understand his original intent. Her deployments of Racine and Mozart, as precursors, establish both James and Duras herself as their artistic descendants. *La Bête dans la jungle* claims the cosmopolitan, multilingual James for continental Europe, but it also represents a form of authorial self-fashioning. As I've explored, Duras's analysis of "The Beast in the Jungle" both is and is not consistent with French readings of her period; in naming herself his heir, Duras marks her own work as consistent with prevalent French interpretations of James, even as she renders that model more unambiguously feminist. Like James, then, she declares herself a self-referential author (French understandings of James in this period, as summarized by Bessière and Symington, find no contradiction in locating the author in his narrators). As I will discuss in more detail in Chap. 5, in the late 1950s James largely was read by the French intellectual elite, who understood him through the lens of postwar French politics. Duras and her leftist contemporaries sought to expose the person (whether themselves, or Henry James, or others) who did the writing—they saw this as a form of resistance to "bourgeois" notions of authorship that disavow the historical complicity of art with capitalism.[27] In her adaptations, Duras suggests that both she and James can and should be known through their work.

In her brief 1983 description of the project in *L'Arc*, Duras reflects that theater allows her to express James's focus on sexual difference in ways that the written page could not. She sees her play as staging the primary conflict in James's plot between gendered binary terms: male and female, city and country, public and private, English and French, writing and music. Her reading relies not only on the assumption but the certainty that the encounter between John Marcher and Catherine Bertram/May Bartram is characterized by heterosexual desire, however failed and incomplete; indeed, she describes James's original story as "*[un] histoire d'amour*" ("*Le Château*" 100, "a love story").[28] Catherine, as a stand-in for women's sexuality, is "the beast," killed by John's inability to see anything but himself as reflected in her (*La Bête* 54). In *La Bête dans la jungle*, Duras encapsulates post-Lacanian feminist understandings of sexual difference as articulated in distinct ways by Cixous, Irigaray, and Kristeva. She also engages in an essentializing heterocentrism. Indeed, she may in fact actively undermine a queer interpretation of the text, as presented to her by James Lord. A gay American who returned to France after his wartime service due to its greater acceptance of homosexuality, Lord associated "The Beast in the Jungle" with the struggle (of another French-speaking, queer American expatriate male author) to express male–male desire. In an unpublished 2006 letter to me, Lord provides his own view of "The Beast in the Jungle."[29]

> The basic, central issue of James's story, I've always felt, is homosexuality, a matter clearly of capital concern to the author...The beast...represents the wild, rampant erotic impulse, an impulse which James found himself incapable of acting upon...Now, one must bear in mind that James's story was written only seven years after the Wilde scandal and trials. All this must have been still uncomfortably present in the awareness of anyone who himself had homosexual inclinations, however buried—entombed!—in the unconscious these may have been. (Lord 2006 3, 4)

Lord regards his decision to adapt "The Beast in the Jungle" for the stage as a sort of public "outing" for both the story and Henry James himself. He and Duras were friends, and he asked her to collaborate on the project.

As she didn't read English, Lord translated his play into French for her; he argues that she made only minor and cosmetic changes to this version. "Her adaptation didn't amount to much: changing May's name to Catherine and tricking up the dialogue here and there with self-conscious Durasisms. These are surely perceptible in the printed text…" (8–9).[30]

Without more substantive proof, we have no way of knowing which tale of the adaptation process is more accurate. Duras biographer Jean Vallier, who also interviewed Lord, summarizes a series of letters between the two concerning the collaboration, which can be interpreted to support either account (*C'était II* 290, 355–357, 823–824).[31] Although Lord's version seems in keeping with the experiences of others who worked with Duras, he benefits from having outlived her—and the reading of "The Beast in the Jungle" that he presented to me in 2006 sounds remarkably like Sedgwick's, which by that point had been widely available in print for two decades. Duras's famously unreliable relationship to her own history or to accounts of her creative process means that the author's contradictory statements about her engagements with Henry James's work prior to and during the adaptations with Lord and with Robert Antelme (see Chap. 5) provide us with little help here. In this case more than most, we can only understand the playwright's perspective through an analysis of the plays themselves.[32] Indeed, Duras's "creative" relationship to her biography and public persona is in part an attempt to emphasize the significance of her work over the "private" individual who authored it, as Vallier and others have noted; Duras seems to suggest that this conflict was centrally important to James as well (see Chap. 6).

But if Lord's version of the play offered what in effect is a queer theoretical analysis *après la lettre*, as he suggests, Duras did in fact engage in more than just minor revisions: as published, *La Bête dans la jungle* examines May Bartram's heterosexual femininity, not John Marcher's queer masculinity. As I've discussed briefly above, Duras's views on gay masculinity were backwards even for that period. Consistent with her presentation of John's struggle in *La Bête dans la jungle*, she believed that homosexuality results from the fear-based repression of a natural, universal male desire for women.[33] It adds to the complex history of this story's critical reception that a queer reading, by a gay male writer, may haunt a feminist theatrical adaptation that undermines that possibility. Duras's interpretation of James is radical for its time—but its feminism relies on a reactionary anti-queer textual politics.

As I will discuss in the next chapter, for twenty-first century readers this suggests a conflict between Duras's progressivism, in some areas, and her consistently retrograde representations of non-normative others. Her adaptations also seem, strangely, more historically distant to us than James's story. When we read *La Bête dans la jungle* today, its version of feminism appears outdated, even heavy-handed. Duras's views reflect her own socio-historical time and place, as do ours. Moreover, as Lora Romero eloquently suggests, "unless one thinks of society as a monolithic whole against which must arise an equally monolithic opposition, then a progressive stance in one arena does not entail a progressive stance in all other arenas" (5). In Chap. 5, I will argue that Duras's deep ambivalence towards French colonialism and the racism that fuels it, her retrograde ideas about queer desire, and her (feminist) essentialism should inform, without undermining, our recognition that her adaptations provide a unique and valuable interpretation of James. We should read Duras's versions of James both on their own terms and critically, as situated examples in an emerging history of feminist claims upon his work.

## Notes

1. All translations are mine unless otherwise noted. Other adaptations include François Truffaut's 1978 film *The Green Room* (*La chambre verte*), which is based on another short story, "The Altar of the Dead" (1895), but incorporates elements from "The Beast in the Jungle"; a 1969 British teleplay; and an experimental American film, 1980's *The Cold Eye (My Darling, Be Careful)*, directed by Babette Mangolte (Griffin 341). Benoît Jacquot made a television version, *La Bête dans la jungle*, based on the Duras play, in 1988.
2. As a further complication, Duras's collaborator in the project, the expatriate American author and biographer James Lord, insists that Duras deliberately erased examinations of closeted gay masculinity from both James's text and his own early version of the play. Duras is listed as the sole author of all three works on the publication's cover and frontispiece. The few scholarly readings of this play include Madeleine Borgomano, Yves Claveron, Carol J. Murphy, and Micéala Symington. Borgomano and Murphy are most interested in the ways that Duras's adaptations might shed light on the sole reference to James in 1987's *Emily L.* (see Chap. 6). Claveron argues that the play's John Marcher is an early version of Duras's ill male character in her better-known 1982 novella, *The Malady of Death*. Jean Bessière and Symington offer a short analysis of the play, and Duras's responses to James, in the course of their larger discussion of French receptions of his work (19–22). Symington's reading of the play, published separately, is discussed briefly below.

3. Critical responses to this story, from James's time to our own, are remarkably unified in seeing John Marcher's perspective as central. Roger Gard provides a typical early review, from 1912 (508); also see Allen Tate (1950), Krishna Vaid (1968, 224–225), Courtney Johnson (1969), and James Ellis (1984) for a range of representative readings that predate the post-Sedgwick focus on this story. Ellis briefly suggests that James's references to ancient ruins provide a coded counter to Marcher's perspective, in that May Bartram can read what he cannot (27–28).
4. The best-known source for Lacan's examination of "*le féminin*"/ "*La Femme*" is Seminar XX, from 1972–73. Representative criticisms of feminist uses of Seminar XX include Linda Martín Alcoff, Michael Hames-García, Alison Reed, Siobhan Somerville, and Kaila Adia Story. As Hames-García argues about the trajectory of queer theory and gender studies that rose in the wake of the French feminists, "theorists have systematically sought to define the newness and uniqueness of their scholarship through a denial of past and ongoing efforts to integrate considerations of class, gender, race, and sexuality...[and] resisted the consequences of a truly substantive, thorough, and ongoing engagement with theories that are centrally concerned with race and class from the other side of a deep epistemological divide" (43).
5. See Coulson's Chapter 3 for a thoughtful counter to this reading of the relationship with Woolson. She argues that Woolson evinces an ambivalence towards heterosexuality that equals James's, for different reasons. "Henry cannot reconcile himself to heterosexual sexuality; Constance, on the other hand, despite her erotic attraction to men, cannot embrace the social and psychological subordination to masculine authority that marriage would entail" (97).
6. In addition to those indicated in this paragraph, see Buelens and Lamm. Silverman briefly addresses "The Beast in the Jungle" at the conclusion of an article on *The Portrait of a Lady*.
7. See Ohi, and also Stevens (*Henry James*), on "queer style." "The general claim of this work on queer temporality is that sexually deviant lives often take a skewed position with respect to normative life narratives: they mature early or late, they don't follow the usual trajectories, they exhibit strange effects of precociousness or belatedness or abnormal pacing, and so forth" (Looby, "Sexuality" 426–427). The "queer temporality" Looby and others have found in James is, for Duras, effectively "women's time," instead (see Julia Kristeva and Emily Apter). Matthew Helmers reads the temporal shifts in the story, and Marcher's relationship to time, as "beyond the play of binaries" and therefore queer. Christopher Lane emphasizes James's "ontologically and homoerotically indeterminate narratives," and gently admonishes Sedgwick in arguing that "criticism of James that attempts to confirm this indeterminacy as homosexual opacity stalls when it argues that

sexual meaning inhabits the narrative subject more visibly than the narrative's frame of reference." Eric Savoy more generally emphasizes the importance of resisting the impulse to equate James with his narrators (Helmers 115; Lane 927–928).
8. See Jean Vallier (*C'etait I*, Chapters 15–20; *Marguerite Duras: La vie...*); please also see Laure Adler, Aliette Armel, Michel David, Colin Davis, and Murphy.
9. In an early biography, Dupee states that James's French "was more than good, it was phenomenal" (78). James regularly wrote French correspondents in their native tongue, and used French phrases in his private notebooks as well as his fiction. In a July 29, 1876 letter to William James, his sense of boredom with Paris is encapsulated by his inability to enjoy even the theater, as "I know the Théâtre Français by heart!" (*Complete Letters 1872–1876* Vol. 3, 160–162).
10. Bessière and Symington author the first chapter of *The Reception of Henry James in Europe*, edited by Annick Duperray; also see that text's invaluable timeline of European editions and translations (xxiv–xlviii) as well as Chapter 2, Angus Wrenn's analysis of Paul Bourget's role in crafting French receptions (36–46). Peter Brooks, Edwin Sill Fussell, Pierre A. Walker, and Wrenn (*Henry James*) all provide English-language explorations of "the 'Frenchness' of James's fiction" (Walker xiii); none mentions Duras's adaptations. See Brooks's Chapter 4 and Wrenn's Chapter 2 for analyses of James's own responses to French literature of the period. Wrenn suggests that James's attitude to Flaubert in fact is "characterized by respect rather than enthusiasm" (*Henry James* ix).
11. Bersani reminds us that the point of view in this passage "is not May Bartram's; it is omniscient but selective" (*Intimacies* 15). He's right, but I want to shift emphasis slightly: James "selectively" offers only Bartram's perspective, and not Marcher's, in this one instance.
12. "[T]he analogy between the art of the painter and the art of the novelist is, so far as I am able to see, complete. Their inspiration is the same, their process (allowing for the different quality of the vehicle) is the same, their success is the same...Their cause is the same..." (James, *The Art* 5). Michael Moon has addressed the prevalence of the word "scene" throughout James's critical writing, and particularly in "The Art of Fiction" (5).
13. Examples can be found in a series of conversations that occur throughout the story (501–505, 523–532).
14. Thanks to Elissa Marder for first pointing out this connection. Contemporary critics supported Duras's claim of a close affinity with Racine (Vallier; *C'était II* 500, 760, 874). James recalls reading Racine's *Phèdre* in 1859 in Geneva, during one of his family's sojourns abroad, under a teacher who "became a friend," and whose account of watching the play in Paris clearly left an impression (*Notes* 243).

15. Ted Hughes translates this as "Be careful, my lord. Your hands / May have eradicated many monsters / And never once failed. But let me say: / Not every monster has been accounted for. / There is one monster you have not recognized— / Your son, my lord, forbids me to say more" (77). See Simon Critchley for a brief overview of critical responses to the play.
16. See *This Sex Which Is Not One*, particularly the essay within of the same title. Irigaray explicitly connects visuality with phallogocentrism. Vision is an important element throughout Duras's corpus, not just in her theatrical and cinematic work; her emphasis on seeing (rather than, for example, the sense of touch) is one way that she differs from Irigaray.
17. Ellipses original.
18. In a third play on words, the set in each *tableau* echoes a medieval religious tableau: three painted panels arranged sequentially, from left to right, in order to make a sacred story accessible to illiterate viewers. Within each panel, however, a number of events often seem to be happening simultaneously, in a manner that violates the left-to-right chronological order of the larger work.
19. From Scene II: "Catherine: *Oui. Vous avez peur ?...Vous avez peur.*" "*Vous avez peur?*" (31).
20. Rowe examines the importance of *Don Giovanni* in 1877's *The American* (*Other* 56–74). Adeline R. Tintner addresses the influence of opera on James's later writing (281–307).
21. According to F. R. Noske, Zerlina's part is characterized by unusual syncopation. "In eighteenth century operatic scores fluent syncopation generally belongs to the refined language of the upper classes. In this opera, however, we find it in the part of a simple peasant girl" (175).
22. Zeiss details how the orchestral music for this aria shifts from a major to a minor chord, subtly violating the standard conventions of the *rondò*, the two-tempo aria form that it most resembles. See also Noske (1970, 168).
23. See Horne ("The Presence") and Van Leer ("Frank and Jim") for a discussion of French New Wave cinematic interest in James; works by James would be adapted for film by Jacques Rivette, Barbet Schroeder, Claude Chabrol, and François Truffaut.
24. Cixous also publishes a 1978 essay on James titled "*L'écriture comme placement ou de le ambiguïté de l'intérêt*" ("Writing as placement; or, of the ambiguity of interest") but her analysis is aligned with some of those Bessière and Symington describe, rather than with Duras's as I present it here. Through her largely psychoanalytic readings of *Portrait of a Lady, Washington Square, What Maisie Knew, The Wings of the Dove*, and (in translation) "The Pupil," "The Figure in the Carpet," and "The Beast in the Jungle," Cixous argues that James's style both reveals and conceals what he himself has repressed. She seems to find no feminist possibilities in his work.

25. See Lacan ("Homage") and Maurice Blanchot on this Durasian term. While in a short chapter of *L'Amitié* (98–101) Blanchot ruminates on Duras's 1969 novel *Détruire, dit-elle* (also made into a film of the same title, that year), he makes a substantive reference to the "hole-word" in "The Narrative Voice (the 'he,' the neutral" (385). A number of readers have noted the connection between *Lol V. Stein* and Gertrude, and Duras deploys a similar reference to Dickinson in *Emily L.* (see Chap. 6). Gertrude Stein's portrait of James in *Four in America* (1947) resonates with Duras's uses of Racine, Mozart, and James himself in *La bête dans la jungle*. Stein famously queers her own as well as American cultural history in this work, ambivalently claiming James as a predecessor while also inserting herself as a crucial interpreter of a male cultural history. See Haralson ("Rereading") and Caramello.
26. Kristeva 190–201. For a brief overview of the feminist discussions of temporality that emerge in the wake of the 1981 translation of Kristeva's essay, see Emily Apter.
27. As better-known examples in this vein, see Cixous's and Blanchot's readings of James.
28. In his discussion of Duras's homophobia, Lucey provides a translated section from a 1981 interview. "Men and women. We are irreconcilable, yet still we try, as we have for centuries, to reconcile ourselves to each other. With each love we do this. This is what I call the fabulous richness of heterosexuality. And, on the other hand, the incommensurable poverty of homosexuality. They love themselves in loving the other. Whereas we love our inverted image. We love our opposite, our antidote, our own hell. That is where the immensity of this richness is to be found" (344, 373 n.10; *Nous, l'homme et la femme. Nous sommes irréconciliables, nous essayons toujours, depuis des millénaires de nous réconcilier. Cela à chaque amour. C'est ça que j'appelle la richesse fabuleuse de l'hétérosexualité. Et par contre l'incommensurable misère de l'homosexualité. Ils s'aiment eux-mêmes en aimant l'autre. Tandis que nous aimons notre image inversée. Nous aimons notre contraire, nous aimons notre antidote, nous aimons notre enfer. Et c'est ça, l'immensité de la richesse*).
29. Best known as a biographer, Lord published *A Giacometti Portrait* (1980), *Giacometti: A Biography* (1985), and the posthumous *My Queer War* (2011). His first of two letters to me, dated October 10, 2006, was in response to my request for information regarding the collaboration with Duras.
30. The discussion of the character's name change is the only specific detail Lord provides about the nature of Duras's changes to his original adaptation. As I suggest above, it does in fact seem significant. In 2009, a couple of weeks before his death, Lord indicated in a second letter that he would send me a copy of the first (English) adaptation that he had brought to Duras in the late 1950s (2009, 1). At the date of this writing, the executor of his estate has not responded to several requests for further information about this document.

31. See also Adler (590, n.917). Both Colin Davis and James S. Williams suggest that although Duras uses collaboration as one way to destabilize notions of authorship, she does not share creative authority, insisting that each text must be publicly acknowledged as her own. Armel reads Duras's relationship to her own biography as an aspect of her creative work; David argues that Duras creates her public image as a version of one of the feminine characters in her own fiction. Colin Davis suggests that Duras's *La Douleur* (1985) appropriates Antelme's *L'Espèce Humain* (1947); Williams ("A Beast") indicates that the author's later collaborations with the young man she renamed "Yann Andréa" undermine his queer voice, and that much of the work of her prolific late period owes a great deal to Yann Andréa's uncredited assistance (582–584).
32. Adler, perhaps Duras's least critical biographer, repeats the author's assertion that "she read all of Henry James's work before adapting 'The Aspern Papers' with Robert Antelme" (565). This seems unlikely when we consider that Duras does not read or write comfortably in English (Lord 2006, 7; see also Colin Davis). By Duras's period, "The Beast in the Jungle" had two separate French translations, first published in 1928 and 1957—but only a few of his other works would have been readily available in French, for several more years after the play was written. Even in 2006 as they are writing, Bessière and Symington emphasize that French translations of James "do not comply with the organization of the New York Edition and do not allow a systematic reading of the short stories or tales" (16–17).
33. Lucey, writing in 2013, suggests that Duras's homophobia stems from both personal and cultural biases, including "hostility to identity politics that was typical of certain strains of leftist discourse [in France] in these years" (347). Crowley argues that later in her work "the male homosexual…becomes the object of a denunciatory attack on what she presents as the sterility of his desire" (659). During Xavière Gauthier's interviews with Duras, published in 1974 as *Les Parleuses*, she states, "*Il y a toujours eu, au départ de l'homosexualité masculine, un accident qui a fait que la voie, la voie de la hétérosexualité été abandonee, hein, toujours*" ("Always, at the inception of male homosexuality, there is an accident that means that the natural path, the path of heterosexuality, is abandoned forever"; 28), although she also concedes that gay men are in alliance with women against "*la class phallique*" ("the phallic class"; 152). Vallier quotes another acquaintance's brief reference to Lord, who tellingly is described as one of "those pederasts who used to go to dinner with Marguerite" (*C'était II* 365 n.57). In Duras's 1987 novel *La vie matérielle* she terms Yann Andréa "*Y.A., homosexuel*" (79). By way of contrast, Williams ("All Her Sons") argues that Duras's interest in outsiders and "anti-literature," as well as her late work with Yann Andréa, might in fact make her writing relevant to gay men; Williams acknowledges that he is writing against critical consensus.

CHAPTER 5

# Gender, Colonialism, and Italian Difference: Duras and *The Aspern Papers*

In 1961, *Les Papiers d'Aspern*, a play based on Henry James's 1888 novella *The Aspern Papers*, runs at the Théâtre des Mathurins-Marcel Herrand in Paris. Later published in the same Gallimard volume with *La Bête dans la jungle*, the play is an "*Adaptation théâtrale de Michael Redgrave d'après la nouvelle* Aspern's Papers. *Adaptation française de Marguerite Duras et Robert Antelme*" (61; Theatrical adaptation by Michael Redgrave, after the novella *Aspern's Papers* [sic]. French adaptation by Marguerite Duras and Robert Antelme). For the most part, French scholars have viewed this play as a direct translation of Redgrave's. Indeed, reading the two together, it is clear that Duras worked from a version of the famous British actor's adaptation as well as James's original, presumably both in translation. Robert Antelme had excellent English, as Duras did not, so his most likely contribution was as her translator of Redgrave's play: Antelme himself always presented *Les Papiers d'Aspern* as her work.[1] As I will argue in this chapter, the French play's departures from Redgrave's script are in fact quite substantive. *Les Papiers d'Aspern* interprets James's novella as an account of gendered racialization and linguistic difference that resonates with the emergence of French and Francophone postcolonial writing in Paris during the late 1950s and early 1960s.

Bessière and Symington focus on different aspects of Duras's plays, seeing them as paradigmatic of her period's interest in authorial reflexivity.[2] However, they share my rejection of the idea that *Les Papiers d'Aspern* is simply a translation, suggesting that "the details she changes must...be measured not simply against the original, but also in comparison with Redgrave's adaptation" (19). This chapter begins with that task, for those interested in Duras's relationship to Henry James or theater; again, more generally, I also argue that Duras's readings of James present a systematic, period-specific analysis that should be considered within the larger histories of both feminist scholarly interpretations and French readings of his work. Additionally, this under-read play merits closer attention in discussions of Duras's portrayals of both colonialism and ethnic gendering. As Bessière and Symington rather equivocally suggest, the Duras adaptations are "the most remarkable and authentic literary inventions through the reading and distortion of James" in 150 years of French responses to his work (22).

*Les Papiers d'Aspern* is a critical revision of Redgrave, who becomes for Duras a stand-in for British theatrical conventions and twentieth-century Anglo-American interpretations of James. Redgrave's adaptation provides Duras with the opportunity to refine—through resistance to the version of James that it presents—her own self-authoring as an avant-garde French feminist artist who consistently frames the position of (white) women under colonial capitalism through comparison with their own others: ethnically- and racially-marked, non-bourgeois, "colonized" subjects. In short, the differences between the two scripts reflect entirely different ideas about Henry James, cultural colonialism, and theatrical representation. On a narrower level, reading *Les Papiers d'Aspern* alongside *La Bête dans la jungle* allows us to conclude that Duras finds in James's overall project (not just in his individual works) a sustained examination of gender, power, and language. Duras does not separate James's published fiction from James the private historical person, but again this is typical for her context. James's depictions of the overdetermined misunderstandings between the American critic and the Bordereau women in Venice enable Duras to frame what will become a consistent motif in her better-known work, including the two titles for which she is most famous outside of France, the 1959 film *Hiroshima mon amour* and the 1984 novel *L'Amant*. Similar themes mark the "India cycle," composed of the novels *Le ravissement de Lol V. Stein* (1964), *Le vice-consul* (1965), and *L'amour* (1971) as well as the films *La femme du Gange* (1974), *India Song* (1964), and *Son nom de Venise dans Calcutta desert* (1976); and the so-called "autobiographical" novels (in addition to *L'Amant*): *Une barrage contre le Pacifique* (1950), *L'Eden Cinema* (1977), and *L'Amant de la Chine due Nord* (1991). Each of these works stages complex encounters between white French and colonized Asian subjects. Duras regularly presents the precarious position of white women living at the lower rungs of patriarchal French colonial societies, or at its margins, as enabling their profound empathy with the Asian men and women with whom they form intimate, familial, and/or sexual connections. For Duras, patriarchal hierarchies of sex mirror and enable colonial hierarchies of ethnicity, gender, language, and nationality.

Duras's "authorial" relationship to her own history has complicated readers' responses to much of her work in this vein. As I have suggested, she encouraged the conflation of her own life with those of her characters: she invented personal details, speaking of herself in the third person as "Duras," the writer.[3] In discussing her background with interviewers, Duras reveals that she thought of herself as both French and "colonial," a hybridized product of French Vietnam, despite the fact that both of her parents were white and French.[4] Jane Bradley Winston explores how, in the wake of the publication of *Un barrage*, Duras was seen by fascinated readers as racially ambiguous. Simone de Beauvoir was under the impression that Duras was "half-white, half-Indochinese," and introduced her as such to a friend. Racial alterity was read by numerous contemporary critics into her face and body as well as her writing (32–33).

Duras's unusual first-person knowledge of the brutalities of French colonialism in Vietnam, her wartime experiences working in the French Resistance, and her status as a member of the leftist intellectual elite all influence her engagements with anti-colonial and anti-Gaullist activism in 1950s and early 1960s Paris. Frantz Fanon's *Peau noire, masques blanques* (*Black Skin, White Masks*) came out in 1952; Fanon's teacher and fellow Martinician Aimé Césaire published *Discours sur le colonialism* (*Discourse on Colonialism*) in 1955. During the Algerian Revolution (1954–62), Jean-Paul Sartre's journal *Les temps modernes* became an important platform for critics of racism at home, and colonialism in Algeria and elsewhere. At a 1956 meeting organized by the short-lived "*Comité d'action des intellectuels contre la pursuit de la guerre en Afrique du Nord*" ("Action Committee of Intellectuals Against the Pursuit of War in North Africa"), both Sartre and Césaire spoke for Algerian independence (Macey 341–342). *Les temps modernes* published a translated version of African American writer Richard Wright's *Black Boy*, serialized in its entirety, from January to June 1947; later, Sartre would write the preface to Fanon's 1961 *Les Damnés de la terre* (*The Wretched of the Earth*). Fanon's work, particularly 1959's *L'an V de la revolution algerienné* (*Year Five of the Algerian Revolution*)—the title deliberately evokes the French Revolutionary Calendar—helped inspire increasing leftist resistance to the war. The subsequent right-wing backlash consolidated in a May 1958 coup that installed Charles de Gaulle's nationalist government. Fanon also served as an inspiration for Dionys Mascolo, Duras's second husband and the father of her son Jean. In 1960, Mascolo—himself the child of Italian immigrants—produced a famous manifesto that described the war as "criminal" and equated French colonialism with Nazism. The connection, again, evokes Césaire, who in *Discourse on Colonialism* traces an ideological genealogy in which capitalism leads inevitably to colonialism and fascism (Césaire 35–50). Duras was one of 121 Parisian artists and intellectuals who signed this document; others included Arthur Adamov, Maurice Blanchot (who probably drafted the manifesto with Mascolo), Pierre Boulez, Françoise Sagan, and Nathalie Sarraute. David Macey describes the *Manifeste de 121* as "the most explosive petition to have been produced since *J'Accuse*," the 1898 open letter Émile Zola wrote to the French government to protest the imprisonment of Alfred Dreyfus. Under the Gaullist government, teachers and civil servants who signed the *Manifeste de 121* were suspended, and state-run media blacklisted the others (444–446).[5]

The crucible of postwar Paris effectively fused, for both Gaullists and the left, what outside of France are regarded as distinct approaches or movements. Duras and her contemporaries thought of Communism, anti-colonialism, and avant-garde art as closely intertwined activities. In part, this relationship to art and politics was forged by a prior generation: the Dadaists and Surrealists, in the 1920s and 1930s, espoused leftist philosophies that combined elements of Marxism and anti-colonialism, and openly mocked rising European fascist movements of the period.[6] The Nazi Occupation and the Resistance had established writers and artists as freedom fighters; alliances formed during this period would influence French political and intellectual life for decades to come. Both pre- and post-1917 Marxisms in Western Europe emphasized the goal of a global revolution of workers: combined with the collective trauma of the Occupation, this sense of a shared ethical and political purpose helped determine the postwar French left's sense that they were the center of a critical resistance to global oppression, under various fascist and anti-worker regimes.

Artists and intellectuals such as Duras and Antelme, who had worked together in the Resistance ten years earlier, now found themselves citizens of a nation that occupied Algeria, Vietnam, and parts of the Caribbean. It is difficult to overstate how profoundly leftist Paris felt the cultural betrayal of Gaullism; inevitably, the French intellectual and artistic elite identified with the colonized rather than with the colonizers represented by their own government. For the French left in the 1950s and 1960s, active and public resistance to French colonialist policy—including but not limited to the war in Algeria—was a vital continuation of work begun during the Occupation. That work would help establish collective commitment to a massive general strike of May 1968, led by workers and students, which paralyzed the country and was a key factor in the overthrow of de Gaulle.

Duras identified as both an anti-racist and a Communist to the end of her life.[7] However, understood in context these views do not necessarily suggest a relationship to racial or ethnic alterity that is consistently "progressive," as that term is defined in the twenty-first century period. Sartre is an indicative example. Over the course of the 1950s and 1960s, he variously understood himself to be an existentialist, an anti-colonialist, and finally a Communist who used Marxist ideas to temper what he would come to view in 1960's *Critique de la raison dialectique* (*Critique of Dialectical Reason*) as the bourgeois individualism of his earlier existentialism. In 1956's "*Le colonialisme est un système*," Sartre argued that the Algerians would free both themselves and France itself from the corrupting system of colonialism. As Frantz Fanon suggests, the French left of the postwar period sometimes seemed "more worried about the damage being done to France's honour and soul than they were about shattered Algerian bodies."[8]

Readers of Duras argue that a similar ambivalence about colonialism and ethnic and/or racial difference is central to her project (Marie-Paul Ha xiv; Holmlund 174–175). In intimate and domestic settings, power flows unevenly back and forth between white and racialized characters—as desire, need, and a shared struggle to survive enable both empathy and exploitation. Christine Anne Holmlund suggests that Duras stages a "politics of marginality" that offers an alternative to masculinist postcolonial approaches and Eurocentric Western feminist discourses; in the films Holmlund discusses, white women and Orientalized others are similarly oppressed by colonial economic and social systems (168). Michael Sheringham admits that Duras's fictional representations "risk reproducing the colonialist worldview they certainly repudiate," as she consistently associates non-Europeans with "absolute alterity" (441).[9] Gabrielle H. Cody, in her reading of Duras's theatrical productions, argues that the stage offers Duras a controlled, "false" solution to the problem of the invisibility of women and colonized others; in her plays, Duras emphasizes the fact that these subjects actively "appear as invisible" (4, 20). As a member of the colonizing class, Duras writes about the intimate brutalities of colonialism, and she describes the oppression experienced by (white) women as echoing the cultural gendering experienced by racial or ethnic others under colonialist systems. This simultaneously suggests both appropriation and a sustained analysis of the irresolvable tensions surrounding gender, race, sexuality, and power in colonial settings.[10]

Duras's *Les Papiers d'Aspern* stages an encounter between two distinct forms of "cosmopolitan" subjectivity. James's narrator becomes a representative of a clubby, literate, privileged, Anglo-American masculinity—the Bordereau women serve as "colonized," impoverished, "Italian" muses for this version of manhood. Anna Despotopoulou might argue that this is an entirely accurate analysis of James, both in *The Aspern Papers* and elsewhere. For her, James's multi-national women characters embody the "precarity of not belonging," as compared to male cosmopolitan characters who are "citizens of the world." In James, women's "cosmopolitanism" is synonymous with domestic and/or other forms of insecurity (146–150). Duras's reading of Italy and the Italian language in James's novella reflects her sense of the cultural and sexual invisibility enforced—equally, or at least comparatively, in her view—on women and non-white subjects under colonial, patriarchal, and/or fascist systems. Unlike the vast majority of her contemporaries, Duras sees the transatlantic, upper-class, multilingual Henry James as allied not with the exploiters who physically resemble him and his narrator, but rather with the exploited—the ethnic/female others whose desperation both he and she emphasize.

Both Sara Blair and Leonardo Buonomo have documented the particular ways that representations of Italy in James's work reflect period-specific understandings of Italy and the Italians as racialized, in ways that Anglo-Americans are not. At the same time, as Blair argues, James's "documentary stance" in his travel writing, and most notably in 1907's *The American Scene*, incorporates both "openness to otherness, [and] anxiety about managing otherness."[11] In her adaptation of *The Aspern Papers*, Duras describes the unnamed American narrator as misreading Italy, Italians, and the Italian language because of his own paternalist views of ethnic and sexual difference. She regards James as empathizing with the perspective of the Italianized Bordereau women, while both Michael Redgrave and the American narrator of *The Aspern Papers*—but, critically, not James himself—represent colonizing, Anglo-American literary and cultural elitism.

Henry James first published *The Aspern Papers* in 1888, and revised it for a 1909 American edition.[12] The origin of the novella lies in an 1887 entry in his *Notebooks*. James hears an anecdote about an American literary critic who tracks down an elderly mistress of the long-dead Shelley, living in Florence with a niece; he lodges with them, hoping that the old woman will die during his stay and provide him with an opportunity to obtain letters written by the poet. James changes small but meaningful details of the story. The setting is shifted to Venice; Shelley is transformed into a fictional American poet, Jeffrey Aspern. Juliana Bordereau and her niece (possibly her daughter with Aspern) Tina become "scarcely respectable Americans—they were believed to have lost in their long exile all national quality, besides being as their name implied of some remoter French affiliation" (1). An unnamed Aspern scholar narrates the story. He travels to Venice to gain access to Juliana Bordereau's home, and perhaps find some of the poet's undiscovered papers. The narrator is repelled by the "avidity" evinced by Aspern's "divine Juliana," now living in poverty in a dilapidated *palazzo*. Her desperation to provide some financial security for the unmarried Tina leads her to charge him an outrageous rent. The climax of the story occurs when the narrator sneaks into Juliana's rooms at night, hoping to steal the letters he imagines are kept there. Surprising him at this task, Juliana declares him a "publishing scoundrel" and collapses into her niece's arms (20, 15, 79). His attempts to insinuate himself into Tina's good graces culminate in her eventual offer, upon her aunt's death, of conditional access to the papers: he must marry her in order to obtain them, as she believes her aunt might have suggested. The narrator reacts with horror to this idea, and Tina subsequently burns the papers. As the story ends, the critic is left with a miniature portrait of Aspern, given to him by Tina. He declares in the last line of the story "that it hangs above my writing table. When I look at it I can hardly bear my loss—I mean of the precious papers" (96). As his modifications to the skeleton of the story in his *Notebooks* suggest, James foregrounds questions of nationality, cultural value, language, and place. The repeated use of Italian in the text emphasizes the differences between the Bordereaus and the American critic. Like later queer theoretical readers, Duras draws out James's relationship to style, narration, dialogue, and linguistic difference: for her, however, these elements are clear evidence of his feminist project.

We have a few precedents in English language scholarship for a feminist analysis of *The Aspern Papers*. Most influentially, Rowe argues that Tina Bordereau's "refusal to accept the insignia...of this patriarchal culture" represents James's own examination of gender and power. Joseph Church and William Veeder both offer psychoanalytic readings based on the unnamed American critic's terror of "phallic" women. Despotopoulou argues that female characters in James's work more generally suggest his sense that women's displaced relationships to national belonging render them innately cosmopolitan, modern, and consequently more interesting subjects (Rowe, *Theoretical* 118; Veeder 22–24; Church 28; Despotopoulou 142–144). Yet as none of these readers shares Duras's focus on questions of gender and language, or the French political-cultural context that is a palpable presence in her adaptation, I'd like to briefly address elements of James's novella that provide a foundation for the reading she produces.

James emphasizes translation or missed translation in this story, which suggests some sort of critical reflection upon the exoticizing Anglo-American fantasies of Italy that were prevalent in his own period. Italian terms arrive with the Bordereaus; initially, the narrator serves as translator for the reader, in introducing their moldering *palazzo*. Clearly not fluent in Italian, he immediately renders words into English for his readers, like a tourist who is proud to have learned a few useful phrases. He describes "the *piano nobile* or most important floor," and "a narrow *riva* or convenient footway on either side" (5).[13] The Bordereaus initially seem off-putting and unplaceably foreign. In this early section, the narrator twice suggests that Aspern is "not a woman's poet" (2, 4). Detailing his friend Mrs. Prest's suggestion that he try to lodge with the Bordereaus, he suggests that "It is not supposed easy for women to rise to the large free view of anything, anything to be done; but they sometimes throw off a bold conception—such as a man would not have risen to—with singular serenity." James may be calling our attention to the narrator's paternalistic assumptions, and the reader begins to sense that this story will present a conflict between what is and what is not "supposed," particularly regarding women. The narrator implies a homosocial, literate brotherhood—composed of himself, the reader, and the dead Jeffrey Aspern—as he describes the poet's relationships with women as reminding him of "Orpheus and the Mænads" (1, 5). At this point, typically for James, we are wholly reliant on the narrator, and forced into alliance with him through a shared language and perspective. Yet the introduction of Italian marks the first sign of another view, which will come to undermine the narrator's sense of cultural superiority.

Immediately after his initial uses of Italian in describing the Bordereaus' home, the narrator's relationship to foreign words changes. French terms are introduced, predominantly by Juliana but also by the narrator; italics gradually are dropped, and he no longer translates words. As Chapter II opens, "*sala*" and "*scagliola*" now are unitalicized, undifferentiated from the English words that surround them; in the last paragraph of Chapter

III, "padrona" is the first Italian word to remain untranslated (9, 8). In part, this tactic provides a distinction between Italian phrases and the French that peppers the text once Juliana Bordereau is introduced. Although nominally American, she is equally comfortable in French and English; in the first sentence she speaks to the narrator, she fluently deploys both languages. He also uses French, but in a series of clichéd phrases that seem artificial and forced by comparison. James directs our attention towards his inconsistent italicization of non-English words. As Juliana states "it's many years since I've been in one of the *gondola*," the narrator immediately comments "She uttered these words as if they designated a curious far-away craft known to her only by hearsay" (17). The gradual but marked disappearance of word and phrase translations, and the increasingly sporadic use of italicization for Italian terms, serves another purpose, as readers gradually are immersed in the Bordereau women's flexibly multilingual perspective.

In his attention to italics, James may be examining the foundations of our ideas about linguistic and cultural difference. The word "italic" originates as an ancient Latin adjective referring to Italian groups beyond the borders of Rome, and connoting barbarism. By the sixteenth century, italics would be deployed within a book that used Roman type to set specific words or phrases apart, and mark them as unreliable or ridiculous.[14] Whether or not James had a history of typesetting handy, his selective use of italics and standard Roman fonts for Italian-language words and phrases in published editions of *The Aspern Papers* parallels a gradual shift away from exclusive reliance on the narrator's perspective.[15] French, English, and Italian run together on the page, alongside the rare Latin phrase. Moreover, James draws parallels between the narrator's ideas about women and his linguistic provincialism; his italicized Italian terms are rendered even more alien by his awkward and increasingly unnecessary translations.

As the narrator enters the house and meets Juliana and Tina Bordereau, James prepares us for an encounter that will explore the consequences of the narrator's sense of (masculine, cultural) entitlement. Early in Chapter III, having already noted that he has managed to make the Bordereaus' maid blush, he twice speaks of having "won my suit" with the unsophisticated Miss Tina, who repeatedly tries to deflect his attentions. The narrator responds with an assertion of his own sense of (masculine) authority. "I saw in a moment my good lady had never before been spoken to in any such fashion—with a kind of humorous firmness that didn't exclude sympathy, that was quite founded on it. She might easily have told me that my sympathy was impertinent, but this by good fortune did not occur to her" (13, 13–14). His treatment of Tina evokes a note of sexualized pressure that becomes less "humorous" as the story develops. Gradually, the narrator gains access to the deeper levels of the women's living quarters: they reside on the first floor, and he is lodged on the second. Initially, he is allowed access only to the *sala*, with the stairs that lead to his own rooms. He longs to reach the more intimate spaces of their quarters beyond, but as he indicates, "I sat in the garden looking up over the top of my book at the closed windows of my hostess…Their motionless shutters became as expressive as eyes consciously closed" (29). Like Juliana, who wears a green eye covering for most of the story, the shuttered house seems unable to force him to leave; both engage in the passive resistance of refusing to acknowledge his presence. While a number of scholars have rightly emphasized the homoeroticism of the narrator's fascination with Aspern, there also is a distinctly heterosexual power dynamic at play as the narrator becomes more forceful in his quest for the papers.[16] He hopes to gain sublimated erotic access to his hero through the equally embodied and feminized vehicles of the elderly Juliana and her crumbling *palazzo*: he fantasizes about rifling through the concealed papers in an orgiastic frenzy. In James's original, the narrator's invasion of the dying Juliana's chambers is described in terms that render it unsettlingly sexualized. His entrance resembles an opportunistic rape, narrowly interrupted—he violates the women's privacy, but also their symbolic bodies, repeatedly conflated throughout the novella with the inner parts of the house itself.

> I had no definite purpose, no bad intention, but felt myself held to the spot by an acute, though absurd, sense of opportunity. Opportunity for what I couldn't have said, inasmuch as it wasn't in my mind that I might proceed to thievery. Even had this tempted me I was confronted with the evident fact that Miss Bordereau didn't leave her secretary, her cupboard, and the drawers of her tables gaping. I had no keys, no tools and no ambition to smash her furniture. None the less it came to me that I was now, perhaps alone, unmolested, at the hour of freedom and safety, nearer to the source of my hopes than I had ever been. I held up my lamp, let the light play upon the different objects as if it could tell me something. Still there came no movement from the other room. If Miss Tina was sleeping she was sleeping sound. Was she doing so—generous creature—on purpose to leave me the field? Did she know I was there and was she just keeping quiet to see what I would do—what I *could* do? (77–78)

The narrator tries to convince himself to commit a crime by fantasizing that Tina is testing his manly resolve. In the following paragraphs, doors, rooms, and furniture stand in for the women's body parts—and those connections become more transparently concrete and sexualized. The narrator "gape[s]" at Juliana's "exposed" desk "grotesquely," noting that she can "no longer mount guard." As he later confesses, "I did something more, for the climax of my crisis...If she [Miss Tina]...wished me to keep away, why hadn't she locked the door of the communication between the sitting-room and the sala? That would have been a definite sign that I was to leave them alone. If I didn't leave them alone she meant me to come for a purpose..." (79). Reaching out to touch a small, clitoral button that he deduces may open the desk, the narrator glances over his shoulder, to sudden alarm: Juliana stands behind him, ghostlike in her nightgown. "For the first, the last, the only time I beheld her extraordinary eyes," which had inspired some of Aspern's best poems, uncovered by their habitual "horrible green shade." As she collapses in shock, he flees (78–79).

Early in the story, James also suggests a division between the house's feminine, private spaces and its more public ones through his representations of Italian and English in the story. Italian terms cross divisions of culture and class; the Bordereaus' Italian maid, Olimpia, figures prominently in the private life of the house. Class boundaries that would separate the three women in an English household of the period are muddled and permeable. Their sole "*serva*," Olimpia at times also becomes a representative of the (feminized) house. She and Miss Tina speak the Italian of native Venetians: as the narrator states disparagingly of Tina, "she had acquired by contact the trick of the familiar soft-sounding almost infantile prattle of the place. I judged her to have imbibed this invertebrate dialect from the natural way the names of things and people—mostly purely local—rose to her lips" (40). The servants speak rarely, but they use Italian words that often remain unitalicized in the text, sharing this mark of fluency with Tina. Juliana's relationship to language is the most cosmopolitan. She uses Italian and French readily; however, her Italian terms often are differentiated, either by Juliana herself or through the use of italics. "Are your rooms too dear?...We can arrange, we can *combinare*, as they say here" (59). Aware of and playful with the concept of linguistic alienation and cultural privilege, Juliana is the story's only true expatriate—again, though, her multilingualism reflects a personal history of transatlantic (sexual) exploitation and abandonment. Elderly, sick, and impoverished, without connections, she is painfully aware of her inability to ensure even a basic level of financial security for Tina.

Unlike Aspern, whom the narrator describes as "essentially American," the two women with the French name "had long ago shed and unlearned any native marks and notes...they might have been Norwegians or Spaniards" (33). In Duras's interpretation of the story, cultural and gender difference are interchangeable markers of alterity, as the narrator is shut out by a mysterious femininity that is simultaneously white and ethnically alien. His scorn for women is paralleled by his distaste for things Venetian; like Tina's "invertebrate dialect," the Bordereaus' home reveals a "low Italian standard" (31, 40). His prejudice ensures a series of dialogic missed encounters, as he states at one point: Tina "looked at me as if I had spoken a strange tongue" (36). Nevertheless, through his encounter with the Bordereaus, with the Italian language, and with the city of Venice, the American critic is changed. Like the damp that seeps quietly in over centuries to undermine the city's foundations, the Venetian atmosphere gradually erodes his sense of cultural and masculine dominance.

At one point, the narrator imagines conversing with Jeffrey Aspern; staring into the painted face of his hero, the narrator waxes romantic in his praise of his hero's "delightful eyes...they were so young and brilliant and yet so wise and so deep." The closest textual parallel, of course, is to Juliana's "extraordinary eyes." The narrator terms Aspern "a god"; again, this description later is repeated by Juliana, Aspern's lover (88, 2, 42). In a move typical of nineteenth-century conceptions of homosexuality as a "hermaphroditism of the soul," James's narrator also plays the role of a womanly supplicant, laden with flowers.[17] Initially, this performed feminization is a deception: he feigns a gushy interest in the Bordereaus' untended garden as a pretext for visiting the house. Yet he in fact proceeds to delight in the "bowers" he cultivates. Juliana maintains (masculine) indifference towards his efforts, terming his interest in flowers not "a manly taste" (47). Impatient but deferential, he waits for her to notice, to thank him for the extravagant bouquets he produces. In the context of the story, his relationship to gardening feminizes him; in a parallel reversal of assumed roles that Duras must have noticed, it also renders the upper-class Anglo-American narrator akin to a household servant, like Olimpia.

The narrator's conversations with Juliana Bordereau also are marked by transgressions of gender-role expectations. He is coy, loquacious; she is logical, pragmatic, annoyed by his prattling (48–50). At the story's conclusion, Tina's proposal of marriage marks the critic as fully unmanned. She has property: she offers it to him in exchange for his hand—and, by implication, his body—in marriage. He recoils from Tina's unwanted advance in visceral horror. Numerous critics have suggested that his response is evidence of his potential homosexuality, and James's text makes it clear that Tina is aware that the narrator's desire is only for Aspern's papers. But Duras's play presents an alternate reading. In another of the novella's series of reversals—in which presumed hierarchies of gender, culture, and power disintegrate in the midst of real encounters between situated individuals—the narrator's sexual phobia also renders him feminized, a virginal girl to the suddenly masculinized Tina's no-nonsense, stereotypically "male" desire. She effectively promises access to Aspern's private documents, on the condition that the narrator marries her. He forgoes the satisfaction of his desire for the papers, because it comes at the price of prostituting himself to Tina.

As in *Daisy Miller* (1878), and echoing the references to Naples in "The Beast in the Jungle," in *The Aspern Papers* an Italian city serves as an almost viral threat—an unsettling sexual, cultural, and linguistic alterity that invades and undermines the narrator's Anglo-American sense of self. Like John Marcher in "The Beast in the Jungle," after he realizes that he has lost the papers forever, the narration shifts points of view. Changing from his usual third- to second-person address, the narrator describes the city of Venice in intimate terms. His metaphors blur spatial boundaries between the domestic and the public, the stage and the city.

> Without streets and vehicles, the uproar of wheels, the brutality of horses, and with its little winding ways where people crowd together, where voices sound as in the corridors of a house, where the human step circulates as if it skirted the angles of furniture and shoes never wear out, the place has the character of an immense collective apartment…And somehow the splendid common domicile, familiar domestic and resonant, also resembles a theatre with its actors clicking over bridges and, in straggling processions, tripping along fondamentas. As you sit in your gondola the footways that in certain parts edge the canals assume to the eye the importance of a stage, meeting it at the same angle, and the Venetian figures, moving to and fro against the battered scenery of their little houses of comedy, strike you as members of an endless dramatic troupe. (93–94)

In this remarkable description, urban life in Venice resembles that of a provincial Italian village. We move inside of Venice, a "theatre," as both audience and actor. What initially seems clearly differentiated, as male or female, English or Italian, public or private, is blended together through the encounter.

## Redgrave's Reading: "The Narrator is the Author Himself"

In 1958, Michael Redgrave completes a theatrical adaptation of *The Aspern Papers*; in addition to changing key plot elements, his version elides moral complexity and uses lower-class Italian characters as comic foils for the Bordereaus and the narrator. Unlike James, he names the narrator, calling him "Henry Jarvis." In order to render his allusion even more obvious, he terms this character "H.J." throughout the text. "Henry Jarvis" still uses a pseudonym; in Redgrave's text as in James's original, he at long last gives his real name to Tina. However, in James the narrator's "true" name remains as unknown to the reader as his false one. Redgrave provides both the narrator's legal name and his pseudonym: "Henry Jessamine." This narrator, twice-over "H.J.," is identified wholly with James himself. Redgrave therefore removes from the text the uncomfortable ambiguity whereby James forces his readers to face their own complicity in the narrator's assumptions. Redgrave's H.J., in his Anglophilia and "pomposity," is a gentle caricature of portrayals of James common in the U.S. and U.K. at the time. As he states in his introduction, "the reader may be pardoned for thinking...that the narrator is the author himself."[18]

Redgrave's play presents the narrator's biases as fact, as is particularly evident in his treatment of issues of language and class. Olimpia is renamed "Assunta"; a much older woman, she plays a larger role in the play than Olimpia does in the novella. Rendered as a stock "stupid servant," this version of the character undermines the critique of the narrator's ideas about class, nationality, gender, and domestic labor that were made possible through James's Olimpia. Indeed, "Olympia" suggests ancient Roman mythology and therefore the foundations of Western thought; "Assunta" suggests an allusion to the impoverished post-World War II nation. Marked as Catholic, ethnic, and other, she is more readily stereotyped by viewers accustomed and perhaps ascribing to long traditions of Anglo-American anti-Catholicism. Assunta's general ignorance is epitomized by her inability to speak any English at all. While his adaptation therefore uses more Italian, Redgrave ignores what Duras will see as the novella's critical engagement with linguistically- and ethnically-marked class difference.

In addition to shoring up these boundaries, Redgrave recuperates H.J. as a moral figure; in this version, James's unethical narrator becomes reliable and authoritative. Through his development of the critic's servant Pasquale, a minor character in James's original, Redgrave splits the

American critic in two: Pasquale is given a number of the lines in the original text in which the narrator had revealed his duplicity and acquisitiveness. Redgrave's H.J. is a harmless, idealistic academic whom Pasquale terms "my lord," believing his employer's pseudonym to be evidence that he is in fact a disguised aristocrat despite the fact that H.J., like a proper American, repeatedly insists that "I am *not* a *lord!*" (75). Pasquale independently steals the trunk containing Aspern's papers, which he believes are letters documenting some personal scandal affecting "milord"; this transforms the climax of the story, in which Juliana discovers the American critic at her desk.

Unlike in James's original, in Redgrave's play Aspern's papers are of unquestionable cultural importance.[19] H.J.'s actions—failures of gallantry, in this version—are conducted in pursuit of significant literary artifacts. Indeed, in his preface Redgrave declares that it is Tina's behavior that is the most unconscionable, if also the most human. As he states, "the last action, the burning of the papers—to my mind the only really 'wicked' one—is the most 'sympathetic' of all" (ix). Redgrave changes Juliana's famous condemnation of "critics" to "scandal-mongers." The shift renders this important moment the paranoid rant of an ill old woman, rather than the justified objection that it seems in James. In addition, it constructs another (gendered) hierarchy between legitimate scholars, like H.J., and untrained, feminized "gossips" (James 60; Redgrave 59). At the play's conclusion, Tina now decides to use H.J.'s misplaced lighter to start the fire in which she will burn the letters: this makes her a scorned woman, behaving out of spite rather than loyalty to her aunt. Reading James as uncritical of his narrator, and engaging in familiar postwar ethnic caricatures of the defeated Italians, Redgrave removes from *The Aspern Papers* all of the means by which James uses the Bordereaus and their Venetian palazzo to undermine the American critic's self-aggrandizing cultural solipsism.

## Duras's *Les Papiers d'Aspern*

James's novella has existed in French translation since 1920, and was included (alongside "The Turn of the Screw") in an influential 1929 collection, reissued several times by different publishers. While an emphasis on James's "internationalism" was standard in French readings during this period, Duras's twist on that theme certainly was not.[20] Again, although it's clear that she used Redgrave's text alongside James's, Duras presents *The Aspern Papers* as a feminist analysis of ethnic and linguistic alterity.

She begins by eliminating much of what Redgrave terms his own "elaborate pastiche of James's manner of speech," and rendering sections of dialogue closer to the original (vii).[21] Duras retains much of the Italian that Redgrave inserts through his development of Pasquale and Assunta; however, her version resonates with the reading of the use of Italian in James's version that I've explored above. She follows Redgrave in providing a name for the narrator, perhaps because this makes the play easier to stage, but the French version always uses H.J.'s full name—"Harry Jarvis"—which effectively undermines any automatic parallel between Henry James and his narrator. In *Les Papiers d'Aspern* as in James's original, the American critic's character and authority are ambiguous; through the use of question marks and ellipses, Duras makes Redgrave's confident man of letters sound halting, unsure of himself. The characterizations of servants draw out James's potential critique of ethnically-marked class categorizations, and Duras presents James's account of the spaces of Venice and the Bordereaus' home as an explicit analysis of gendered relationships to space and language.

Early in Duras's adaptation, Harry Jarvis and Mme. Prest discuss Aspern's romance with Juliana. The section culminates in the line from James's original, in which it appears twice, that Aspern "was not a woman's poet." While the dialogue is lifted nearly word-for-word from Redgrave's play, Duras edits it in order to place emphasis on sections from James's original that Redgrave downplays. By way of comparison, Redgrave writes:

| | |
|---|---|
| H.J.: | I have reason to believe that Aspern did not cherish obscurity. *He* took no pains to conceal anything. On the contrary. As for her, until five months ago her secret was safe. But when we stumbled on those papers in the attic in Philadelphia, we uncovered the fragments of a genius. When Aspern discovered Italy he discovered himself. He sounded the depth of his own obliquity and he was appalled. But he never lacked courage and he clung to that. Finally he sought expiation. The last group of poems are like burnt-offerings whose smoke still rises to the gods, long after the tide of battle has sunk without trace into the earth. |
| MRS. PREST (with gentle irony): | Bravo, Harry, that was splendid! |

| | |
|---|---|
| H.J.: | Believe me, Helen, to us Americans he will be our morning star. When these poems are published he will hang high in the heaven of literature for all the world to see. He will be part of the light by which we walk. Who knows what treasures of his later genius are not hidden in this house? As for her...there hovers about her name...how shall I say? |
| MRS. PREST: | An intimation of immorality? |
| H.J. (wincing slightly): | A perfume of impenitent passion! (12–13) |

Mrs. Prest's last line plays on the title of Wordsworth's 1807 "Ode: Intimations of Immortality from Recollections of Early Childhood." Elements of the exchange are original to James: in describing Juliana, James's narrator reflects that "There hovered about her name a perfume of impenitent passion, an intimation that she had not been exactly as the respectable young person in general." Two sentences later, Aspern's "works immortal through their beauty" are paired with the narrator's unsupported hypothesis that the poet's "divine Juliana" likely "had had a foreign lover...before her meeting with Jeffrey Aspern" (31–32). Redgrave uses James's phrases to change the characterizations: putting the words in Mrs. Prest's mouth makes her, rather than the "wincing" H.J., an ungenerous gossip. Recognizing a reference to Wordsworth's poem, Redgrave makes it more obvious while also eliminating the critical engagement with literary "immortality" suggested by James's switches between referents. James's unreliable narrator believes that Juliana is "immoral," but the "intimation" of Wordsworth's "Ode" reminds a literate reader of the "immortality" that will be presented in a couple of lines, as a description of Aspern himself: the "immortal" poet may be the truly "immoral" character, in a story that explores what happens to the cast-off female muses of literary men. In Redgrave's version, the younger Juliana Bordereau was both sexually promiscuous and entirely culpable. Just like H.J.'s servant Pasquale, who voices mercenary ideas that belong to the American narrator in James's original, Redgrave's Mrs. Prest, the only female outsider in the text, becomes the repository of lines that had made James's male narrator seem ignoble, as well as potentially feminized.

Duras modifies this passage from Redgrave, removing the long speech that Redgrave inserts to establish H.J. as an idealistic man of letters. She also removes the feminine praise, ironic or no, that generally follows these monologues in Redgrave's version.

HARRY JARVIS: *À coup sûr. Écoutez Helen, lorsque nous sommes tombés sur ce paquet dans le grenier de Philadelphie, nous avons mis au jour des textes de génie. Nous les devons sans doute à sa découverte prestigieuse des poètes américains. Qui sait quels trésors peuvent être cachés dans cette maison. Saviez-vous que sa légende n'est pas sans ombre...il a provoqué des passions redoutables...on a même pu l'accuser d'immoralité.* (77)

HARRY JARVIS: Of course. Helen, while we were holed up with that packet of papers in that attic in Philadelphia, we found the works of a genius. Beyond a doubt, we discovered the work of the most prestigious of American poets. Who knows what treasures might be hidden in that house? You know that his reputation wasn't without shadows...he provoked powerful passions...one could even accuse him of immorality."

Duras seems to recognize Redgrave's switches of speaker and implied responsibility, but she goes further than simply reinstating the ambiguities of James's original. Her Harry Jarvis indicates that it was Aspern who was unethical, in the relationship with Juliana: "*on a même pu l'accuser d'immoralité.*" This is a possible reading of James's original depiction—as James emphasizes, Aspern "had 'treated her badly'." But both the qualifying punctuation of his sentence and the quote-marks around this phrase leave it open to interpretation (5). Redgrave's H.J. makes statements or gives orders—in Duras's version, Harry Jarvis speaks in question marks and ellipses, particularly when in dialogue with Pasquale or Tina. Duras's Mlle. Tina asks fewer questions of Jarvis than Redgrave's Miss Tina does of H.J.[22] For Duras, Harry Jarvis's experience with the Bordereau women represents a transformative encounter between Anglo-American masculine certainty and the ambiguity of a culturally and linguistically alien femininity. Each interpretation is a selective reading of James, and each eliminates the ambiguities of his phrasing in order to settle the story, somewhat violently, on just one clear set of concerns and arguments.

The difference between these two plays is most marked in their respective treatments of the Italian language. Although she keeps Redgrave's name change, Duras's version of the Bordereaus' Italian maid speaks correct and concise French; she eliminates the misunderstandings and translation errors that made Assunta a comic stereotype. Pasquale's insistence on speaking English while Assunta responds in their shared native tongue becomes a mark of his class pretensions; his snobbery, not Assunta's provincialism, is the joke (100–103). In *Les Papiers d'Aspern* Mlle. Tina and her maid communicate almost entirely in Italian. For comparison, Redgrave inserts some Italian in the important section in Act I in which we are introduced to Miss Tina. This is one of only two scenes in his version in which we see Tina and Assunta alone together. Tina's speech is authoritative, preemptory; Assunta speaks, as usual, in broken English while referring to the American critic and Mrs. Prest.

| | |
|---|---|
| MISS TINA: | Assunta! (*Almost at the same moment* ASSUNTA *appears*) Assunta, why are the shutters...? |
| | ... |
| MISS TINA (*whispering*): | But I heard the door slam, I thought they had gone. |
| ASSUNTA (*also whispering*): | One gone. One stay. (17, ellipses original) |

Redgrave's Assunta appears instantaneously because she's been eavesdropping. For Duras, by contrast, Assunta's rapid arrival is the result of an intuitive sympathy that she shares with Tina. In this version, Assunta takes charge by ordering Tina to be silent: the relationship is familial rather than strictly hierarchical. Here and throughout Duras's adaptation, Assunta's simple French nevertheless is spoken in complete, grammatical sentences.

| | |
|---|---|
| *MLLE. TINA*, presque au meme moment, Assunta paraît: | *Assunta, pourquoi les volets sont-ils...?* |
| | ... |
| *ASSUNTA:* | *Chut! Il est dans le jardin.* |
| *MLLE. TINA*, chuchotant: | *Mais j'ai entendu la porte claquer, je le croyais parti.* |
| *ASSUNTA*, chuchotant aussi: MISS TINA, *almost at the same moment, Assunta appears*: | *Madame est partie, Monsieur est resté. (81)* Assunta, why are the shutters...? |

| | |
|---|---|
| ASSUNTA: | Shush! He's in the garden. |
| MISS TINA, *whispering*: | But I heard the door slam, and I thought he'd left. |
| ASSUNTA, *also whispering*: | Madame has left, Monsieur has remained. |

Duras most revises Redgrave's text into greater conformity with her reading of James's original in Act II, scene iii. This is the moment when Juliana discovers the American critic attempting to steal the letters. Prior to this scene, Duras has begun to undermine Redgrave's reading of this key event. In Act II, scene ii, Duras's Tina is more clearly opposed to Jarvis's scheme to obtain the papers: Mademoiselle Tina makes no promises to assist him, and Duras removes the section in which Redgrave's H.J. defensively reacts to Juliana's attack on his masculinity. Her Harry Jarvis does not respond, as Redgrave's H.J. does, that "there is nothing unmanly in a love of flowers" (55). Her additions to Redgrave's Act II, scene iii are lifted directly from James. Again, though, Duras's portrayal goes further—she inserts ellipses and repetition into Tina's speech that suggest the languidity of sleepiness or sexual arousal. In her version, Harry Jarvis is cynically manipulating an inexperienced and lonely woman.

| | |
|---|---|
| *MLLE. TINA*, lentement, souriant: | *Vous parlez de ces choses si aisément, c'est comme le flot qui continue...Cette soirée était si belle...si belle pour moi...C'est tellement...différent naturellement...J'ai l'impression que ça me change moi-même...Mais le reste n'a pas changé, ici rien n'a bougé, vous voyez, ces portes, le même silence...* |
| *HARRY JARVIS*, éveillé: | *Votre tante doit dormir?* |
| *MLLE. TINA*, lentement: | *Dormir ou ne pas dormir, on ne distingue pas toujours.* |
| MISS TINA, *softly, smiling*: | You speak of these things so easily, like a flowing wave...This night is so lovely...so lovely to me...It's so very... different naturally...I have the impression that it's changing me...But the rest doesn't change, here nothing moves, you see, the doors, the same silence... |

GENDER, COLONIALISM, AND ITALIAN DIFFERENCE: DURAS... 133

| HARRY JARVIS, *wide awake*: | Your aunt should be asleep by now? |
|---|---|
| MISS TINA, *slowly*: | Sleeping or not sleeping, one can't always tell. (All ellipses original) |

In Redgrave, Juliana begins an incoherent monologue in which it is clear that she is remembering Aspern, and Jarvis orders Tina to *"Let her talk!"* (71). Tina's response, again a direct quote from the James story ("How can you? Can't you see she's ill?") seems excessive, almost hysterical in the context of Redgrave's adaptation. By contrast, Duras implies that Juliana has just suffered the final in a series of debilitating strokes, and the old woman dies soon afterwards. Harry Jarvis is risking Juliana's life when he urges Tina not to call the doctor, to *"Laissez-la parler!"* (136). While everyone else's attention is diverted, Jarvis and Pasquale conspire to steal the papers from the green trunk.

Redgrave introduces an improbable exchange between H.J. and Tina, not found in James, in which the critic confesses to feeling guilty over his interest in the papers; he admits that he is using a false name, thereby reestablishing his moral rectitude and (Anglo-American, masculine) authority.

| H.J.: | Yes, I feel very guilty. I have sailed under false colors. But now you shall know the truth...I don't like gardens and flowers any more than the next man. Even my name is not my own. My sole reason for being in Venice this summer is to see what she has of Jeffrey Aspern's papers. That, believe me, believe me, is the whole truth! |
|---|---|
| MISS TINA: | What is your name? |
| H.J.: | Jarvis. Henry Jarvis. |
| MISS TINA *(amazed)*: | Gracious! (*She pauses*) I like your own name best. I feel I can trust you better as Mr. Jarvis. |
| H.J.: | Then you will look and see what is in that trunk? |
| MISS TINA: | The trunk isn't there! (73–74) |

Alternately, Duras emphasizes Tina's preoccupation with her aunt at this moment, and removes any reference to the calm conversation in which H.J. unburdens his conscience before asking for the trunk.

| | |
|---|---|
| *MLLE TINA*, elle crie: | *Vous pouvez laisser la porte ouverte!* (À Harry Jarvis.) *C'est une attaque. La plus grave qu'elle ait jamais eue.* (Une pause.) *Ces moments sont abominables. Ces paroles mélanges. Ça s'est produit quelquefois ainsi. Elle ne parle que dans la folie. Autrement c'est le silence...Et ces choses me concernent, et je ne comprends pas.* (Accablée.) *Quelle prison! Nous sommes deux pauvres femmes enfermées, c'est vrai!* (Légère pause.) |
| *HARRY JARVIS:* | *Je suis navré, mais...Mais il faudrait peut-être... savoir...Ne pouvez-vous voir ce qu'il y a dans cette malle?* |
| *MLLE. TINA*, vivement: | *La malle n'est pas là.* (137–138) |
| MISS TINA, *shouting*: | You can leave the door open! (*To Harry Jarvis.*) It's an attack. The worst she's ever had. (*A pause*). These moments are horrible. The mixed-up words. It's sometimes been like that. She talks crazily. Otherwise there is silence. And these things concern me, and I don't understand. (*Overwhelmed.*) What a prison! We are two poor sick women, it's true. (*Slight pause*). |
| HARRY JARVIS: | I'm sorry, but...But is it possible...to know... Can't you see what is in that trunk? |
| MISS TINA, *sharply*: | The trunk isn't there. |

Read in context, the exclamation point at the end of Redgrave's final sentence quoted above ("The trunk isn't there!") suggests surprise and alarm, indicating as elsewhere in his adaptation that Tina secretly sympathizes with H.J.'s quest for the papers. Duras's terrified Mlle. Tina dismisses a request that seems worse than insensitive. This time it is Jarvis, not Tina, whose speech is marked by ellipses: he knows his inquiry is inappropriate, but he can't stop himself from asking about the papers yet again. Jarvis, not Tina, is the supplicant; Tina is authoritative, even angry. Again, while both Redgrave's and Duras's interpretations are supported by James's ambiguous text, Redgrave justifies the masculine narrator's position, downplays the elements of the original story that indicate a critique of Anglo-American masculine cultural privilege, and makes characters conform to (hetero)normative gender, sexual, and class categories. Duras's Harry Jarvis uses specifically sexualized power in an attempt to dominate Tina Bordereau. At the same time, just like John Marcher in her reading of "The Beast in the Jungle," her version of James's anonymous narrator gradually will become self-alienated through his encounter with femininity, as revealed in the changes in his use of language over the course of her play.

The stage set for *Les Papiers d'Aspern* suggests other parallels with *La Bête dans la jungle*. It consists entirely of Juliana Bordereau's *sala*, the space in the novella in which most of the action occurs. This room is the public face of the *palazzo* and the area used both by the Bordereau women and by the narrator; it represents a site of confrontation, as Duras's set design suggests.

*Le troisième panneau fait face au public et comporte l'élément principal de la pièce: une haute et lourde porte à deux battants qui s'ouvre vers l'extérieur sur le boudoir et la chambre de Mlle. Bordereau. Lorsque cette porte est ouverte, on voit une autre porte également à deux battants capitonnée de cuir...Lorsque cette seconde porte est ouverte, on voit des éléments suggérant une grand pièce: paravent de laque, lustre entouré de gaze, atmosphère obscure.* (66)

The third panel should face the audience and represent the principal element of the set: a tall and heavy door with two panels that opens onto the bedchamber and sitting room of Miss Bordereau. When this door is open, one can see another door also of two panels upholstered in leather...When that second door is open, one sees elements suggesting a very large room: lacquered screens, chandeliers covered in gauze, a dim atmosphere.

The set design evokes postwar French feminist symbolizations of female genitalia in other fictional, philosophical, and activist writing—the inner and outer doors, sheathed in skin; the exotic mystery of the expansive, dark interior. Although this move is typical of Duras (see Chap. 4), it isn't her invention: the set is a visual elaboration on James's suggestion that the house is an extension of Juliana's body. Throughout the play, the door is opened and closed, and occasionally left half-open as the women pass in and out. Duras describes a scene in which the American critic tries to force the door open, and then is discovered by Pasquale attempting to peer through the keyhole. In fact, as Tina informs him later, there is no key: the door is unlocked, but there is a trick to opening it (103–104, 106). Assunta and Tina manage the door throughout the play, but Jarvis never succeeds despite his attempts to force his way through. Again, this is a relatively clear sexualized metaphor, as the play's only upper-class, heterosexual male fails to understand the complexity of feminine arousal. Meanwhile, women approach the door with the familiarity that comes from permission, and readily enter. These shifts aren't coincidental, as Duras emphasizes that the door is never locked, eliminating a passage from Redgrave in which Assunta carefully "makes the inner, double door fast" before allowing H.J. and Mrs. Prest into the house (Redgrave 2). In this, Duras renders more explicit, and explicitly feminist, the corporeal symbolism of James's representation of Juliana's inner sanctum; and she elaborates on the clitoral symbolism suggested by the desk that may (or may not) open if the correct button is pushed in just the right way.

The stairs, a minor element in James's novella, similarly become a key site in Duras's play. A landing that connects the sets of stairs that ascend from the *sala* and descend from the second floor, connecting sites associated with the different characters, becomes a place of confrontation between Mlle. Tina and Harry Jarvis, and between servants and their employers. As suggested by the use of Italian, these moments are comparatively egalitarian. In a revision of both James and Redgrave, Duras concludes the play with Mlle. Tina and Assunta, together on the stairway. This is the only time that we see the two alone, in a private domestic setting, after the exchange from Act I (also on the stairs) in which Tina tries to avoid meeting Mrs. Prest and Harry Jarvis. As the French audience would have experienced Assunta's Italian as a foreign language, I've left it untranslated.

ASSUNTA:     Fa più fresco.
MLLE. TINA:   Oui...Il fait même presque froid tout d'un coup. (Elle frissonne.) Assunta, je crois que nous allons allumer le poéle. Apportez du bois, voulez-vous ?
ASSUNTA:     La Signorina ha freddo perchè non mangia. J'apporte du bois et du papier.
MLLE. TINA:   Non, du bois seulement.
ASSUNTA:     Fa più fresco.
MLLE. TINA:   Yes, it's gotten cold suddenly (*She shivers*). Assunta, I believe we should light the stove. Bring some wood, will you?
ASSUNTA:     La Signorina ha freddo perchè non mangia. I'll bring some wood and some paper.
MLLE. TINA:   No, just some wood.

The information that Tina needs no paper—she's about to burn Aspern's letters—is provided in French for the audience. Otherwise, linguistic difference actually enables communication between two women of distinct backgrounds. We are invited to witness their intimacy, but non-Italian-speaking members of Duras's French audience cannot readily participate. This final scene in *Les Papiers d'Aspern* emphasizes that Duras's women characters embody fluid relationships with class, culture, and language. At the same time, her conclusion undermines the evocative play between public and private spaces that closes James's story. Rather than projecting intimacy outside as he does, into the "apartment" of the city of Venice, Duras leaves us indoors, in a definitively feminine domestic place.

The relationship between Tina and Assunta will remind readers of other cross-linguistic, cross-cultural feminine pairings in Duras's corpus: the familial alliance between the mother and the Vietnamese servant Dô in the "autobiographical" novels is a key example. Dô takes on a position of authority in the household; she is the mother's ally in their shared resistance against the petty tyranny of the regional French colonial government. Again, however, these domestic parities between white women and their ethnically and linguistically "othered" servants do not present a consistent or public challenge to hierarchical systems of race, ethnicity, class, and language. Like Dô and the mother in *Un Barrage contre la Pacifique*, Assunta and Mlle. Tina carve out a fragile interior space together at the impoverished margins of a society that, it seems, will never know of their relationship. Just as the mother hopelessly tries to stop the sea from consuming her small plot of doomed land, Tina's burning of the papers seems a vain struggle against an inevitable fate. She and Assunta will continue to live together in increasing poverty, as the palazzo molders around them. At the end, just as Juliana feared, Tina is left without real means or protection.

Duras is a colonizer who writes about colonialism, a white Western woman who equates feminist with anti-colonialist struggles, a Communist who romanticizes the relationships between servants and employers. Reading Duras's depictions of ethnically "other" characters as themselves post- or anti-colonial would force us into all sorts of unsustainable political and ethical compromises. But I'm also unwilling to grant that an author—one whose work examines the private and public structures of domination; stages the muddled encounters between white and ethnically-marked characters; and unsettles clear hierarchies of linguistic, cultural, and sexual authority—should *not* be read through a feminist postcolonial critical lens, solely because of her whiteness and Frenchness. Regardless of our discomfort with her artistic and political equivocations, Duras's fictional portrayals are both anti-colonialist and deeply essentializing. Choosing to examine her out of social and historical context—through, for example, the psychoanalytic feminist readings that dominate feminist readings of her work—is to fail both her and her subjects. Moreover, Duras's sustained focus on race, language, sex, and power in her writing is inseparable from her very public relationship to French leftism, including the anti-colonialism and anti-fascism of her period.

In *Postcolonial Duras: Cultural Memory in Postwar Europe*, Winston similarly examines the divergence between scholarly feminist constructions of Duras and the author herself, asking:

> How did Duras, a lower-class *colon* [colonial] offspring, Communist activist, and revolutionary intellectual of the groupe de la rue Saint-Benoît, come to stand in our perception as *Duras*, a woman writer obsessed solely with sentimental issues, especially and increasingly, sexuality and desire? What is the social function of the icon *Duras*? What is its part, if any, in the silencing of disruptive cultural, political, and historical meanings in Duras's work and more broadly in the postwar French cultural and literary fields? (3)

Although we should recall that Duras herself was the architect of "Duras," the great French writer, we also cannot dismiss the fact that throughout her corpus (including in *Les Papiers d'Aspern*) Duras presents nuanced, consistently challenging explorations of what happens when ethnically or culturally dominant groups encounter their own others.

This, of course, evokes Frantz Fanon's critique of the French left as more concerned with the soul of the French nation than with the real, lived suffering of Algerians fighting and dying under French military rule. Even as we acknowledge the accuracy of that critique, a reader of postwar French society should recognize the uniqueness of Duras's examination of the "universal" Western subject as itself ethnically marked—as much a product of the contingencies of language, culture, and class as any other. In the land of Descartes, Duras turns her back on Enlightenment notions of universal (European) subjectivity. Without terming her a postcolonialist, then, perhaps we can explore more fully the ways that postcolonialisms—not just the Western feminist discourses that so regularly have been deployed to explain her work—help us to understand her depiction of French subjectivity, as situated in and forever changed by a confrontation with its own colonialist history. Like the 1950s French left's interpermeable commitments to Communism, anti-colonialism, and avant-garde artistic production, Duras blurs together forms of gendered and cultural alterity in order to communicate her sense of political urgency. The fact that she chooses the expatriate, transatlantic, multi-lingual, Anglo-American Henry James as the vessel into which to pour her own explosive, period-specific mixture of feminism, anti-humanism, and anti-colonialism is another provocation. She appropriates his ambiguous prose for the cause of her resistance to paternalistic fantasies of French nationalism—and she claims his relationship to writing and meaning as an inspiration for her own complexly feminist authorship.

## NOTES

1. Most biographers of both Duras and Antelme—best known for his Resistance work and his published account of his wartime internment at Dachau, 1947's *L'Espèce Humain* (*The Human Race*)—present their working relationship as jointly supportive. Colin Davis, however, uses textual evidence to argue that she was the dominant partner in their working relationship (see Duperray xl; Adler Chapters 6–9; Vallier, *C'était II*, Chapters 2–5).
2. The authors find no feminist possibilities in either Duras's play or James's original; for them, Duras sees James as a stylistic precursor to the French *nouveau roman*. According to this analysis, her readings are in keeping with Maurice Blanchot's (particularly in 1959's *Le livre à venir*) as well as Nathalie Sarraute's (in the 1956 essay "*Ce que voient les oiseaux*"), in which Sarraute compares James's relationship to narration to Proust's (22, 29–30).
3. Duras, Lamy, and Roy 37; Chalonge 185–188; Adler 13. Although Duras would not have seen it this way, this is akin to the "queer nostalgia" that Probyn discusses—a creative, resistant, empowered relationship to one's own origins. However, numerous scholars have accused her of simply lying, and indeed her "real" history is difficult to pin down. See Vallier (*C'était I*, Chs. 1–7) for a critical analysis of Duras's childhood and its role in her later storytelling.
4. See Vallier (*C'était I*, Ch. 1); Vircondelet Chs. 1–2; Adler Chs. 1–3. Gabrielle H. Cody is one of several interviewers who states that Duras spoke fluent Vietnamese (4; see also Leslie Garis); Julia Waters remarks upon Duras's repeated assertions in interviews that she understood her "non-French origins" to be essential to her work as well as her personal identity (*Duras and Indochina* vi). Adler, among others, mentions her skill at cooking Vietnamese food (228). As Duras often serves as the sole source in these accounts, we should treat them with some skepticism.

5. Unpublishable in French newspapers due to concerns about government reprisals, the document was circulated as an open secret. As Macey indicates, its existence was made fully public in *Le Monde*'s September 4, 1960 edition, via a strategically-headlined story: "121 Writers and Artists Sign a Declaration on the Right to *insoumission* (conscientious objection to military service) in the War in Algeria." "The names of the signatories and the nature of the text were soon widely known" (445).
6. See, for example, "Murderous Humanitarianism," Samuel Beckett's translation of a 1932 statement by the Surrealist Group of France, signed by eleven Surrealist artists (including André Breton, René Crevel, and Paul Éluard). The Surrealists argue that colonialism destroys indigenous cultures and creates a bourgeois (native) elite marked by a "counterfeit liberalism" that simply copies European society (67). Beckett's translation was first published in *Negro Anthology*, a 1934 collection edited by Nancy Cunard that included work by Langston Hughes, Zora Neale Hurston, and others. These fusions were obvious and necessary to Duras and her contemporaries.
7. In the late 1980s, Duras recorded with her old friend and fellow Resistance fighter a series of conversations published in 2009 as *Entretiens inédits de Marguerite Duras et François Mitterand*, which includes a four-minute discussion titled *Le fondements du racisme*. Duras's continued Communism, even after she'd left the French Communist party, is well-documented (see Adler 175–184; Garis).
8. "les Algériens ont raison de s'attaquer *politiquement d'abord* à ce système économique, social et politique et pourquoi leur libération et *celle de la France* ne peut sortir que de l'éclatement de la colonization" (The Algerians are right to attack *politically first of all* this economic, social and political system, because their liberation and *that of France* depend on the shattering of colonialism) (Sartre, *"Le colonialisme"* 1372). Fanon is quoted in Macey (343).
9. Waters argues that the fact that the lovers of the young Frenchwoman in *L'Amant* and *L'Amant de la chine de nord* are Chinese rather than Vietnamese complicates readings of these novels as engaging in an essentialized "Orientalism" of all Asian peoples. At the same time, in her view Duras's work does little to challenge the system of colonialism. "China's status as an imperial power in its own right establishes the lover's credentials as a worthy match and adversary for the young white girl of French origins." At the conclusion of *L'Amant de la chine de nord*, "the departure of the French does not signal the return of Indochina to the indigenous population but, rather, its inevitable and unspoken handing back to its former colonizers" ("'Cholen'" 188). See also Lucy Stone McNeese, and the essays contained in the collection *Orient(s) de Marguerite Duras*,

edited by Florence de Chalonge et al.—of particular interest are those by Elena Ciocoiu, Osama Hayashi, and Yann Mével, which present thoughtful readings of Duras's exoticization of "the Orient."
10. In an interesting twist, Chamika Kalupahana suggests that *The Europeans* (see Chap. 3) stages anxieties about whiteness, through racially ambiguous descriptions of Felix's sister Eugenia. It seems unlikely Duras would have read this novel, but perhaps Kalupahana provides further fodder for Duras's argument, and vice versa, about James.
11. Blair 3, 19–20, 172. Buonomo, *Immigration* 177–179; *Backward* 92–99. See Salter and Maine for readings of the representation of Italy in this novella or in James's writing more generally. See Zorzi for James's possible motives for placing *The Aspern Papers* in Venice. James devotes nearly a quarter of *Italian Hours*, his 1909 collection of travel essays dating from 1872 onwards, to his reflections on Venice. See also Warren.
12. One key difference between the 1888 and 1909 editions is that "Tita" will be renamed "Tina." In 1888's Chapter IV James refers to Juliana Bordereau's "reckless passion" (New Directions 44); by 1909, this has become "impenitent passion." Redgrave uses "Tita," but otherwise seems to be using the 1909 edition (see "impenitent" below as one example). Duras could have had access to two separate French translations of James, but it's not clear which one she used (Bessière and Symington 16–17).
13. See Buonomo (*Backward* 11–24) for an introduction to period-specific fantasies of Italy. James's Italian was passable but not fluent. As Robert Gale, an early reader, states "James dots both his letters and his notebooks with *ecco's*, *basta's*, *pazienza's*, *speriamo's* and the like; but when he is seriously questioning a literary problem in the privacy of his notebook he uses, if not English, only French" (166 n.41). In *Italian Hours* James recounts attending in April 1873 "a comedy…in Venetian dialect," which he could "but half follow" (189). The quote both disparages the Italian spoken in Venice and suggests he had comprehension problems when faced with regional variants.
14. According to Geoffrey Dowding, an historian of printing, the italic type was invented in 1500 and modeled on Italian handwriting conventions. In the sixteenth century, it was a typeset for popular texts, rather than the formal Roman-type block letters used for more serious subjects (Dowding 43–58; see also Updike 125–132). In 1733's "On Poetry: A Rhapsody," Jonathan Swift writes: "To statesmen would you give a wipe, / You print it in *Italic type*. / When letters are in vulgar shapes, / 'Tis ten to one the wit escapes" (Swift 537, ll. 95–98). My thanks to Frank T. Boyle, years ago, for this context.
15. Another suggestive example, in the final chapter, occurs when the narrator asks his Venetian servant, Pasquale, about Juliana, only to learn that she is

dead. "'When was the funeral?'" the narrator inquires, and Pasquale replies in a mix of awkward English, italicized but untranslated Italian phrases, and unitalicized single Italian words: "'The other yesterday. But a funeral you could scarcely call it, signore: *roba da niente—un piccolo passeggio brutto* of two gondolas. Poveretta!'" (italics original, 81).

16. Rowe suggests that the narrator of *The Aspern Papers* is "one in a long list of male characters in James's fiction who express in one way or another their desires" for other men. Elsewhere, he will term the American critic's "passion" for Jeffrey Aspern as an example of the "disguised male-male (sexual) relations" described in James's work during this period (*Other* 27, 207 n.27). See also Savoy and Robert L. Caserio.
17. See Introduction, note 5, above.
18. Although Redgrave then immediately clarifies "I do not intend him, of course, as a portrait of his great progenitor" (viii), it is hard to read H.J. as anything but.
19. James makes it possible to read his narrator as a delusional fanatic, obsessed with researching a mediocre and largely-forgotten poet. At the inception of the story, in describing his many co-authored publications about Aspern, he states "some people now consider I believe that we have overdone them" (5). The structure of the phrase is open-ended: "some people now consider" and "I believe" both modify "we have overdone them." As the second modifying phrase is unmarked by commas, the narrator's insistence on obtaining the material for yet another publication about Aspern may in fact be a defense against a realization that this work is of little real interest or importance.
20. Bessière and Symington 17–19.
21. For a representative example of the French play's reinstitution of important dialogue from James's text, compare Duras 78–79 to James 1–3 and Redgrave 14.
22. For example, see the series of questions that comprise Jarvis's dialogue with Pasquale, Duras 105–106, as compared to the same section in Redgrave (40–41).

CHAPTER 6

# Conclusion: Towards a Queer Feminist James

In 1987, a quarter-century after her theatrical adaptations of "The Beast in the Jungle" and *The Aspern Papers* were staged, Marguerite Duras makes the only other reference in her extensive corpus to Henry James. It occurs near the end of *Emily L.*, a short novel about women and authorship organized around a poem, "Winter Afternoons," Duras's revision of Emily Dickinson's "There's a certain slant of light."[1] Written by the titular female character, and subsequently destroyed by her husband, the half-remembered poem haunts this story of thwarted feminine artistic potential. As Vicki Mistacco suggests, "Emily L.'s lot reconfigures the perennial situation of the woman writer; indeed, she evokes other Emilies, Emily Dickinson whose poem she rewrites…If she is *Elle*, the archetype of the woman writer in history, she also affords a pretext for telling the narrator's and Duras's modern-day story of writing" (77). At the conclusion of the novel, the unnamed woman novelist tells her lover, "You'll understand the story like Henry James's heroes—when it's over" (100). We are invited to conflate Duras with the alcoholic, elderly woman author who voices this bit of dialogue, thereby also linking her with Emily L. (the silenced poet), Emily Dickinson, and a transhistorical version of "Elle" ("She"), the woman writer. The line also harks back to Duras's reading of John Marcher's experience at the conclusion of "The Beast in the Jungle." By implication, Henry James, too, becomes an insider who "knows," as only women/writers can.

Bessière and Symington argue that Duras's adaptations are both "distortions" and "readings" (22). Yet her versions of James are no more selective than other interpretations of his work. Scholarly images of James transform from generation to generation: the suspect cosmopolitan described by T. W. Higginson and other turn-of-the-century readers develops into the brilliant but old-fashioned stylist affectionately referenced by modernists.[2] Later, the repressed (but definitively heterosexual) aesthete of postwar scholarship shifts, as the century closes, into a paragon of queer male *fin-de-siècle* culture. Winding through the composition of these dominant depictions, the trajectory that I've sketched in *Henry James's Feminist Afterlives* functions like a dissonant note—one that will be picked up by twentieth-century feminist writers of various stripes, including Marianne Moore, Gertrude Stein, Leslie Marmon Silko, and Cynthia Ozick.[3] Insistently repeated, a note becomes a theme. This one suggests the limitations of analyses that continue to insist that the potential feminism so many women authors, writing in different times and places, have found in James's work is an external imposition by scholars trying to force him into conformity with late twentieth-, early twenty-first century sensibilities.

In her critique of feminist readings of James that emerged in the 1980s and early 1990s (including those by Castle, Fetterley, and Walton), Martha Banta concedes that "there is little or nothing in Henry James's mind that is *not* about social relations between women and men; every issue is ultimately gendered." But for her, "[i]t will not do to think of James as protofeminist...See James for what he is: author of tales mainly about upper-class unmarried women involved in various courtship rituals and marriage rites with upper-class men at the private level, and recorder of the social splits that separate males from females in the nation's public life" (21, 23). There seems a basic category mistake here—first, Banta could be describing any of a number of "drawing room" authors (Jane Austen, Charlotte Brontë, George Eliot, Edith Wharton) who, because female, evidently are more unequivocally "feminist" despite, in several cases, their arguably more conservative fictional stances regarding gender roles. If Banta objects to the inherently bourgeois nature of James's predominant interest in the privacy of his upper-class women characters, perhaps her argument should lie along Marxist lines—by couching her critique as a feminist one understood broadly, she fails to acknowledge that there is no single valid form of feminism. Annie Fields and her genteel American activist peers, and French feminists like Irigaray and Kristeva, share little in common other than their "feminist" commitment, as they understand that term—and each finds ways to express her certainty that feminism is not by definition synonymous with living a conventionally public life, or attaining professional success. Whether or not we agree with their clearly bourgeois relationships to feminine authorship, Fields, Dickinson, and Duras all find different ways of rejecting the "Wollstonecraft dilemma" that Banta seems uncritically to reiterate. Rather than looking for agency and achievement via avenues that their societies consider to be predominantly "male" and public, each finds access to an alternate, "feminine" system of self-expression that also is distinctly feminist—by which I mean simply that each asserts the right to determine her own relationship to authorship, in ways that are meaningful for her. Instead of reversing the terms of a hierarchical binary, each of these women writers engages in the more radical work of unsettling and evacuating the binary itself. James notes that the very public Dr. Prance, for example, is incapable of asking Basil Ransom a personal question, although she would have been comfortable delving "with precision" into the causes of "a sore throat" (346). It is valid to argue that one need not be Dr. Prance in order to be recognizably feminist; indeed, that character from *The Bostonians*, whom twenty-first century feminists seem most comfortable embracing as one of their own, has little use for her own period's feminist causes.

In a manner wholly determined by his own and his society's contingent ideas about masculinity and femininity, James repeatedly stages a conflict between individual agency and the constraints that come with being physically and socially embodied as female in the turn-of-the century period. While perhaps not "feminist," this focus certainly qualifies as "proto-feminist." Indeed, I can think of fewer more succinct definitions of that troublesome term than the conviction that Banta attributes to James's work: "every issue is ultimately gendered" in his writing, by structural rather than just personal forces, and this fact consistently allows some of his characters greater agency than others. Queer theorists long ago stopped apologizing for Eve Sedgwick's attempts to find a biographical basis for the queerness she and they see in James: as Savoy, Lane, Looby, and Stevens emphasize, we don't need James to be recognizably or actively "gay" for his writing to be queer. Feminist readers might learn from this example. James doesn't have to be "a feminist," in a way that resembles our definitions of that term, for his writing to articulate what are specifically, and perhaps even uniquely, feminist concerns.

Duras's analysis of James does undermine the complex ambivalence of his engagements with femininity, and thereby risks limiting the relevance of her adaptations to the postwar French setting out of which they emerge. By comparison, James's own gender-transgressive sympathies with real women, and his female characters, offer a more compellingly open-ended alternative. The pitfalls inherent to Duras's readings become clear in her evocation of the author in *Emily L*.: individual women who write are incarnations of a universal and anonymous "She." This ahistorical representation fails to recognize the ways that notions of womanhood—and of authorship—transform profoundly from the period of Emily Dickinson to *Emily L*. Reading Annie Fields, Emily Dickinson, Marguerite Duras, and Henry James together, in their separate contexts, suggests the near-incompatibility between different views of women's writing, from 1879 to 1987. Yet when encountering the work of white, middle-class, Western women, we still seem more likely to assume universals than note differences. The women authors I address in *Henry James's Feminist Afterlives* are not only not "universal" simply because all three are white and Western: each is formed through highly-specific regional, national, and historical constructs. Scratching the surface of Duras's "*Elle*" reveals, productively, that it has never existed for any (woman) writer.

Beyond the fact that they are based on shorter works by Henry James, *La Bête dans la jungle* and *Les Papiers d'Aspern* share other parallels: both are Duras's adaptations of earlier adaptations by queer, English-speaking male members of a transatlantic literary-artistic community. James Lord reads "The Beast in the Jungle" as an analysis of male homosexuality; by contrast, Michael Redgrave, the celebrated and closeted British actor, uses theatrical cues to undermine potentially homoerotic elements in *The Aspern Papers*.[4] For Redgrave, James's unnamed narrator is a sympathetic representation of literate, upper-class, presumably straight, Anglo-American culture; his well-meaning paternalism may lead him to commit grave errors, but it also helps civilize the ignorant, Italian-speaking, feminized others of the text. Lord, in his 2006 and 2010 letters to me, seems to recognize himself in James, and in James's narrator. The overall tone of the 2006 letter, in which he describes Duras's contributions ("tricking up the dialogue here and there with self-conscious Durasisms") reveals the sense of betrayal still felt, fifty-five years later, by a gay author whose work, in his view, was stolen by a trusted and powerful (heterosexual) friend. Yet like Redgrave's version of *The Aspern Papers*, Lord's letter also suggests a clichéd version of mid-twentieth-century gay male scorn towards women, and an indifference to the possibility of feminist readings of James.

Even as long-standing feminist political commitments may make feminist literary scholars more likely to whitewash differences among (white) women than to find in them productive fodder for comparative historiographical analysis, so queer theory has been slow to integrate historically-specific queer masculinities that seem in alliance with versions of normative femininity. Queer theory has been at the vanguard of emphasizing the constructed nature of sex and sexuality. At the same time, an understandable desire for the benefits accrued when one's basic humanity is acknowledged too often seems to lead to the jettisoning of those whose lack of whiteness, health, wealth, clear citizenship, sexual respectability, etc., make them liabilities to a movement focused primarily on obtaining rights for monogamously coupled, white, Western, middle-class gays and lesbians. Synonymous with this political and ethical conflict has been an emphasis on the (normative) manhood of gay men—and a reluctance in recent years to explore gender transgression in queer, cisgender male authors. To indulge in an overgeneralizing heuristic, feminist readings of James often have suggested either the ahistorical, universal femininity of his female characters, or the author's paternalistic appropriation of their experiences. Queer theoretical readings have focused on ways that James's style and his relationship to his characters, male and female, expresses queer manhood in one form or another. Missing is an approach that enables James, the queer male author, to ambivalently identify with his own era's ideals of femininity, and all of the associated concepts of privacy, domesticity, etc. that that idea also represented for him, in ways that are both determined by and resistant to normative nineteenth-century paradigms.

We read James in the wake of a long history of shifting socio-political and intellectual interactions between feminists and queer men. The habit of mistrust between feminisms and queer theories, learned through painful experiences of feminist homophobia and transphobia as well as gay male misogyny, tells us that our analyses of potentially queer/feminist elements in James necessarily are exclusive. Writing just prior to Sedgwick, as Foucault is first translated into English, Marilyn Frye argues the necessity of a division between women's and gay rights movements. In her view, "gay rights" simply seeks the benefits of male privilege for gay men. In 1987, Leo Bersani infamously echoes Susan Sontag in describing drag as a sexist "parody of women." In the post-2000 era, Janet Halley follows Sedgwick and Gayle Rubin in arguing that queer theory and feminism are necessarily "split" (Frye 128–151; Bersani, "Rectum" 208; Halley 3). According to this logic, either gender or sexuality is the exclusive focus of each methodology—and each civil rights movement. Literary scholars must choose which critical lens to apply, activists which flag to fly; presumably, those decisions reflect an individual's personal identity claims, defined as either one or the other.

The easiest counter to this false choice—what if more than one lens, flag, or "identity" applies?—misses the broader point: more than one always applies, regardless of the subject. Voices at the margins of these movements have long argued that feminisms and queer theories share the same basic mission,[5] but that's not the critique of the dominant versions of these approaches that I'd like to explore briefly. In 2014 Michael Hames-García provocatively claims Audre Lorde, Cherríe Moraga, Adrienne Rich, and Gloria Anzaldúa as his intellectual and political predecessors, thereby rejecting "white queer theory" and its origin story in the work of scholars like Michel Foucault and Eve Sedgwick. Rather than arguing that feminism and queer theory need each other, Hames-García calls out the false assumptions of universality and neutrality inherent to dominant Western traditions (135–136). This approach is quite distinct from Halley's "split" between two monolithic movements and schools of thought—Hames-García points towards the self-evident existence of a multiplicity of differently-directed, often-opposed, sometimes-intertwined feminisms and queer theories. He is part of a long line of scholar-activists who argue that partisan differences—as indissoluble points of conflict— are productive, not just unavoidable.

What does any of this mean for the approach to upper-class, white, transatlantic Henry James that I've articulated throughout these chapters? The queer feminist trajectories evoked by Hames-García emphasize racial, ethnic, and cultural specificity, as a means of rejecting the claims to universality that undergird many predominant approaches. Similarly, I argue that scholarship on James has for too long simply noted in passing—as a given that need not be examined further—the situated nature of his relationship to what we now call gender and sexuality. James's partisanship, and the limited perspective it provides, instead must be at the heart of our analyses of the queer/feminist potential in his work. His female characters invite feminist inquiry precisely because they are not "all women everywhere": they are exemplars of a fixed time and place, and they anchor his consistent critique of late nineteenth-century capitalism and the rigged game of its notions of "individualism," as differentially available to men and women. At the same time, and in opposition to Hames-García's approach, I emphasize a consistent set of foci, perspectives, and preoccupations—a recognizably proto-feminist *something* in James—that cuts across the distinctions of time, place, language, and so on. Late nineteenth-century Anglo-American and twentieth-century French feminisms share significant racial (and other) commonalities, of course; but I hope that I have emphasized the ways that in fact, reading Duras, Dickinson, and Fields as "the same" simply because all three are white and Western is a profound error, a means of undercutting the productive value of their differences in service to an anxious, and false, assertion of feminist universality. But they, and I, share certain basic principles that define our approaches as feminist. That commonality finds shared expression, for each of us, in Henry James and his fiction.

James was not consciously critical, or even necessarily aware, of the historically-contingent nature of his ideas about women. What I have called his "gender-transgressive" identifications with women who looked and acted like Annie Fields would not have extended to other women. This also seems self-evident, considering some of his depictions. At the same time, he startlingly and consistently reaches beyond his own situated ideas. In an essay first published in 1882, later included in 1909's *Italian Hours*, James describes the first memory that comes to mind when he thinks of the city of Venice. He begins by evoking the great architectural and artistic marvels of the city, but only through negation. "It is not of the Great Square that I think, with its strange basilica and its high arcades, nor of the wide mouth of the Grand Canal, with the stately steps and the well-poised dome of the Salute; it is not of the low lagoon, nor the sweet Piazzetta, nor the dark chambers of St. Mark's." In an intimate description that parallels his image of Venice as an "immense collective apartment," at the conclusion of *The Aspern Papers*, he states:

> I simply see a narrow canal in the heart of the city—a patch of green water and a surface of pink wall. The gondola moves slowly; it gives a great smooth swerve, passes under a bridge, and the gondolier's cry, carried over the quiet water, makes a kind of splash in the stillness. A girl crosses the little bridge… you see her against the sky as you float beneath. The pink of the old wall seems to fill the whole place; it sinks even into the opaque water…On the other side of this small water-way is a great shabby façade of Gothic windows and balconies—balconies on which dirty clothes are hung and under which a cavernous-looking doorway opens from a low flight of slimy water-steps. It is very hot and still, the canal has a queer smell, and the whole place is enchanting. (16–17)

In opening her 1999 book, Lyndall Gordon focuses on the story, possibly apocryphal, of James's unsuccessful attempts to use a gondolier's pole to submerge Constance Fenimore Woolson's clothing in a canal, while helping to clear her apartment a few months after her 1894 suicide. Others have argued that gondoliers serve as homoerotic ideals in James: in 1875's

*Roderick Hudson* the title character, a sculptor, lies on his back watching "a brown-breasted gondolier making superb muscular movements, in high relief, against the sky of the Adriatic." Indeed, a few pages after the description quoted above in the essay on Venice, James comments on the physical beauty of his gondolier, interestingly named Pasquale (Gordon 1–2, 289, 290n.; Yoder 477–479; Bartel 70; James, *Roderick* 227, *Italian* 22). As a figure invested with homoerotic potential, or as a possible facilitator and witness—as Gordon has it—to James's unsuccessful attempts to push out of sight the material remnants of a woman central to his own appropriative relationship with femininity, Venetian gondoliers are hard to ignore in James. But, as in Duras's adaptation of "The Beast in the Jungle," in focusing on the male figure in the scene, we miss the full story.

In the city that he describes in *The Aspern Papers* as a great stage, this memory is a theatrical moment—made real, and therefore even more potent, through the presence of dirty laundry, slime, heat, and unpleasant smells. The star of the living play of Venice is a girl crossing a quiet bridge far from the crowds at St. Mark's and the Piazzetta. James emphasizes her typicality—he describes her as both "characteristic and charming"—but she is also more specific and immediately memorable than the city's famous architecture or fine paintings. Even the "handsome" gondolier, who will later be named as she never is, serves as her backdrop; his shout is another of the watery noises that "splash" around them, to announce her arrival on stage, and James's. She is aestheticized and anonymized—simultaneously, she is more human and alive than anything else around her. This girl and the chance moment of public privacy that she represents for James encapsulate his ambivalent identifications with women.

Rendered as typically Italian and therefore "other," she and James seem to just miss encountering each other. From his situated location, as he glides through the canals of Venice, James comes into her world, recognizes her, and then moves on. But the fact that it is *this* memory that most evokes Venice for him suggests that, in this instance at least, his intense sympathetic connection reflects more than just a sense that she is "characteristic." At this moment of witnessed urban privacy, she is another human presence—the only one?—"at the heart" of the great city, and she shares with James the status of an observer. To extend the analogy, it is by means of the gondolier, and his mediating shout, that James reaches across the water to her. Through his own queerness, and the liminal social position that it represents, James first and always—if equivocally—recognizes his kinship with women, in the shifting and complexly-colored world that surrounds and determines them both.

Although his account of the Venetian girl on the bridge has the ring of truth, and elements of this memory recur in *The Aspern Papers* and elsewhere, we can't know if she really existed. As Gordon emphasizes, "everything in James—fictions, reviews, and memoirs—suggests that documentary truth is limited and needs the complement of imaginative truth" (370). The imaginative truth he sketches in *Italian Hours*, and throughout his corpus, transgresses clear categories of gender, and indeed at times other boundaries as well. We need only look to the readers of James I've examined throughout this book—women who practiced ambivalent relationships to their own period's ideas about femininity, publicity, privacy, and writing—to find a series of feminist approaches that, when regarded as a whole, provide no singular definition of what feminist authorship is or does. Revising our concept of Henry James in light of these and other responses to his work by women writers, we can begin to explore the complex solidarity that he has with women as a sense of shared, if not identical, purpose. Like Annie Fields and the Venetian girl, women are fellow-travelers in James's queer version of late nineteenth-century transatlantic community: however far away, they are both always foreign and, somehow, also at home.

NOTES

1. "There's a certain slant of light" is F320A in Franklin.
2. Virginia Woolf wrote four separate essays on James, which were published in the posthumous collections *The Death of the Moth* (1942) and *Granite and Rainbow* (1958). Woolf concludes the review "Henry James's Ghost Stories," first published in the *Times Literary Supplement* on December 22, 1921 as follows: "We must admit that Henry James has conquered. That courtly, worldly, sentimental old gentleman can still make us afraid of the dark" (292). On the responses of Woolf and other modernists to James, see Maud Ellmann, Chaps. 3 and 4.
3. In addition to Stein's *Four in America* (1947), see Moore's poem "An Octopus," first published in 1924; Silko's 2000 novel *Gardens in the Dunes* as well as the 2012 article in the *HJR* in which she cites James as an influence for that work; and Cynthia Ozick's 2010 novel *Foreign Bodies*.
4. In a 1996 memoir Corin Redgrave recalls his father's difficulty acknowledging to his son the open secret of his bisexuality, which he attributes to "a split personality," in a manner reminiscent of the pre-twentieth-century pseudoscientific conceptions of spiritual "hermaphroditism" that Reis dis-

cusses. Corin sometimes describes his father as "gay." While writing his adaptation of James, Michael Redgrave is in a long-term relationship with a man, installed nearby and closely integrated into the actor's family life, with his wife and children (17–19, 27–28, 104, 106–109).

5. Way back in 1972, gay rights activist Carl Wittman argued that the "women's liberation movement" is the "closest ally" of gay men (39). Barbara Smith, writing in 1990, reminds feminists that "the major 'isms' *including* homophobia are intimately and violently intertwined" (100).

# Works Cited

L *The Letters of Emily Dickinson*. Ed. Thomas H. Johnson and Theodora Ward. 3 vols. Cambridge, MA: Harvard University Press, 1958. Citation by letter number.

Adler, Laure. *Marguerite Duras*. Paris: Gallimard, 1998.

Alcoff, Linda Martín. *Visible Identities: Race, Gender, and the Self*. New York: Oxford University Press, 2005.

Allen, Elizabeth. *A Woman's Place in the Novels of Henry James*. London: Macmillan, 1984.

Anderson, Linda. "Autobiographical Travesties: The Nostalgic Self in Queer Writing." *Territories of Desire in Queer Culture: Refiguring Contemporary Boundaries*. Ed. David Alderson and Linda Anderson. New York: Manchester University Press, 2000. 68–81.

Anesko, Michael. *Letters, Fictions, Lives: Henry James and William Dean Howells*. New York: Oxford University Press, 1997.

Anesko, Michael and Greg W. Zacharias, Eds. *The Complete Letters of Henry James, 1880–1883*. Lincoln, NE: University of Nebraska Press, 2016–2017.

Apter, Emily. "'Women's Time' in Theory." *Differences* 21.1 (2010): 1–18.

Armel, Aliette. *Marguerite Duras et l'autobiographie*. Paris: Le Castor Astral, 1990.

Auchincloss, Louis. *Reading Henry James*. Minneapolis: University of Minnesota Press, 1975.

Banta, Martha. "Men, Women, and the American Way." *The Cambridge Companion to Henry James*. Ed. Jonathan Freedman. New York: Cambridge University Press, 1998. 21–40.

Barnett, Louise K. "Jamesian Feminism: Women in Daisy Miller." *Studies in Short Fiction* 16 (1979): 281–287.

Bartel, Kim. "Unmoored from 'the Shore of the Real': Henry James, Roderick Hudson, and the Advent of the Modern in Nineteenth-Century Painting." *The Henry James Review* 26.2 (2005): 168–188.

Bateman, Benjamin. "Species Performance, or, Henry James's Beastly Sense." *MFS* 60.3 (Fall 2014): 464–483.

Bellonby, Diana. "The Surrogate Author-Function in *The Portrait of a Lady*: A Theory of Influence." *Criticism* 55.2 (2013): 203–231.

Bennett, Paula Bernat. *Emily Dickinson: Woman Poet*. Iowa City: University of Iowa Press, 1990.

———. *My Life, A Loaded Gun*. Boston: Beacon Press, 1986.

———. "'The Negro never knew': Emily Dickinson and Racial Typology in the Nineteenth Century." *Legacy* 19.1 (2002): 53–61.

———. "'The Orient is in the West': Emily Dickinson's Reading of *Antony and Cleopatra*." *Women's Revisions of Shakespeare*. Ed. Marianne Novy. Urbana, IL: University of Illinois Press, 1990. 108–122.

———. "'The Pea that Duty Locks': Lesbian and Feminist-Heterosexual Readings of Emily Dickinson's Poetry." *Lesbian Texts and Contexts: Radical Revisions*. Ed. Karla Jay and Joanne Glasgow. New York: New York University Press, 1990. 104–125.

Berman, Jessica. "Feminizing the Nation: Woman as Cultural Icon in Late James." *The Henry James Review* 17.1 (1996): 58–76.

Bersani, Leo. *A Future for Astyanax: Character and Desire in Literature*. Boston: Little, Brown, 1976.

———. "Is the Rectum a Grave?" *October* 43 (1987): 197–222.

Bersani, Leo and Adam Phillips. *Intimacies*. Chicago: University of Chicago Press, 2008.

Bessière, Jean and Micéala Symington. "The French Reception of Henry James." *The Reception of Henry James in Europe*. Ed. Annick Duperray. New York: Continuum, 2006. 19–22.

Bianchi, Martha Dickinson. *Emily Dickinson Face to Face*. New York: Houghton Mifflin, 1932.

Blair, Sara. *Henry James and the Writing of Race and Nation*. New York: Cambridge University Press, 1996.

Blanchot, Maurice. "The Narrative Voice (the 'he,' the neutral)." *The Infinite Conversation*. Trans. Susan Hanson. Minneapolis: University of Minnesota Press, 1993. 379–387.

Borgomano, Madeleine. "Henry James chez Duras ou l'image dans le tapis...." *Les lecteurs de Marguerite Duras*. Ed. Alexandra Saemmer and Stéphane Patrice. Lyon: Presse universitaire de Lyon, 2005. 81–92.

Bray, Alan. *Homosexuality in Renaissance England*. New York: Columbia University Press, 1996.

Brooks, Peter. *Henry James Goes to Paris.* Princeton, NJ: Princeton University Press, 2007.
Browner, Stephanie. "Gender, Medicine, and Literature in Postbellum Fiction." *Profound Science and Elegant Literature.* Philadelphia: University of Pennsylvania Press, 2012. 135–181.
Buelens, Gert. "In Possession of a Secret: Rhythms of Mastery and Surrender in 'The Beast in the Jungle'." *The Henry James Review* 19.1 (1998): 17–35.
Buonomo, Leonardo. *Backward Glances: Exploring Italy, Reinterpreting America (1831–1866).* Teaneck, NJ: Fairleigh Dickinson University Press, 1996.
———. *Immigration, Ethnicity, and Class in American Writing 1830–1860: Reading the Stranger.* Teaneck, NJ: Fairleigh Dickinson University Press, 2014.
Butler, Judith. *Bodies That Matter.* New York: Routledge, 1993.
———. *Undoing Gender.* New York: Routledge, 2004.
Caesar, Judith. "James's *The Europeans.*" *The Explicator* 62.3 (2004): 151–153.
Cameron, Sharon. *Choosing Not Choosing: Dickinson's Fascicles.* Chicago: University of Chicago Press, 1993.
———. *Thinking in Henry James.* Chicago: University of Chicago Press, 1989.
Campbell, Sarah. "Saying 'Nothing' and Meaning 'Everything' in *The Golden Bowl.*" *Arizona Quarterly* 67.2 (2011): 101–125.
Cannon, Kelly. *Henry James and Masculinity.* New York: St. Martin's Press, 1994.
Capps, Jack L. *Emily Dickinson's Reading.* Cambridge, MA: Harvard University Press, 1966.
Caramello, Charles. *Henry James, Gertrude Stein, and the Biographical Act.* Chapel Hill: University of North Carolina Press, 1996.
Cary, Richard, Ed. *Sarah Orne Jewett Letters.* Waterville, ME: Colby College Press, 1967.
Caserio, Robert L. "Anti-Social James." *The Henry James Review* 31.1 (2010): 7–13.
Castle, Terry. "Haunted by Olive Chancellor." *The Apparitional Lesbian.* New York: Columbia University Press, 1993. 150–185.
Cesaire, Aimé. *Discourse on Colonialism.* New York: Monthly Review Press, 2000.
Chalonge, Florence de. "Genre, texte, sujet: quelques enjeux de l'écriture durassienne durant les années 70." *Marguerite Duras, La Tentation du poétique.* Ed. Bernard Alazet et al. Paris: Presses Sorbonne Nouvelle, 2002. 177–188.
———, Yann Mével, and Akiko Ueda, Eds. *Orient(s) de Marguerite Duras.* New York: Rodopi, 2014.
Church, Joseph. "Writing and the Dispossession of Woman in *The Aspern Papers.*" *American Imago* 47 (1990): 23–42.
Cixous, Hélène. "The Laugh of the Medusa." Trans. Keith Cohen and Paula Cohen. *Signs* 1.4 (1976): 875–893.
———. "L'écriture comme placement ou de le ambiguïté de l'intérêt." *L'Art de la fiction: Henry James.* Ed. Michel Zéraffa. Paris: Klincksieck, 1978. 203–222.

Claveron, Yves. "L'adaptation théâtrale de *La Bête dans la jungle* par Marguerite Duras; une figure de l'homme blesse ou *La maladie du mort*." *Frontières et passages; les échanges culturels et littéraires XXVIII*, Rouen: Publications de l'Université de Rouen, 1999. 266–274.

Cody, Gabrielle H. *Impossible Performances: Duras as Dramatist*. New York: Peter Lang, 2000.

Comment, Kristin M. "Dickinson's Bawdy: Shakespeare and Sexual Symbolism in Emily Dickinson's Writing to Susan Dickinson." *Legacy* 18.2 (2001): 167–181.

Coulson, Victoria. *Henry James, Women and Realism*. New York: Cambridge University Press, 2007.

Critchley, Simon. "I Want to Die, I Hate My Life—Phaedra's Malaise." *NLH* 35.1 (2004): 17–40.

Crowley, Martin. "'C'est curieux un mort': Duras on Homosexuality." *The Modern Language Review* 93.3 (July 1998): 659–677.

Daugherty, Sarah B. "Henry James, George Sand, and *The Bostonians*: Another Curious Chapter in the Literary History of Feminism." *The Henry James Review* 10.1 (Winter 1989): 42–49.

David, Michel. *Le Ravissement de Marguerite Duras*. Paris: L'Harmattan, 2005.

Davis, Colin. "Duras, Antelme and the Ethics of Writing." *Comparative Literature Studies* 34 (1997): 170–183.

Davis, Sara de Saussure. "Feminist Sources in *The Bostonians*." American Literature 50 (1979): 570–589.

Decker, William Merrill. *Epistolary Practices: Letter-Writing in America Before Telecommunications*. Chapel Hill: University of North Carolina Press, 1998.

Despotopoulou, Anna. "Girls on Film: Postmodern Renderings of Jane Austen and Henry James." *Yearbook of English Studies* 36.1 (2006): 115–130.

———. "'No Natural Place Anywhere': Women's Precarious Mobility and Cosmopolitanism in James's Novels." *The Henry James Review* 35.2 (2014): 141–156.

Dowding, Geoffrey. *An Introduction to the History of Printing Types*. New Castle, DE: Oak Knoll Press, 1998.

Dreger, Alice Domurat. *Hermaphrodites and the Medical Invention of Sex*. Cambridge, MA: Harvard University Press, 1998.

DuBois, Ellen Carol. *Elizabeth Cady Stanton/Susan B. Anthony: Correspondence, Writings, Speeches*. New York: Schocken, 1981.

Dupee, F. W. *Henry James*. Westport, CT: Greenwood Press, 1993.

Duperray, Annick. *The Reception of Henry James in Europe*. New York: Continuum, 2006.

Duras, Marguerite. *La Bête dans la jungle*. *Théâtre III*. Paris: Gallimard, 1984. 9–60.

———. "*Le Chateau de Weatherend: 'La Bête dans la jungle'*." *L'Arc* 89 (1983): 100–102.

---. *Emily L.* Paris: Minuit, 1987.
---. *Emily L.* Trans. Barbara Bray. New York: Pantheon, 1989.
---. *Les papiers d'Aspern. Théâtre III.* Paris: Gallimard, 1984. 61–166.
---. *The Ravishing of Lol Stein.* Trans. Richard Seaver. New York: Pantheon, 1966.
---. *La vie matérielle.* Paris: POV, 1987.
Duras, Marguerite and Xavière Gauthier. *Les Parleuses.* Paris: Minuit, 1974.
Duras, Marguerite, Suzanne Lamy, and André Roy. *Marguerite Duras à Montréal.* Montréal: Éditions Spirale, 1981.
Eberwein, Jane Donahue. "'Is Immortality True?': Salvaging Faith in an Age of Upheavals." *A Historical Guide to Emily Dickinson.* Ed. Vivian R. Pollak. New York: Oxford University Press, 2004. 67–102.
Edel, Leon. *Henry James: The Middle Years: 1882–1895.* New York: Avon, 1962.
---. *Henry James: The Master: 1901–1916.* New York: Avon, 1972.
Edelman, Lee. "Homographesis." *Homographesis: Essays in Gay Literary and Cultural Theory.* New York: Routledge, 1994. 3–23.
Ellis, James. "The Archaeology of Ancient Rome: Sexual Metaphor in 'The Beast in the Jungle'." *The Henry James Review* 6.1 (1984): 27–31.
Ellman, Maud. *The Nets of Modernism: Henry James, Virginia Woolf, James Joyce, and Sigmund Freud.* New York: Cambridge University Press, 2010.
Ellman, Richard. *Oscar Wilde.* New York: Vintage, 1988.
Erkkila, Betsy. "Dickinson and the Art of Politics." *A Historical Guide to Emily Dickinson.* Ed. Vivian R. Pollak. New York: Oxford University Press, 2004. 133–174.
---. "Emily Dickinson and Class." *American Literary History* 4.1 (1992): 1–27.
Esdale, Logan. "Dickinson's Epistolary 'Naturalness'." *The Emily Dickinson Journal* 14.1 (2004): 1–23.
Faderman, Lillian. *Surpassing the Love of Men: Romantic Friendship & Love Between Women from the Renaissance to the Present.* New York: Harper, 2001.
Fahrenberg, Heike. *Framing and Reframing the Ladies: Viewing Attitudes in* The Portrait of a Lady *and Its Cinematic Counterpart.* Oxford: Peter Lang, 2010.
Farr, Judith. *The Passion of Emily Dickinson.* Cambridge, MA: Harvard University Press, 1992.
Fausto-Sterling, Anne. *Sexing the Body: Gender Politics and the Construction of Sexuality.* New York: Basic Books, 2000.
Fetterley, Judith. "*The Bostonians*: Henry James's Eternal Triangle." *The Resisting Reader: A Feminist Approach to American Fiction.* Bloomington: Indiana University Press, 1978. 101–153.
Fields, Annie, Ed. *Diary of a trip to France, 1898.* 12 September 1898 entry. Annie Adams Fields Papers. P-281, Reel 2. Massachusetts Historical Society. Boston, MA.

———. *Letters of Sarah Orne Jewett.* Boston: Houghton Mifflin, 1911.
Finnerty, Páraic. *Emily Dickinson's Shakespeare.* Amherst: University of Massachusetts Press, 2008.
Fisher, Paul. *House of Wits: An Intimate Portrait of the James Family.* New York: Holt, 2008a.
Fisher, Will. "The Sexual Politics of Victorian Historiographical Writing about the 'Renaissance'." *GLQ: A Journal of Lesbian and Gay Studies* 14.1 (2008b): 41–67.
Foss, Chris. "Female Innocence as Other in *The Portrait of a Lady* and *What Maisie Knew*: Reassessing the Feminist Recuperation of Henry James." *Essays in Literature* 22.2 (1995): 253–268.
Foucault, Michel. *The History of Sexuality, An Introduction: Volume I.* Trans. Robert Hurley. New York: Vintage, 1990.
Franklin, R. W., Ed. *The Poems of Emily Dickinson: Variorum Edition.* Cambridge, MA: Harvard University Press, 1998.
Freedman, Jonathan L. *Professions of Taste: Henry James, British Aestheticism, and Commodity Culture.* Stanford, CA: Stanford University Press, 1990.
Fritzsche, Peter. "Specters of History: On Nostalgia, Exile, and Modernity." *The American Historical Review* 106.5 (Dec. 2001): 1587–1618.
Frye, Marilyn. "Lesbian Feminism and the Gay Rights Movement: Another View of Male Supremacy, Another Separatism." *The Politics of Reality: Essays in Feminist Theory.* Berkeley, CA: The Crossing Press, 1983. 128–151.
Fulton, Valerie. "Rewriting the Necessary Woman: Marriage and Professionalism in James, Jewett, and Phelps." *The Henry James Review* 15.3 (1994): 242–256.
Fussell, Edwin Sill. *The French Side of Henry James.* New York: Columbia University Press, 1990.
Gale, Robert L. "Henry James and Italy." *Nineteenth-Century Fiction* 14.2 (1959): 157–170.
Gard, Roger, Ed. *Henry James: The Critical Heritage.* New York: Barnes & Noble, 1968.
Garis, Leslie. "The Lives and Loves of Marguerite Duras." *The New York Times,* October 20, 1991. Web. January 6, 2016.
Gates, Joanne E. "Henry James's Dictation Letter to Elizabeth Robins: 'The Suffragette Movement Hot from the Oven'." *The Henry James Review* 31.3 (2010): 254–263.
Geary, Edward A. "*The Europeans*: A Centennial Essay." *The Henry James Review* 4.1 (1982): 31–49.
Gollin, Rita K. *Annie Adams Fields: Woman of Letters.* Amherst, MA: University of Massachusetts Press, 2002.
Goodman, Susan. *Republic of Words: The* Atlantic Monthly *and Its Writers, 1857–1925.* Hanover, NH: University Press of New England, 2011.
Gordon, Lyndall. *A Private Life of Henry James: Two Women and His Art.* New York: Vintage, 1999.

Graham, Wendy. *Henry James's Thwarted Love*. Stanford, CA: Stanford University Press, 1999.

Griffin, Susan M., Ed. *Henry James Goes to the Movies*. Lexington, KY: University Press of Kentucky, 2002.

Gunter, Susan E. *Alice in Jamesland: The Story of Alice Howe Gibbens James*. Lincoln: University of Nebraska Press, 2009.

———., Ed. *Dear Munificent Friends: Henry James's Letters to Four Women*. Ann Arbor: University of Michigan Press, 2000.

———. and Stephen H. Jobe, Eds. *Dearly Beloved Friends: Henry James's Letters to Younger Men*. Ann Arbor: University of Michigan Press, 2001.

Ha, Marie-Paul. *Figuring the East: Segalen, Malraux, Duras, and Barthes*. Albany, NY: SUNY Press, 2000.

Habegger, Alfred. *The Father: A Life of Henry James, Sr*. Amherst, MA: University of Massachusetts Press, 2001.

———. *Henry James and the "Woman Business."* Cambridge: Cambridge University Press, 1989.

———. *My Wars Are Laid Away in Books: The Life of Emily Dickinson*. New York: Modern Library, 2002.

Hadley, Tessa. *Henry James and the Imagination of Pleasure*. New York: Cambridge University Press, 2002.

Halberstam, Judith. *Female Masculinity*. Durham, NC: Duke University Press, 1998.

Halley, Janet. *Split Decisions: How and Why to Take a Break from Feminism*. Princeton, NJ: Princeton University Press, 2006.

Hames-García, Michael. "Jotería Studies, or the Political is Personal." *Aztlan: A Journal of Chicano Studies* 39:1 (Spring 2014): 135–141.

Haralson, Eric. *Henry James and Queer Modernity*. New York: Cambridge University Press, 2003.

———. "Rereading Gertrude Stein Rereading Henry James (After a Fashion)." *The Henry James Review* 25.3 (2004): 239–245.

Harris, Susan K. *The Cultural Work of the Late Nineteenth-Century Hostess: Annie Adams Fields and Mary Gladstone Drew*. New York: Palgrave Macmillan, 2002.

Hart, Ellen Louise and Martha Nell Smith, Eds. *Open Me Carefully: Emily Dickinson's Intimate Letters to Susan Huntington Dickinson*. Ashfield, MA: Paris Press, 1998.

Hayes, Kevin J., Ed. *Henry James: The Contemporary Reviews*. New York: Cambridge University Press, 1996.

Helmers, Matthew. "Possibly Queer Time: Paranoia, Subjectivity, and 'The Beast in the Jungle'." *The Henry James Review* 32.2 (2011): 101–117.

Henneberg, Sylvia. "Neither Lesbian Nor Straight: Multiple *Eroticisms* in Emily Dickinson's Love Poetry." *The Emily Dickinson Journal* 4.2 (1995): 1–19.

Herford, Oliver. *Henry James's Style of Retrospect: Late Personal Writings 1890–1915*. New York: Oxford University Press, 2016.

Higginson, T. W. "Cheerful Yesterdays." *The Atlantic Monthly* 79.475 (1897): 665–678.

———. "Emily Dickinson." "A Letter to a Young Contributor." *The Magnificent Activist: The Writings of Thomas Wentworth Higginson (1823–1911)*. Ed. Howard N. Meyer. New York: Da Capo, 2000. 543–564, 528–542.

———. "Henry James, Jr." "Howells." *Short Studies of American Authors*. New York: Charles T. Dillingham, 1880. 51–60, 32–39. Nabu Public Domain Reprints.

———. "James Russell Lowell." *The Heath Readers, Sixth Edition*. New York: Heath, 1904. 45–50. Biblio Bazaar, LLC, 2008.

———. "Literature as an Art." *The Atlantic Monthly* 20.122 (1867): 745–755.

———. "Unmanly Manhood." *The Woman's Journal* 13.5 (1882): 1.

———. "Women and Men: The Victory of the Weak." *Harper's Bazar* 20.13 (1887): 214–215.

Hobsbawm, Eric. *The Age of Empire: 1875–1914*. New York: Vintage, 1989.

Holly, Carol. "'Absolutely Acclaimed': The Cure for Depression in James's Final Phase." *The Henry James Review* 8.2 (Winter 1987): 126–138.

Holmlund, Christine Anne. "Displacing Limits of Difference: Gender, Race, and Colonialism in Edward Said and Homi Bhabha's Theoretical Models and Marguerite Duras's Experimental Films." *Edward Said*. Ed. Patrick Williams. Vol. 3. Thousand Oaks, CA: Sage, 2001. 159–183 (first published 1991).

Horne, Philip. *Henry James: A Life in Letters*. New York: Viking, 1999.

———. "The Presence of Henry James in European Cinema." *The Reception of Henry James in Europe*. Ed. Annick Duperray. New York: Continuum, 2006. 260–282.

———. "Where Are Our Moral Foundations?: Emily Dickinson and Henry James." *Studies in Victorian and Modern Literature: A Tribute to John Sutherland*. Ed. William Baker. Lanham, MD: Fairleigh Dickinson University Press, 2015. 243–262.

Howe, Helen. *The Gentle Americans 1864–1960: Biography of a Breed*. New York: Harper, 1965.

Howe, M. A. DeWolfe. *Memories of a Hostess: A Chronicle of Eminent Friendships, Drawn Chiefly from the Diaries of Mrs. James T. Fields*. Boston: Atlantic Monthly Press, 1922.

Howells, William Dean. *Selected Letters Vol. 6: 1912–1920*. Ed. William M. Gibson and Christoph K. Lohmann. Boston: Twayne, 1983.

Hutchison, Hazel. "'An Embroidered Veil of Sound': The Word in the Machine in Henry James's *In the Cage*." *The Henry James Review* 34.2 (2013): 147–162.

Irigaray, Luce. *An Ethics of Sexual Difference*. Trans. Carolyn Burke and Gillian C. Gill. Ithaca, NY: Cornell University Press, 1993.

———. *This Sex Which Is Not One*. Trans. Catherine Porter. Ithaca, NY: Cornell University Press, 1985.

Irmscher, Christoph. "When Harry Met Annie." *Raritan* 26.4 (Spring 2007): 155–179.

Irving, Washington. *The Sketchbook of Geoffrey Crayon, Gent.* New York: Signet, 1981.

Izzo, Donatella. "The Silence of the Sphinx: 'The Beast in the Jungle'." *Portraying the Lady: Technologies of Gender in the Short Stories of Henry James.* Lincoln: University of Nebraska Press, 2001. 226–243.

James, Alice. *The Diary of Alice James.* Ed. Leon Edel. New York: Dodd, Mead, 1964.

James, Henry. "The Art of Fiction." *The Art of Fiction and Other Essays.* New York: Oxford University Press, 1948. 3–23.

———. *The Aspern Papers. The Aspern Papers and Other Stories.* New York: Oxford University Press, 2000.

———. *The Aspern Papers. The Aspern Papers/The Europeans.* Norfolk, CT: New Directions, 1950 (reprint of 1888 edition).

———. *Autobiographies.* Ed. Philip Horne. New York: Library of America, 2016.

———. "The Beast in the Jungle." *Complete Stories: 1898–1910.* New York: Library of America, 1996. 496–541.

———. "Boston." *The American Scene.* New York: Penguin, 1994.

———. *The Bostonians.* New York: Penguin, 1986.

———. *Complete Letters.* Ed. Pierre A. Walker and Greg W. Zacharias. 9 vols. Lincoln, NE: University of Nebraska Press, 2006–2015.

———. *Complete Letters: 1880–1883.* Ed. Michael Anesko and Greg W. Zacharias. Lincoln, NE: University of Nebraska Press, 2016.

———. *The Complete Notebooks of Henry James.* Ed. Leon Edel and Lyall H. Powers. New York: Oxford University Press, 1987.

———. *The Europeans. Henry James: Novels 1871–1880.* New York: Library of America, 1983. 875–1038.

———. *European Writers and the Prefaces.* New York: Library of America, 1984.

———. *Henry James: Letters.* Ed. Leon Edel. 4 vols. Cambridge, MA: Belknap, 1974–1984.

———. *Italian Hours.* New York: Penguin, 1995.

———. "Letter to Annie Adams Fields Sept. 3 1882." 1882. MS. Huntington Library, San Marino, CA. PDF.

———. "Letter to Annie Adams Fields June 15 1883." 1883. MS. Huntington Library, San Marino, CA. PDF.

———. "Letter to Annie Adams Fields Jan. 26 1892." 1892. MS. Huntington Library, San Marino, CA. PDF.

———. "Letter to Annie Adams Fields Aug. 20 1898." 1898. MS. Huntington Library, San Marino, CA. PDF.

———. "Letter to Annie Adams Fields Sept. 5 1898." 1898. MS. Huntington Library, San Marino, CA. PDF.

———. "Letter to Annie Adams Fields Sept. 12 1898." 1898. MS. Huntington Library, San Marino, CA. PDF.
———. "Letter to Annie Adams Fields Sept. 23 1898." 1898. MS. Huntington Library, San Marino, CA. PDF.
———. "Letter to Annie Adams Fields Oct. 24 1900." 1900. MS. Huntington Library, San Marino, CA. PDF.
———. "Letter to Annie Adams Fields Sept. 5 1904." 1904. MS. Huntington Library, San Marino, CA. PDF.
———. "Letter to Annie Adams Fields Feb. 24 1905." 1905. MS. Miller Library, Colby College, Waterville, Maine. PDF.
———. "Letter to Annie Adams Fields Aug. 25 1909." 1909. MS. Houghton Library, Harvard University, Cambridge, MA. PDF.
———. "Letter to Annie Adams Fields Jan. 2 1910." 1910. MS. Huntington Library, San Marino, CA. PDF.
———. "Letter to Annie Adams Fields Feb. 16 1911." 1911. MS. Huntington Library, San Marino, CA. PDF.
———. "Letter to Annie Adams Fields July 25 1914." 1914. MS. Houghton Library, Harvard University, Cambridge, MA. PDF.
———. "Mr. and Mrs. James T. Fields." *The American Essays*. Princeton, NJ: Princeton University Press, 1956.
———. "Preface." In Rupert Brooke, *Letters from America*. New York: Scribner's, 1916. ix–xlii.
———. *Roderick Hudson. Novels 1871–1880*. New York: Library of America, 1983. 167–511.
———. *Selected Letters*. Ed. Leon Edel. Cambridge, MA: Belknap, 1974.
James, William. *Varieties of Religious Experience*. New York: Touchstone, 1997.
Jewett, Sarah Orne. "Letter to Annie Adams Fields. December 1882." Letters from Sarah Orne Jewett, Folder 72, Burton Trafton Jewett Research Collection. Maine Women Writers Collection. Abplanalp Library, University of New England, Portland, ME.
———. "Letter to Annie Adams Fields. 5 June 1883." Letters from Sarah Orne Jewett, folder 63, Burton Trafton Jewett Research Collection. Maine Women Writers Collection. Abplanalp Library, University of New England, Portland, ME.
——— to William Dean Howells. May–June 1905." Folder 72, Burton Trafton Jewett Research Collection. Maine Women Writers Collection. Letters from Sarah Orne Jewett, Abplanalp Library, University of New England, Portland, ME.
Johnson, Courtney. "John Marcher and the Paradox of the 'Unfortunate' Fall." *Studies in Short Fiction* 6 (1969): 121–135.
Johnson, Kendal. *Henry James and the Visual*. Cambridge: Cambridge University Press, 2007.

Kalupahana, Chamika. "*Les beaux jours sont passés*': Staging Whiteness and Postcolonial Ambivalence in *The Europeans* by Henry James." *Canadian Review of American Studies/Revue canadienne d'études américaines* 33.2 (2003): 119–138.

Kaplan, Fred. *Henry James: The Imagination of Genius*. New York: Morrow, 1992.

Kelly, Mike. "Nostalgia: 100th Anniversary of the National Miners' Strike." *The Journal*, 26 March 2012. Web. June 3, 2015.

Koppelman, Susan. "Introduction." *Two Friends and Other Nineteenth-Century Lesbian Stories by American Women Writers*. New York: Plume, 1994. 9–15.

Koski, Lena. "Sexual Metaphors in Emily Dickinson's Letters to Susan Gilbert." *The Emily Dickinson Journal* 5.2 (1996): 26–31.

Kristeva, Julia. "Women's Time." Trans. Alice Jardine and Harry Blake. *The Kristeva Reader*. Ed. Toril Moi. New York: Blackwell, 1986. 187–214.

Lacan, Jacques. "Homage to Marguerite Duras, on *Le ravissement de Lol V. Stein*." In Marguerite Duras, *Marguerite Duras*. Trans. Peter Connor. San Francisco, CA: City Light Books, 1987. 122–129.

Lamm, Kimberly. "A Future for Isabel Archer: Jamesian Feminism, Leo Bersani, and Aesthetic Subjectivity." *The Henry James Review* 33.3 (Fall 2011): 249–258.

Landry, H. Jordan. "Animal/Insectual/Lesbian Sex: Dickinson's Queer Version of the Birds and the Bees." *The Emily Dickinson Journal* 9.2 (2000): 42–54.

Lane, Christopher. "Framing Fears, Reading Designs: The Homosexual Art of Painting in James, Wilde, and Beerbohm." *ELH* 61.4 (1994): 923–954.

Lewis, R. W. B. *The Jameses: A Family Narrative*. New York: Farrar, 1991.

Loeffelholz, Mary. *Dickinson and the Boundaries of Feminist Theory*. Urbana: University of Illinois Press, 1991.

———. "Dickinson's Decoration." *ELH* 72.3 (2005): 663–689.

———. *From School to Salon: Reading Nineteenth-Century American Women's Poetry*. Princeton, NJ: Princeton University Press, 2004.

Looby, Christopher. "John Marcher's Queer Timing." *The Henry James Review* 33.3 (2012): 265–271.

———. "Sexuality and American Literary Studies." *A Companion to American Literary Studies*. Ed. Caroline F. Levander and Robert S. Levine. Malden, MA: Wiley-Blackwell, 2011. 422–436.

Lord, James. Letter to the author, October 10, 2006.

———. Letter to the author, August 12, 2009.

Lucey, Michael. "The Contexts of Marguerite Duras's Homophobia." *GLQ: A Journal of Gay and Lesbian Studies* 19.3 (2013): 341–379.

Macey, David. *Frantz Fanon: A Biography*. New York: Verso, 2012.

Maher, Jane. *Biography of Broken Fortunes: Wilkie and Bob, Brothers of William, Henry, and Alice James*. Hamden: Archon, 1986.

Maine, Barry. "Picture and Text: Venetian Interiors by Henry James and John Singer Sargent." *The Henry James Review* 23.2 (2002): 136–156.

Malone, Katherine. "Anne Thackeray Ritchie's Links with the Past: Nostalgic for Progress." *English Literature in Transition, 1880–1920* 54.4 (2011): 470–493.
Matheson, Neill. "Talking Horrors: James, Euphemism, and the Specter of Wilde." *American Literature* 71.4 (1999): 709–750.
Matthiessen, F. O. *The James Family*. New York: Vintage-Random, 1980.
McColley, Kathleen. "Claiming Center Stage: Speaking Out for Homoerotic Empowerment in *The Bostonians*." *The Henry James Review* 21.2 (Spring 2000): 151–169.
McCormack, Peggy. *Questioning the Master: Gender and Sexuality in Henry James's Writings*. Newark, NJ: University of Delaware Press, 2010.
McIntosh, James. *Nimble Believing: Dickinson and the Unknown*. Ann Arbor: University of Michigan Press, 2000.
McNeese, Lucy Stone. "Postcolonial Culture: A Postmodern Oxymoron?" *Art and Politics in Duras' "India Cycle."* Tampa, FL: University Press of Florida, 1996.
McWhirter, David, Ed. *Henry James in Context*. New York: Cambridge University Press, 2010.
Mellor, Anne K. *Mothers of the Nation: Women's Political Writing in England, 1780–1830*. Bloomington: Indiana University Press, 2002.
Melton, Jeffrey Alan. "Touring Decay: Nineteenth-Century American Travel Writers in Europe." *PLL* 35.2 (Spring 1999): 206–222.
Messmer, Marietta. *A Vice for Voices: Reading Emily Dickinson's Correspondence*. Amherst: University of Massachusetts Press, 2001.
Meyer, Howard N., Ed. *The Magnificent Activist: The Writings of Thomas Wentworth Higginson (1823–1911)*. New York: Da Capo, 2000.
Michaels, Walter Benn. "Jim Crow Henry James?" *The Henry James Review* 16.3 (1995): 286–291.
Miller, Christanne. *Reading in Time: Emily Dickinson in the Nineteenth Century*. Amherst, MA: University of Massachusetts Press, 2012.
Mistacco, Vicki. "Plus ça change…: The Critical Reception of Emily L." *The French Review* 66.1 (October 1992): 77–88.
Mitchell, Juliet. "What Maisie Knew: Portrait of the Artist as a Young Girl." *The Air of Reality: New Essays on Henry James*. Ed. John Goode. London: Methuen, 1972. 168–189.
Moon, Michael. *A Small Boy and Others: Imitation and Initiation in American Culture*. Durham, NC: Duke University Press, 1998.
Moore, Marianne. "Henry James as a Characteristic American." *Hound & Horn* 7 (April–May–June 1934): 363–372.
Morrison, Toni. *Playing in the Dark: Whiteness and the Literary Imagination*. Cambridge, MA: Harvard University Press, 1990.
Murphy, Carol J. "Duras's 'Beast in the Jungle': Writing Fear, or Fear of Writing, in *Emily L*." *Neophilologus* 75.4 (1991): 539–547.

Nelson, Robert K. and Kenneth M. Price. "Debating Manliness: Thomas Wentworth Higginson, William Sloane Kennedy, and the Question of Masculinity." *American Literature* 73.3 (2001): 497–524.
Nixon, Nicola. "The Reading Gaol of Henry James's *In the Cage*." *ELH* 66.1 (1999): 179–201.
Noske, F. R. "Don Giovanni: Musical Affinities and Dramatic Structure." *Studia Musicologica Academiae Scientiarum Hungaricae* 12 (1970): 167–203.
Ohi, Kevin. *Henry James and the Queerness of Style*. Minneapolis: University of Minnesota Press, 2006.
Otten, Thomas. *A Superficial Reading of Henry James*. Columbus: Ohio State University Press, 2007.
Padva, Gilad. *Queer Nostalgia in Cinema and Pop Culture*. New York: Palgrave Macmillan, 2014.
Parkinson, R. B. "'Homosexual' Desire and Middle Kingdom Literature." *The Journal of Egyptian Archaeology* 81 (1995): 57–76.
Pateman, Carole. *The Disorder of Women: Democracy, Feminism, and Political Theory*. Stanford, CA: Stanford University Press, 1989.
Patterson, Rebecca. *The Riddle of Emily Dickinson*. New York: Houghton Mifflin, 1951.
Person, Leland. *Henry James and the Suspense of Masculinity*. Philadelphia: University of Pennsylvania Press, 2003.
Petrino, Elizabeth. *Emily Dickinson and Her Contemporaries: Women's Verse in America, 1820–1885*. Hanover: University Press of New England, 1998.
Pippin, Robert. *Henry James and Modern Moral Life*. New York: Cambridge University Press, 2001.
Pollak, Vivian R. *Dickinson: The Anxiety of Gender*. Ithaca, NY: Cornell University Press, 1984.
———. "Dickinson and the Poetics of Whiteness." *The Emily Dickinson Journal* 9.2 (2000): 84–95.
———. "Introduction." *New Essays on Daisy Miller and "The Turn of the Screw."* New York: Cambridge University Press, 1993. 1–34.
Probyn, Elspeth. "Suspended Beginnings: Of Childhood and Nostalgia." *GLQ: Journal of Gay and Lesbian Studies* 2.4 (1995): 439–465.
Racine, Jean. *Phèdre*. Paris: Pocket, 1992.
———. *Phèdre*. Trans. Ted Hughes. New York: Farrar, Straus, 1998.
Redgrave, Corin. *Michael Redgrave: My Father*. New York: Richard Cohen, 1996.
Redgrave, Michael. *The Aspern Papers*. London: Windmill Press, 1959.
Reed, Alison. "The Whiter the Bread, The Quicker You're Dead: Spectacular Absence in (White) Queer Theory." *No Tea, No Shade: New Writings in Black Queer Studies*. Ed. E. Patrick Johnson. Durham, NC: Duke University Press, 2016. 48–64.

Reeder, Greg. "Same-Sex Desire, Conjugal Constructs, and the Tomb of Niankhkhnum and Khnumhotep." *World Archaeology* 32.2 (October 2000): 193–208.
Reis, Elizabeth. *Bodies in Doubt: An American History of Intersex.* Baltimore, MD: Johns Hopkins University Press, 2010.
Roberts, Nancy. "Changing Places: Gender and Identity in *The Portrait of a Lady.*" *Schools of Sympathy: Gender and Identification Through the Novel.* Montreal: McGill-Queen's University Press, 1997. 70–88.
Roman, Judith A. *Annie Adams Fields: The Spirit of Charles Street.* Bloomington: Indiana University Press, 1990.
Romero, Lora. *Home Fronts: Domesticity and Its Critics in the Antebellum United States.* Durham, NC: Duke University Press, 1997.
Rosenberg, Joseph Elkanah. "Tangible Objects: Grasping 'The Aspern Papers'." *The Henry James Review* 27.3 (2006): 256–263.
Rowe, John Carlos. *The Other Henry James.* Durham, NC: Duke University Press, 1998.
———. *The Theoretical Dimensions of Henry James.* Madison: University of Wisconsin Press, 1984.
Rubin, Gayle. "Thinking Sex: Notes for a Radical Theory of the Politics of Sexuality." *The Lesbian and Gay Studies Reader.* Ed. Henry Abelove et al. New York: Routledge, 1993. 3–44.
Sadie, Stanley. *The New Grove Mozart.* New York: Grove, 1983.
Salamensky, Shelley. "Henry James, Oscar Wilde, and '*Fin-de-Siècle* Talk': A Brief Reading." *The Henry James Review* 20.3 (1999): 275–281.
Salska, Agnieszka. "Dickinson's Letters." *The Emily Dickinson Handbook.* Ed. Gudrun Grabher, Roland Hagenbüchle, and Christanne Miller. Amherst: University of Massachusetts Press, 1998. 163–180.
Salter, Sarah. "Scratching at the Surface: Understanding History through Style in James's Italy." *The Henry James Review* 35.3 (2014): 240–246.
Sartre, Jean-Paul. "Le colonialisme est un système." *Les temps modernes* 123 (March–April 1956): 1371–1386.
Savoy, Eric. "*Entre Chien et Loup*: Henry James, Queer Theory, and the Biographical Imperative." *Palgrave Advances in Henry James Studies.* Ed. Peter Rawlings. New York: Palgrave Macmillan, 2007. 100–125.
Schmidt, Barbara Quinn. "*Cornhill Magazine.*" In *British Literary Magazines: The Modern Age, 1914–1984.* Ed. Alvin Sullivan. Westport, CT: Greenwood Press, 1986. 103–110.
Sedgwick, Eve Kosofsky. *Epistemology of the Closet.* Los Angeles: University of California Press, 1990.
Shakespeare, William. *Othello.* New York: Penguin, 2001.
Sheringham, Michael. "Space, Identity, and Difference in Contemporary Fiction: Duras, Genet, Ndiaye." *French Global: A New Approach to Literary History.* Ed. Christie McDonald and Susan Rubin Suleiman. New York: Columbia University Press, 2010. 437–452.

Silko, Leslie Marmon. "Delight: An Appreciation of Henry James." *The Henry James Review* 33 (2012): 205–215.
Silverman, Kaja. "Too Early/Too Late: Male Subjectivity and the Primal Scene." *Male Subjectivity at the Margins*. New York: Routledge, 1992. 157–184.
Simon, Linda. *The Critical Reception of Henry James: Creating a Master*. Rochester, NY: Camden House, 2007.
Skrupskelis, Ignas K. and Elizabeth M. Berkeley, Eds. *The Correspondence of William James. Vol. 3: William and Henry 1987–1910*. Charlottesville: University of Virginia Press, 1994.
Smith, Barbara. "Homophobia: Why Bring it Up?" *The Lesbian and Gay Studies Reader*. Ed. Henry Abelove, Michèle Aina Barale, and David M. Halperin. New York: Routledge, 1993. 99–102.
Smith, Paula. "A Wilde Subtext for *The Awkward Age*." *The Henry James Review* 9.3 (Fall 1988): 199–208.
Sofer, Naomi Z. "Why 'different vibrations...walk hand in hand': Homosocial Bonds in *Roderick Hudson*." *The Henry James Review* 20.2 (Spring 1999): 185–205.
Somerville, Siobhan. *Queering the Color Line: Race and the Invention of Homosexuality in American Culture*. Durham, NC: Duke University Press, 2000.
Sonstegard, Adam. "'A Merely *Pictorial* Subject': *The Turn of the Screw*" *SAF* 33.1 (2005): 59–85.
Sontag, Susan. *Alice in Bed*. New York: Farrar, Straus, 1993.
Stevens, Hugh. *Henry James and Sexuality*. New York: Cambridge University Press, 1998.
———. "Queer Henry *In the Cage*." *The Cambridge Companion to Henry James Studies*. Ed. Jonathan Freedman. New York: Cambridge University Press, 1998. 120–138.
Story, Kaila Adia. "On the Cusp of Deviance: Respectability Politics and the Cultural Marketplace of Sameness." *No Tea, No Shade: New Writings in Black Queer Studies*. Ed. E. Patrick Johnson. Durham, NC: Duke University Press, 2016. 362–379.
Strickland, Georgiana. "Emily Dickinson's Philadelphia." *The Emily Dickinson Journal* 13.2 (2004): 79–115.
Strouse, Jean. *Alice James: A Biography*. Cambridge, MA: Harvard University Press, 1980.
Sumner, Nan and Nathan Sumner. "A Dickinson–James Parallel." *Research Studies* 39 (1971): 144–146.
Surrealist Group of France. "Murderous Humanitarianism." 1932. Reprinted in *Surrealism*. Special issue of *Race Traitor* 9 (1998): 67–69.
Swift, Jonathan. "On Poetry: A Rhapsody." *The Oxford Authors: Jonathan Swift*. New York: Oxford University Press, 1984.

Symington, Micéala. "From Realist to 'Avant-Garde': Henry James in France." *E-rea: Revue électronique d'études sur le monde anglophone* 3.2 (2005): 23 pars. (January 6, 2013). http://erea.revues.org/558.

Tanner, Tony. *Henry James: The Writer and His Work*. Amherst: University of Massachusetts Press, 1985.

Tate, Allen. "Three Commentaries: Poe, James, Joyce." *Sewanee Review* 58 (1950): 1–15.

Tate, Carolyn. "Interrogating the Legibility of Queer Female Subjectivity: Rethinking May Bartram's 'Bracketed' Character in 'The Beast in the Jungle'." *The Henry James Review* 33.1 (2012): 17–29.

Taylor, Andrew. *Henry James and the Father Question*. New York: Cambridge University Press, 2002.

Tintner, Adeline R. *The Cosmopolitan World of Henry James*. Baton Rouge: Louisiana State University Press, 1991.

Updike, Daniel Berkeley. *Printing Types: Their History, Forms, and Use*. 2 vols. Cambridge, MA: Harvard University Press, 1937.

Vaid, Krishna. *Technique in the Tales of Henry James*. Cambridge, MA: Harvard University Press, 1964.

Vallier, Jean. *C'était Marguerite Duras*. 2 vols. Paris: Fayard, 2006, 2010.

———. *Marguerite Duras: La vie comme un roman*. Paris: Textuel, 2006.

Van Leer, David. "Frank and Jim Go Boating: Henry James and the French New Wave." *Henry James on the Stage and Screen*. Ed. John R. Bradley. New York: Palgrave Macmillan, 2000. 84–102.

———. "A World of Female Friendship: The Bostonians." *Henry James and Homo-Erotic Desire*. Ed. John R. Bradley. New York: Macmillan, 1999. 93–109.

Vann, J. Don. "*Cornhill Magazine*." *British Literary Magazines: The Victorian and Edwardian Age, 1837–1913*. Ed. Alvin Sullivan. Westport, CT: Greenwood Press, 1984. 82–85.

Veeder, William. "The Aspern Portrait." *The Henry James Review* 20.1 (1999): 22–42.

———. "The Portrait of a Lack." *New Essays on* The Portrait of a Lady. Ed. Joel Porte. New York: Cambridge University Press, 1990. 95–121.

Vinson, Steve. "They-Who-Must-Be-Obeyed: Arsake, Rhadopis, and Tabubue; Ihweret and Charikleia." *Comparative Literature Studies* 45.3 (2008): 289–315.

Vircondelet, Alain. *Duras: A Biography*. Trans. Thomas Buckley. Normal, IL: Dalkey Archive Press, 1994.

Walker, Pierre A. *Reading Henry James in French Cultural Contexts*. DeKalb, IL: Northern Illinois University Press, 1995.

Walton, Priscilla. *The Disruption of the Feminine in Henry James*. Toronto: University of Toronto Press, 1992.

Warren, Kenneth W. "Race." *Henry James in Context*. Ed. David McWhirter. New York: Cambridge University Press, 2010. 280–291.
Waters, Julia. "'Cholen, la capital chinoise de l'Indochine française': Rereading Marguerite Duras's (Indo)Chinese Novels." *France and Indochina: Cultural Representations*. Ed. Kathryn Robson and Jennifer Yee. New York: Lexington, 2005. 179–192.
———. *Duras and Indochina: Postcolonial Perspectives*. Liverpool: Society for Francophone Postcolonial Studies, 2006.
Wells, Anna Mary. *Dear Preceptor: The Life and Times of Thomas Wentworth Higginson*. Boston: Houghton Mifflin, 1963.
Williams, Gary. "Speaking with the Voices of Others: Julia Ward Howe's Laurence." Julia Ward Howe, *The Hermaphrodite*. Lincoln, NE: University of Nebraska Press, 2004. ix–xliv.
Williams, James S. "A Beast of a Closet: The Sexual Differences of Literary Collaboration in the Work of Marguerite Duras and Yann Andréa." *Modern Language Review* 87.3 (July 1992): 576–584.
———. "All Her Sons: Marguerite Duras, Antiliterature, and the Outside." *YFS* 90 (1996): 47–70.
Wineapple, Brenda. *White Heat: The Friendship of Emily Dickinson & Thomas Wentworth Higginson*. New York: Knopf, 2008.
Winston, Jane Bradley. *Postcolonial Duras: Cultural Memory in Postwar Europe*. New York: Palgrave Macmillan, 2001.
Wittman, Carl. "A Gay Manifesto." *Feminism & Masculinities*. Ed. Peter F. Murphy. New York: Oxford University Press, 2009. 28–40.
Woolf, Virginia. *Collected Essays Vol. I*. Ed. Leonard Woolf. Toronto: Clarke, Irwin, 1966.
Wrenn, Angus. *Henry James and the Second Empire*. London: Legenda, 2009.
Yeazell, Ruth Bernard. *The Death and Letters of Alice James*. Oakland: University of California Press, 1983.
Yoder, Edwin M., Jr. "Sad Rags: Tales of Enchanted Dresses." *Sewanee Review* 122.3 (2014): 478–483.
Zeiss, Laurel Elizabeth. "Permeable Boundaries in Mozart's 'Don Giovanni'." *Cambridge Opera Journal* 13.2 (2001): 115–139.
Zorzi, Rosella Mamoli. "*The Aspern Papers*: From Florence to an Intertextual City, Venice." *Henry James's Europe: Heritage and Transfer*. Ed. Dennis Tredy, Annick Duperray, and Adrian Harding. New York: Cambridge University Press, 2011. 103–112.

# Index[1]

**A**
Algerian Revolution, 10, 115
Allen, Elizabeth, 12n3
Anesko, Michael, 2, 13n7, 53n17, 53n21, 53n22
Antelme, Robert
  as Duras's probable translator, 113
  *L'Espèce Humain*, 112n31, 139n1
*Aspern Papers*, The (work by James, Henry)
  depictions of Venice, 141n11, 149–151
  depictions of women, 10, 86, 87, 118–120, 127, 137
  use of Italian in, 98, 113–139
  use of italics and translation in, 113
Assunta (character in Redgrave's The *Aspern Papers* and Duras's *Les Papiers d'Aspern*), 126, 128, 131, 135–137
  *See also* Olimpia (character in James's *The Aspern Papers*)

*Atlantic Monthly, The*
  and Fields, Annie, 5, 18, 21
  under Fields, James T., as editor, 15, 20–22, 47, 73
  under Howells, William Dean, as editor, 73

**B**
Banta, Martha, 12n3, 144, 145
Bartram, May (character from "The Beast in the Jungle")
  as Bertram, Catherine (*see* Duras, Marguerite: works, *Bête dans la jungle, La*)
  feminist readings, 85, 88, 90, 106
  Sedgwick's reading, 85, 88, 89, 91
  "silence,", 88
"Beast in the Jungle, The"
  adaptations of, 85
  Duras's reading of, 10, 90
  Lord, James and, 105, 106, 146

---

[1] Note: Page numbers followed by 'n' refer to notes.

"Beast in the Jungle, The" (*cont.*)
 publication history, U.S., U.K., and
  France, 85, 112n32, 146
 Sedgwick's reading of, 85
Bellonby, Diana, 51n6
Bennett, Paula, 80n3, 82n21, 83n25
 on Dickinson's homoerotics, 60, 61,
  63, 68, 79, 80n4
Bersani, Leo, 3, 12n4, 93, 109n11, 147
 on "The Beast in the Jungle,",
  88, 89
Bianchi, Martha Dickinson, 60, 68
Blanchot, Maurice, 111n25, 116, 139n2
 on James, 111n27
Bordereau, Juliana (character from *The Aspern Papers*), 119–124,
  127–130, 132, 133, 135, 137,
  141n12, 141n15
Bordereau, Tina (character from *The Aspern Papers*), 119, 121–127,
  130–137, 141n12
Boston
 chapter in_ *The American Scene*_,
  17, 45, 47
 Fields, Annie home in, 15
 James's relationship to, 8, 9, 18, 36
Brand, Mr. (character from *The Europeans*), 62, 65–68
Browner, Stephanie T., 24, 26
Buonomo, Leonardo,
  118, 141n11, 141n13

C
Cameron, Sharon
 on Dickinson, 80n5
 on James, 7, 16, 61
Castle, Terry, 23, 24, 27, 144
Chalonge, Florence de, 139n3, 141n9
Chancellor, Olive (character from *The Bostonians*), 19, 23–26, 28,
  49, 52n10

Cixous, Hélène
 on Duras, 89, 90, 104, 105, 110n24
 on James, 86, 110n24, 111n27
"*Comité d'action des intellectuels contre la pursuit de la guerre en Afrique du Nord*,", 115
*Cornhill Magazine*, 47, 55n33
Coulson, Victoria, 5, 13n8, 13n9,
  86, 108n5

D
Dante (Dante Alighieri)
 "Dante Club, The,", 16
 Fields, Annie and, 15, 16, 44
 James, Henry references to, 13n8,
  15, 16, 51n2
 Longfellow's translation of, 16
Despotopoulou, Anna, 118–120
Dickinson, Austin, 79
 marriage to Gilbert, Susan, 79
Dickinson, Emily
 and epistolary writing, 6, 61, 64
 feminist scholarship on, 11, 58,
  60, 80n4
 homoeroticism, potential lesbianism,
  60, 61
 letters; to Higginson, T.W., 65,
  67–70, 80n7; to Holland,
  Elizabeth, 9, 57, 58, 61–64,
  66, 68, 69, 78; to others, 62,
  66, 69, 73, 78, 79
 privacy and publication,
  62, 80n5
 reference to Desdemona and
  Brabantio (characters from
  *Othello*), 76, 77 (*see also*
  Finnerty, Páraic)
 relationship with Dickinson, Susan
  Gilbert, 58, 60, 80n3
 relationship with Higginson, T.W.,
  10, 69–72

relationship with Holland,
     Elizabeth, 9, 10, 58, 61–64, 69
revisions of others' poetry, 78
Dickinson, Susan Gilbert
  marriage to Dickinson, Austin, 79
  relationship with Dickinson, Emily,
     58, 60, 80n3
*Don Giovanni* (opera by Mozart), 97,
  99, 110n20
Duras, Marguerite
  childhood, 139n3
  Communism, 116, 140n7
  as feminist, 10, 11, 85–107
  friendship with Lord, James,
     105, 107n2
  homophobia, 111n28, 112n33
  lack of English, 106
  and literary collaboration, 105,
     107n2, 112n31
  Orientalism in, 117, 140n9
  postcolonial readings of,
     117, 137, 138
  relationship to biography and public
     persona, 106, 138
  relationship to French colonialism,
     10, 11, 107, 113–139
  relationship to theatrical
     production, 10
  and Vietnam, 10, 90, 115
  work in the Resistance,
     90, 116, 140n7
  works:; *barrage contre le Pacifique,
     Une*, 114; *Bête dans la jungle,
     La*; city of Naples, 96; epilogue
     and third-person narration, 93,
     100, 102, 103; lighting, 86,
     97; opera and music, 90, 91,
     93, 99, 102, 110n22; painting,
     93, 95; set design, 10, 86,
     93–95, 97, 104; *"Chateau de
     Weatherend, Le,"*, 92; *Emily L.*;
     and Dickinson's poetry,
     111n25; reference to James,
     107n2, 143; *Hiroshima mon
     amour*, 89, 114; *India Song*,
     96, 114; *L'Amant*, 114,
     140n9; *Moderato cantabile*, 89,
     96; *Papiers d'Aspern, Les*;
     changes to Redgrave's
     adaptation, 114, 128; and
     colonialism, 10, 114; set design
     and vaginal imagery, 135; use
     of Italian, 98; *Ravissement de
     Lol V. Stein, Le*, 104, 114; and
     the "hole-word,", 104, 111n25

E
Eberwein, Jane Donahue, 69
*écriture féminine*, 10, 85, 89
Edel, Leon, 54n25
  as editor of James's letters, 51n3,
     52n14, 54n26
Erkkila, Betsy, 83n25

F
Faderman, Lillian, 31, 53n18, 60, 80n3
Fanon, Frantz, 115–117, 138, 140n8
Fetterley, Judith, 23, 52n10, 144
Fields, Annie Adams
  as author, 5, 9, 15
  "Boston marriage" with Jewett,
     Sarah Orne, 1, 27, 28
  and "Charles Street," in James's
     memory, 23
  and Dante, 15
  as diarist, 5, 43, 52n11, 52n15
  as editor of Jewett's letters, 43,
     51n1, 53n20
  as hostess, 5, 20
  James's letters to, 9, 15–18, 28–30,
     35–39, 41–44, 67
  marriage to Fields, James T., 20
  and transatlantic literary culture,
     21, 29
  travels, 17, 52n11
  visit to Lamb House, 29
  as women's rights activist and
     "conservative feminist,", 20

Fields, James
  as Annie's husband, 20
  as editor of *Atlantic Monthly*, 20, 73
  responses to Henry James, 22
Finnerty, Páraic, 82n21
Flaubert, Gustave (as James's predecessor, in French readings), 109n10
Foucault, Michel, 4, 12n5, 147, 148
Frye, Marilyn, 147

G
Gaulle, Charles de, 10, 116, 117
  See also Algerian Revolution; May '68; *Manifeste de 121*
Gollin, Rita K., 16, 21, 32, 47, 52n9
Goodman, Susan, 20, 22
Gordon, Lyndall, 5, 13n6, 149–151
Graham, Wendy, 17, 54n30
"Great Awakening, The"
  and Dickinson's relationship to Christianity, 69
  in *The Europeans*, 64, 65
  Lyon, Mary and Mount Holyoke Female Seminary, 69
"Great Unrest, The,", 2
Griffin, Susan M., 12n3, 107n1
Gunter, Susan E., 13n7, 13n9

H
Ha, Marie-Paul, 117
Habegger, Alfred
  on Dickinson, 59–62
  on James, 12n3, 13n6, 13n9
Halberstam, Jack, 4
  See also "Perverse presentism"
Halley, Janet, 147, 148
Hames-García, Michael, 108n4, 148
Haralson, Eric, 3, 12n4, 17, 111n25

Harris, Susan K., 20, 21, 29, 30, 52n8
*Hermaphrodite, The* (unfinished novel by Howe, Julia Ward), 12n5
"Hermaphroditism", spiritual, 4, 124, 151n4
Higginson, T.W. (Thomas Wentworth)
  Civil War service and social activism, 70
  described in James, Alice diary, 81n15
  Dickinson's revision of his "Decoration,", 79
  as editor for *The Nation*, 70, 72
  on Howells, William Dean ("Howells"), 74
  ideas about literary style, 70, 71
  ideas about manhood, 73–75
  on Jackson, Helen Hunt, 70, 72
  on James, Henry ("James, Henry Jr."), 73–75
  poetry, 9, 79
  as possible model for Mr. Wentworth (*The Europeans*), 81n15
  relationship with Dickinson, Emily, 58, 70, 71
  on Whitman, Walt, 74, 75, 82n18
  on Wilde, Oscar, 82n18
  works:; *Army Life in a Black Regiment*, 70; "Cheerful Yesterdays,", 82n18; "Dickinson, Emily,", 10, 57, 70–72; "Letter to a Young Contributor, A,", 70; "Literature as an Art,", 82n18; "Lowell, James Russell,", 78, 82n22; *Short Studies of American Authors*; "James, Henry, Jr.,", 69, 73, 75, 81n15; "Howells,", 69; "Unmanly Manhood,", 82n18; "Women and Men: The Victory of the Weak,", 74

INDEX    175

Holland, Susan (Mrs. Josiah)
  correspondence with Dickinson,
    Emily, 62, 63, 66, 69, 78
  ideas about femininity, 62, 63, 68
  views on women's rights, 61
Holmlund, Christine Anne, 117
Horne, Philip
  on Dickinson, 10
  on James's letters, 30, 34,
    52n12, 54n23
Howe, Helen, 23, 32, 53n21
Howe, M.A. DeWolfe
  friendship with Fields, Annie, 43
  *Memories of a Hostess*, 32
  response to Fields-Jewett
    relationship, 23
Howells, William Dean
  as editor of the *Atlantic Monthly*, 73
  friendship with James, Henry, 2, 22,
    23, 74
  friendship with Jewett, Sarah Orne,
    32, 34, 35, 53n21
  time in Maine, 32

I
Individual works, 114
Irigaray, Luce, 86, 90, 94, 104, 105,
  110n16, 144
Irving, Washington, 81n12
Izzo, Donatella, 88, 91

J
Jackson, Helen Hunt, 69, 70, 72, 75–78
James, Alice
  diary, 54n24
  epitaph on gravestone, 7 (*see also*
    Cameron, Sharon)
  health, 7, 8 (*see also* Strouse, Jean)
  on Higginson, T.W., 81n15
  partnership with Loring, Katharine,
    7, 13n9, 23, 32, 54n24
  relationship with brothers, 23, 40
  relationship with family, 8, 13n9
  response to Dickinson's poetry, 83n24
James, Henry
  and American travel writing, 118
  and Civil War, 47, 48
  contemporary reviews of, 11, 58,
    73, 81n11
  "cosmopolitanism,", 118
  Dickinson's readings of (*see*
    Dickinson, Emily, letters)
  Duras's readings of (*see* Duras,
    Marguerite:works,*Bête dans la
    jungle, La* ;Duras,
    Marguerite:works:"*Chateau de
    Weatherend, Le*"; Duras,
    Marguerite:works:*Papiers
    d'Aspern, Les*)
  expatriation, 6, 18, 45, 79, 139
  family, 13n9, 40, 45
  feminist readings of, 3, 12n3, 12n4,
    86, 119, 120, 144, 146, 147
  French scholarly readings of,
    104, 109n10
  French translations of, 90, 107n2,
    112n32, 127, 141n12
  "gender-transgressive" identifications,
    3, 4, 19, 145, 149
  letters:; *The Complete Letters* (U. of
    Nebraska Press), 51n3, 109n9;
    to Fields, Annie; 1882–1892,
    9, 17, 18, 28; 1898, 29, 30,
    35, 36; 1900, 37, 67;
    1904–1905, 38; 1909, 16,
    37–39, 44; 1910, 41–43; 1914,
    9, 15; to Howells, William
    Dean, 2, 33, 53n17, 53n21; to
    Jewett, Sarah Orne, 33, 34, 37,
    41, 53n21; to others, 53n17

James, Henry (*cont.*)
Lord, James reading of "The Beast in the Jungle,", 85, 105, 146
nostalgia in, 18, 37
"obscure hurt" (back trouble), 75, 82n20
on Pankhurst, Emmeline and women's rights, 2, 3
on privacy and burning of letters, 41, 54n26
queer theoretical readings, 3, 12n4, 147, 151
Redgrave, Michael adaptation of, 113, 114, 126, 129, 133
relationship to late-nineteenth-century capitalism, 5
relationship to masculinity, 12n4, 86, 145
in twentieth-century scholarship, 6, 81n11 (*see also* Edel, Leon; Sedgwick, Eve; Simon, Linda)
use of French language, 90, 104, 109n9
use of Italian language, 104, 118, 141n13
use of italics, 121
works (essays):; "Boston,", 9, 17, 47; "Mr. and Mrs. James T. Fields,", 8, 15, 17, 18, 22, 23, 27, 36, 38, 47, 48, 50; "Venice,", 150; *See also* Individual works
works (fiction):; *Aspern Papers, The*, 9, 10, 26, 29, 41, 86, 113–139, 143, 146, 149–151; "Beast in the Jungle, The,", 9, 10, 36, 85, 87–91, 97, 99, 103–105, 107n1, 108n6, 110n24, 112n32, 125, 135, 143, 146, 150; *Bostonians, The*, 19, 23–26, 36, 49, 51n6, 145; *Daisy Miller*, 47, 125; *Europeans, The*, 6, 9, 10, 57–59, 63–65, 68, 69, 73, 78, 79, 81n9, 81n16; *Portrait of a Lady*, 12n3, 29, 51n6,
108n6, 110n24; *Princess Casamassima, The*, 23; *Roderick Hudson*, 81n16, 150; *See also* Individual works
works (other); *Notebooks*, 7, 79, 87, 118, 119; *Notes of a Son and Brother*, 44, 82n20; *A Small Boy and Others*, 81n10
and World War I, 48
James, Henry (father), 44, 81n10
James, William, 44, 54n24, 54n29, 73, 81n10, 81n17, 109n9
Jewett, Sarah Orne
"Boston marriage" with Fields, Annie, 1, 27, 28
Fields's editorship of letters, 22
friendship with Howells and 1905 letter, 32, 34, 53n22
letters from James; 1899, 33, 34, 37, 41; 1901, 33; unlocated (1905 or 1906, 1909), 33, 53n21
letters to Fields, 35
responses to James, 35
visits with James; 1882 (London), 28; 1898 (Rye), 29, 49; 1905 (Maine), 34, 53n22
works:; *Country of the Pointed Firs*, 30, 33, 41, 43; *The Queen's Twin and Other Stories*, 33; *The Tory Lover*, 32–35

K

Kristeva, Julia, 86, 90, 104, 105, 108n7, 111n26, 144
*See also* "Women's time"

L

Lacan, Jacques, 89, 108n4, 111n25
Loeffelholz, Mary
on Civil War in Dickinson and James, 61
on Dickinson, 61, 72, 78, 79

Looby, Christopher, 3, 17, 18, 31,
     108n7, 145
  *See also* "Queer temporality"
Lord, James
  account of collaboration with Duras,
     92, 107n2, 111n29, 111n30
  adaptation of "The Beast in the
     Jungle", 85, 105
  letters to author, 106
  sexuality, 105, 146
  World War II service, 105
Lowell, James Russell
  Dickinson's revision of poem "After
     the Burial,", 78
  Higginson's views of, 78, 82n22

**M**
Major, Charles (author of *When
  Knighthood Was in Flower*), 35
*Manifeste de* 121, 116
March 1912 coal strike (U.K.), 2
Marcher, John (character from "The
  Beast in the Jungle" and *La Bête
  dans la jungle*), 85, 87–93, 95,
  96, 99, 101–103, 105, 106,
  107n2, 108n3, 108n7, 109n11,
  125, 135, 143
Mascolo, Dionys, 116
May '68, 117
Messmer, Marietta, 58, 61, 62, 69,
  72, 80n7
Miller, Christanne, ix, 71, 83n25
Moore, Marianne, 144, 151n3
Münster, Baroness Eugenia (character
  from *The Europeans*),
  66, 81n11, 141n10

**O**
Ohi, Kevin, 3, 17, 55n32, 108n7
Olimpia (character in James's *The
  Aspern Papers*), 123, 124, 126
Ozick, Cynthia, 144, 151n3

**P**
Pankhurst, Emmeline, 25, 49
  1912 "window-breaking" campaign,
     2, 3
Pasquale (character in *The Aspern
  Papers* and *Les Papiers d'Aspern*),
     126–131, 133, 135, 141n15,
     142n22, 150
Person, Leland, 5, 12n4
"Perverse presentism", *see* Halberstam
*Phèdre* (play by Racine, Jean), 93, 94,
     109n14
Pippin, Robert, 83n23
Pirie, Jane (1811 libel case), 31
  *See also* Faderman, Lillian
Pollak, Vivian R., 12n3, 80n3, 83n25
Prance, Dr. Mary (character from *The
  Bostonians*), 24, 26, 145
Probyn, Elspeth, 17, 18, 36,
     51n4, 139n3
  *See also* "Queer nostalgia"

**Q**
"Queer nostalgia,", 17, 139n3
"Queer temporality,", 89, 108n7

**R**
Racine, Jean, 93, 94, 97, 104,
     109n14, 111n25
Ransom, Basil (character from *The
  Bostonians*), 25–27, 145
Redgrave, Michael
  adaptation of *The Aspern Papers*;
     renaming of characters, 126;
  use of Italian, 118, 126
  depiction of James, Henry as
     "H.J.,", 126, 127
  sexuality, 134, 146
Reis, Elizabeth, 4, 12n5, 151n4
Rowe, John Carlos, 12n1, 110n20,
     119, 120, 142n16
Ruth, Book of, 35

## S

Sand, George
  James's writing on,
    19, 51n6
  as potential source for *The Bostonians*, 19, 51n6
Sartre, Jean-Paul
  turn towards Marxism, 117
  writing on Algeria, 115, 117
Sedgwick, Eve
  "The Beast in the Closet" (reading of James, Henry), 3, 85, 88
  queer theoretical critiques of, 17, 89, 145, 147, 148
Silko, Leslie Marmon, 144, 151n3
Simon, Linda, 12n3
Stein, Gertrude, 4, 111n25, 144, 151n3
Stevens, Hugh, 12n4, 17, 54n30, 55n32, 108n7, 145
Strouse, Jean, 7, 13n9, 54n24, 81n10
Surrealist Group of France, The, 140n6
Symington, Micéala, 90, 103, 104, 107n2, 109n10, 110n24, 112n32, 113, 114, 141n12, 142n20, 144

## T

Tarrant, Verena (character from *The Bostonians*), 19, 23, 25
*temps modernes, les*, 115

## V

Venice/Venetians, 10, 114, 119, 123–125, 127, 128, 133, 137, 141n11, 141n13, 141n15, 149–151

## W

Wadsworth, Reverend Charles, 59, 60, 62
Walker, Pierre A., 109n10
Walton, Priscilla, 86, 87, 92, 94, 144
Warren, Kenneth W., 55n35, 141n11
Webster, Noah, 44, 54n30
Wentworth, Charlotte (character from *The Europeans*), 66–69
Wentworth, Gertrude (character from *The Europeans*), 62, 64–69, 79
Wentworth, Mr. (character from *The Europeans*), 59, 62–67, 69, 81n9
Wharton, Edith, 2, 4, 5, 144
Wilde, Oscar
  Higginson's writing on, 82n18
  James's writing on, 46, 105
  as public figure, 19, 46
  trials, 19, 31, 46, 105
Winston, Jane Bradley, 115, 138
"Wollstonecraft dilemma,", 74, 145
Woods, Marianne (1811 libel case), 31, 53n18
  *See also* Faderman, Lillian
Woolf, Virginia, 151n2
Woolson, Constance Fenimore, 4, 5, 13n6, 88, 108n5, 149
"Women's time,", 104, 108n7

## Y

Young, Felix (character from *The Europeans*), 64–68

## Z

Zacharias, Greg, *see* James, Henry, letters: *The Complete Letters* (U. of Nebraska Press)

The manufacturer's authorised representative in the EU is Springer Nature Customer Service Centre GmbH, Europaplatz 3, 69115 Heidelberg, Germany. If you have any concerns regarding our products, please contact ProductSafety@springernature.com

Printed and bound by CPI Group (UK) Ltd, Croydon, CR0 4YY

23/03/2026

02076668-0001